Visual Merchandising

The Business of Merchandise Presentation

Delmar Publishers' Online Services

To access Delmar on the World Wide Web, point your browser to:

http://www.delmar.com/delmar.html

To access through Gopher: gopher://gopher.delmar.com
(Delmar Online is part of "thomson.com", an Internet site
with information on more than 30 publishers
of the International Thomson Publishing organization.)

For information on our products and services:
email: info@delmar.com
or call:
800-347-7707

Visual Merchandising

The Business of Merchandise Presentation

Robert Colborne

Delmar Publishers

I(T)P An International Thomson Publishing Company

Albany • Bonn • Boston • Cincinnati • Detroit • London • Madrid • Melbourne
Mexico City • New York • Pacific Grove • Paris • San Francisco • Singapore
Tokyo • Toronto • Washington

NOTICE TO THE READER

Cover design: Marjolaine Arsenault, Idée Design

Delmar Staff

Acquisitions Editor:	Christopher Anzalone	Production Coordinator:	Jennifer Gaines
Developmental Editor:	Jeffrey D. Litton	Art Design Coordinator:	Douglas J. Hyldelund
Project Editor:	Eugenia L. Orlandi		

COPYRIGHT © 1996
By Delmar Publishers
a division of International Thomson Publishing Inc.
The ITP logo is a trademark under license

Printed in the United States of America.

For more information, contact:

Delmar Publishers
3 Columbia Circle, Box 15015
Albany, New York 12212-5015

International Thomson Editores
Campos Eliseos 385, Piso 7
Col Polanco
11560 Mexico D F Mexico

International Thomson Publishing Europe
Berkshire House 168 - 173
High Holborn
London WC1V7AA
England

International Thomson Publishing GmbH
Konigswinterer Strasse 418
53227 Bonn
Germany

Thomas Nelson Australia
102 Dodds Street
South Melbourne, 3205
Victoria, Australia

International Thomson Publishing Asia
221 Henderson Road
#05 - 10 Henderson Building
Singapore 0315

Nelson Canada
1120 Birchmount Road
Scarborough, Ontario
Canada M1K5G4

International Thomson Publishing - Japan
Hirakawacho Kyowa Building, 3F
2-2-1 Hirakawacho
Chiyoda-ku, Tokoyo 102
Japan

1 2 3 4 5 6 7 8 9 10 XXX 00 99 98 97 96 95

Library of Congress Cataloging-in-Publication Data

Colborne, Robert.
    Visual merchandising : the business of merchandise presentation/Robert Colborne.
        p. cm.
    Includes index.
    ISBN 0-8273-5759-1
    1. Display of merchandise.   2. Show windows.   I. Title.
HF5845.C667   1996
659.1'57—dc20

95-10179
CIP

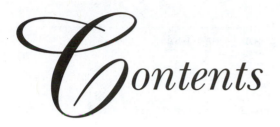

Contents

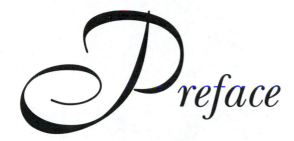

Preface

Retailers compete intensely with each other to gain market share. They constantly scrutinize all retail functions to search for new ways to increase sales. Presentation is a most effective sales generator. Since the beginning of retail, how the merchant presented the product to the customer has been very valuable.

Visual merchandising (VM) or merchandising presentation is an effective means of substantially increasing business and sales. Successful executives understand the value of VM. They understand how to organize and implement it.

Examples of VM abound. From the orderly stalls of vegetables and fruits on Ile-Saint-Louis at Aux Fruits de France to the booths of antiques and collectibles at Marché aux Puces de St. Ouen in Paris; to the flea markets in Kane County, Illinois; to the street vendors on New York's Lower East Side; merchants display their products to enhance their desirability. The merchants achieve order by presenting merchandise by beauty, classification, price, style, utility, or some other method. Because markets differ, retailers and vendors create their own signature styles of presentation to appeal to a variety of customers. The Farmer's Market in Cincinnati presents rows of fresh vegetables in ways that make them irresistible. The boutique Dior in Paris and Macy's in New York present merchandise stylishly to create a buying atmosphere for their target market. Every local, regional, or national retailer, regardless of size, budgets money and time for presentation. A retailer's first activity of the day is to attractively present merchandise.

When creating presentation styles, retailers and vendors are guided by locations of the merchandise and the customer's needs. For example, vegetables and fruits in Paris require one presentation style; Dior requires another.

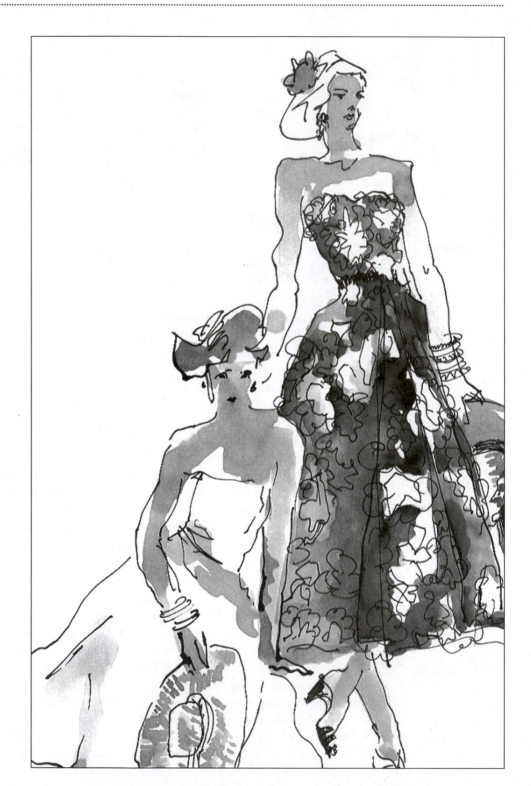

Presentation may

be based on beauty.

Nontraditional or flea market vendors may create presentation styles based on the simplest method, such as classifying by beauty, price, or identity. Sophisticated world boutiques and specialty stores use complex presentation methods to send buying messages to their power customers. Neiman-Marcus sells a diverse class of merchandise to a large and sophisticated customer segment which requires complex and multiple presentation styles. Neiman-Marcus's presentation produces an identity that is its signature.

Some retail managers erroneously think that presentation consists only of setting up the selling floor. However, presentation includes creating atmosphere, coordinating fashions, merchandising, and managing personnel. It requires understanding store fixtures, store operations, fine art, and design.

As you read each chapter, you will discover and learn about the fascinating business and profession of VM. Although each retailer requires applications, the basic methodologies of presentation are presented in this book.

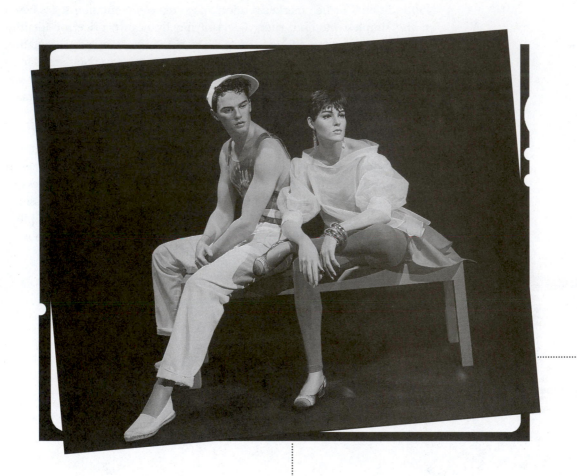
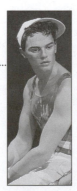
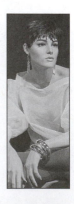

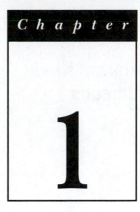
Image

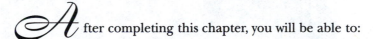

$\mathcal{A}$fter completing this chapter, you will be able to:

1. Discuss the importance of the right store image.

2. Discuss how the wrong image can be destructive.

3. Explain how image is created.

4. Describe the importance of the four *P*s of marketing and explain how a visual merchandiser (VM) implements them.

5. Describe how price affects image.

6. Understand how promotion establishes image.

7. Identify the target customer and understand how to create a comfortable shopping environment for the target customer through image.

Different Kinds of Images

Different consumers want and need different kinds of retailers. Some consumers' shopping needs are satisfied by **fashion-forward** (retailers who have an innovative fashion philosophy), high-ticket stores, while others' needs are satisfied by stores that concentrate on price and value. Hundreds of retailers ranging from car dealers to food markets to fashion apparel stores project many degrees of **social class** appeal with many looks and many styles. See Figure 1–1.

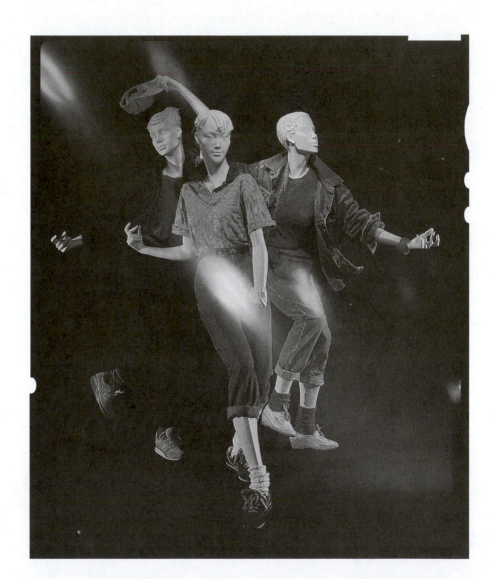

FIGURE 1–1

Some prefer the appeal of fashion–forward stores; others prefer price and value. (Courtesy of Adel Rootstein USA, New York.)

For example, Rolls-Royce dealers create an image of comfort and luxury in their showrooms, while other car dealers provide only minimal comfort. Neiman-Marcus strives for an **upper-class** image, while Wal-Mart seeks a broader **target market** realizing that its customers could feel out of place in a high-end environment such as a typical interior style of an expensive retail unit, such as Tiffany, New York. Wal-Mart and Sam's Club customers are interested primarily in price and product reliability. Consumers are interested in a product at any price level that is identified clearly by the prevailing world fashion. The many kinds of retail operations vary widely from national to regional levels and in classifications such as department, specialty, mass, and local.

A retailer distinguishes itself from its competitors by creating visual **image**. Customers respond to an overall image that projects the best possible selection, price, service, **quality**, style/fashion, advertising, **shopping environment**, region, and presentation.

Although each customer perceives image differently, a common image can be established within retail groups such as city stores, country stores, upper-end stores, lower-end stores, boutiques, and mass merchandisers. Retailers must know their customers before they can create and establish an image plan. Knowing customers is much easier for a small retailer because sales **associates** and managers are more in touch with their customers. Personnel in small stores see customers weekly, greet them by name, and engage them in light conversation. These activities enable associates to know the customers' needs and wants. Each retailer must have a distinct presence to showcase its name, and serve as a means of keeping its recognition alive.

A retailer's employees creates its **internal image. External image** is created by location, merchandise, architecture, design, interiors, **advertising**, signage, and promotional activities. The **visual merchandiser (VM)** creates the store's look, which is reinforced by great advertisements quality merchandise, special promotions, and the friendly smiles of the sales associates. All departments should project and maintain a consistent image because customers are irritated by an uneven image. A store with a stylish interior selling mediocre merchandise creates a jarring effect, as does a store that runs ordinary ads with fashion-forward merchandise.

The VM plays a key role in creating an exciting shopping interior and exciting displays and in presenting merchandise in a knock-dead style. The VM sets the knock-dead mood for the customer and the merchandise. See Figure 1–2.

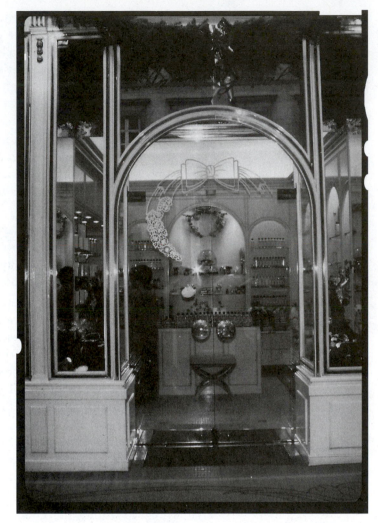

FIGURE 1–2

The merchandise

and customer are

in harmony at

A. Geautal perfumes,

Paris, France.

The Four *P*s
of Marketing

Successful strategies include the four *P*s of marketing: place, product, price, and promotion. As a key player on the retailing team, the VM is involved in each of these strategies. We will review them one by one.

PLACE

Place is defined as location, facilities, size, and **layout**. It is the key strategy for which VMs are responsible. The VM primarily focuses on place, but product, price, and promotion also help fulfill the VM's strategies. The VM's responsibilities include presenting all of the merchandise and creating a pleasant shopping environment for the customer. K-Mart, Wal-Mart, and Sam's Club focus on impulse shoppers.

PRODUCT

Product refers to the merchandise carried by the store. The VM's responsibilities here include how and where to present all of the merchandise. "You can't be all things to all people" is an old but true saying. It applies to those retailers who confuse customers and employees with an array of assorted merchandise representing too many price points, divergent lifestyles, and widely differing social needs. Consumers are turned away by merchandise classifications that do not interest them. Therefore, a narrow merchandising plan can be beneficial. As an example, magazines, a narrow merchandise classification, are positioned next to the cash register point of sale (POS) in supermarkets for impulse sales. The VM develops special display racks and chooses their locations with the merchandise manager (MM). Target positions, merchandise locations where product is presented to generate large sales increases, and loss leaders are often placed next to high-priced goods with the expectation that the customer will trade up. **Loss leaders** are brand-name products that are advertised at low, low prices, often at wholesale prices, to encourage impulse buying.

Vast merchandise assortments make promotion difficult because it is costly and hard to focus on many categories at once. A store's size can only comfortably accommodate so much merchandise. Therefore, adequate room should be appropriated for meaningful merchandise classifications and presentations.

PRICE

The **price** of a product determines the retailer's basic retail philosophy. Store design must match the price of the merchandise. Some designer looks fit $400 items and others fit $20 items. To concentrate on $20 items, one would design a low-end looking store with a well-organized mass-merchandising style interior. All merchandise would be roughly within this low-end price range. "Giveaway merchandise" would be displayed on end caps in bulk to lure customers. The sales associates would dress and present the merchandise with the low-end customer in mind. Displays, signs, colors, fixtures, promotions, advertising, and presentation would fit and project an image that reflects the mean price range of the store.

Selling is not the only road to company profits, however. Marketing research is needed to identify customers. When many retailers carry the same product, success often depends on image and presentation. The same fashion may sell successfully in one store and flop in another. Controlling this variable provides sales success. Discount stores rely on heavily advertised loss leaders to encourage impulse buying. The VM designs fixtures and locates merchandise on the floor for impact and makes signs that tell the customer about the products' value and benefit.

PROMOTION

Promotion includes selling, advertising, **special events,** publicity, and window and **interior displays**. Many store associates are involved in these promotional activities. Sales associates help present promotional merchandise and finalize sales generated by events. **Advertising managers** are involved in publicizing an event, describing it, and informing the public about its location and time. The VM utilizes window and specific interior displays to hype and reinforce the event. In a sense, all interior and window displays are promotional tools. The promotional department organizes all special events, by establishing times, locations, merchandise classifications, and celebrity guest participants. The VM creates the environment for each event.

For example, the food department in a large **flagship** department **store** might feature a celebrity chef one week. A celebrity designer might promote better dresses with a **trunk show** in the store, which is a show of designer clothes that moves from store to store and is sometimes accompanied by the designer or sales Vice President (VP) and a model. The designer salon in a department store might stage a fashion show, and the book department might hold an autographing session. Any special occasion that can herald merchandise can be the core of an event, as well as an image booster.

Store Design

Store design is a key factor in developing an image. The Limited may appeal to a young group, while Lerner's management creates an image that appeals to an older **market segment**. Although both stores are owned by the same conglomerate, each has a different market. To maximize sales, a retailer must understand its design philosophy completely and supply an image that satisfies its market segment's social needs. **Social needs** are concerns about love, friendship, image, group attitudes, status, esteem, and lifestyle. Price, style, and age are additional social needs; others include gender and emotion. See Figures 1–3A and 1–3B.

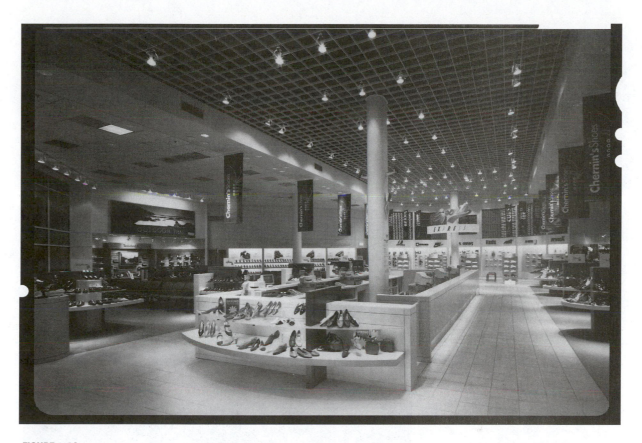

FIGURE 1–3A

A vivid price, style, and

sexy image is established

by this presentation

at Chennion Shoes.

(Courtesy of Charles

Sparks + Company,

Westchester, IL.)

Department stores sell 80 percent of their men's apparel to women buying for men. Stores in malls that cater to young men, however, sell 80 percent of their men's apparel to men. Young men prefer buying their own apparel. They want to select their own styles and are concerned about correct fit. Young men also prefer the accessibility of stores in malls. A store's image must therefore be created to satisfy the emotional needs of young men. That image includes bright colors, active lighting, and vivid graphics. Remember, however, that in time this young men's market will change and so must the store's image.

It would be difficult to attract customers to a Wal-Mart store that looked like Bloomingdale's. A VM must not confuse the customer's perception of the store. It takes years of external and internal image building to get a store's image right. These image-building activities are planned and implemented by the store staff and consultants. New management teams who guess at and then implement image development, instead of doing their homework, can destroy a business in a year or two by projecting the wrong image.

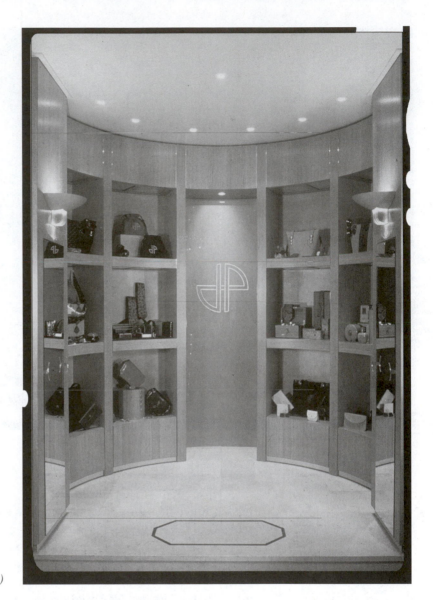

FIGURE 1–3B

Specific emotional

needs are satisfied by

this boutique interior.

(Courtesy of Patou

Boutique, Paris, France.)

Neiman-Marcus stores are identified by specific architecture that consists of deluxe building materials and design—marble, brass, exotic woods, luxury textiles, complicated color **palettes**, and great detail—and can be spotted easily from across a parking lot. Mass merchants, on the other hand, use plastic, chrome, formica that resembles marble, simple color palettes, and little detail to construct their buildings. Most of their building materials have a basic criterion—they must be maintenance free.

Window Displays

Quality design, **mannequins**, and merchandise in **window displays** signal class. Class stores, **regional** or local, always present the newest international fashions and are enhanced with the most current **decorative elements**. Any signage in the window displays is discreet and is integrated into the window presentation. There is complete unity of purpose and appearance. See Figure 1–4.

Creative VMs can design and produce looks that range in appeal to consumers at both the low end or at the upper end buying range. They must constantly control their efforts to produce displays and environment that fit the store's image. Their design criteria must be finely tuned to fulfill the social needs of their target customers.

FIGURE 1–4

Integration of style and appearance is a decorative goal. (Courtesy of Saberny, Paris, France.)

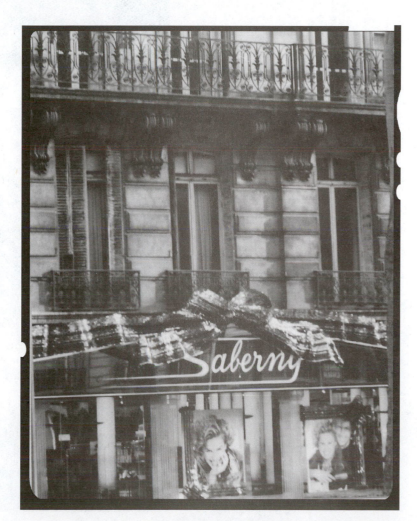

Store management should have a clear business philosophy about marketing to two kinds of target customers: current customers and potential customers. Busy shoppers sail through malls, glancing quickly at displays and storefronts and evaluating appearance and image to determine which stores to enter. A store's appearance must signal its point clearly and quickly. If it does not, customers keep on walking—and looking—in search of their idea of the perfect place to shop. See Figure 1–5.

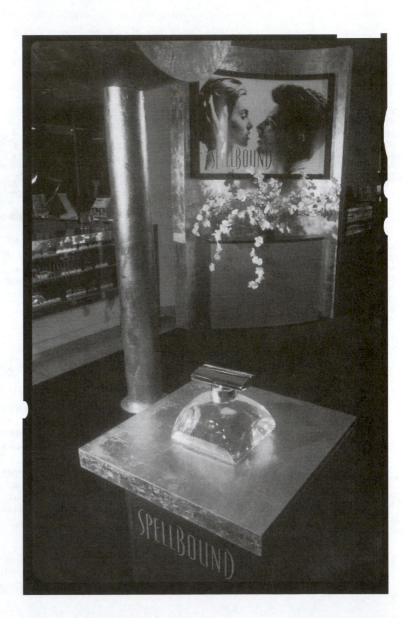

FIGURE 1–5

Busy customers glance quickly at displays—make sure yours invite a second glance. (Courtesy of Niedermaier Store Design, Chicago IL.)

Interior Displays

Most customers would not feel comfortable buying fine fashion jewelry in a store with an interior that looks like a tire store. Some products may look out of place in an environment where there is disregard for the fixtures and the atmosphere necessary to present such merchandise.

There are looks that the customer wants, and others that the merchandise requires. The VMs who balance these looks can create strong sales increases. See Figure 1–6.

Many **vendors** and designers who do **licensing**, franchise, and exclusive agreements look carefully at stores' appearances and images before signing deals with them. If a store's *appearance* is wrong, the merchandise will never be shipped. See Figure 1–7.

FIGURE 1–6

Image is so strong that one can identify the fashion and merchandising style from across the street. (Courtesy of Adel Rootstein USA, New York.)

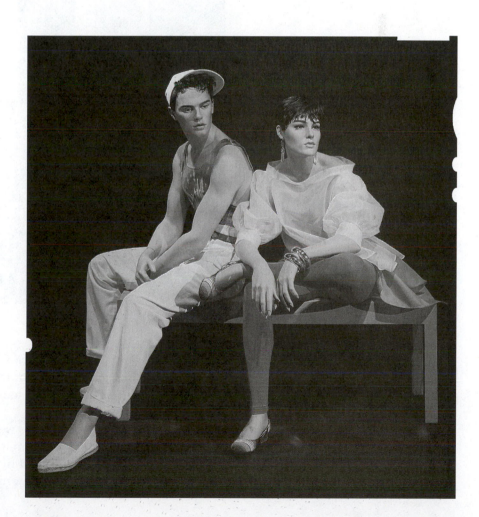

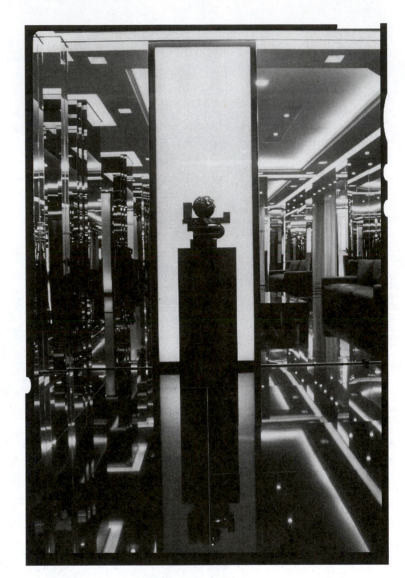

FIGURE 1–7

Most vendors would be very

happy to see their merchan-

dise presented in this manner.

(Courtesy of Louis Scherrer,

Paris, France.)

Image Changes

Change is an important factor to which retailers must respond. Retailers must constantly fine-tune their images to meet the social and economic factors that drive their customers.

Some retail leaders believe that consumers were most unpredictable after the 1960s. They felt that the traditional family had become a minority and they blamed poor sales performance and the demise of the department store on the decline of the family. This view may indicate the laziness or the short-term opinions of those retail gurus, but marketing is not easy. It is costly and somewhat new in fashion retailing. With each era, change is inevitable. Retailers just have to work harder at knowing and fulfilling their customers' needs. If department store giants satisfy consumer needs, they may regain a strong consumer base.

Because customers have formulated some perception of a store's image, and because their social behavior might be affected by any change, one should know the target market completely before creating a new image. Buyers must be careful when buying new product lines to be consistent and to choose products that meet their customers' needs. Generating new market data is extremely costly. To implement new strategies is even more costly.

Style

Top high-priced, **high-fashion** stores reflect an image established in Paris, New York, and other international centers. Highly visible celebrity designers are style leaders. Retailers that specialize in designer clothes can create images based on the designer's collections. Fashion magazines and the fashion press cover the designer's collections completely and reinforce the images to facilitate customer recognition. When discriminating, fashion-conscious customers see a designer's garment in a window, they recognize the designer instantly without signage or labels.

The designers have established the international criteria for style and image. The window displays of such high-fashion stores worldwide are always connected to fashion at the early stage of the fashion bell curve. The bell curve is shaped like a bell or mound that records the fashion life span. The beginning of the curve, the left side (lower left side), measures the beginning or acceptance period of the fashion cycle. The peak measures mass acceptance and the axis of the curve. The right side (down to the bottom right) of the curve measures the decline period of the fashion cycle. The stores that create images that fit the bell curve are marketing fashion beyond just selling.

Menswear Feature:
Projecting the Correct Image?

Following is an interview with Joe Silverberg, chief executive officer (CEO) and president of Bigsby & Kruthers, Inc., an upscale, upper-end group of eight Chicago men's clothing stores specializing in selling suits. Although men's suits are trending out or losing popularity, and many department stores are downsizing these parts of their businesses, Bigsby & Kruthers, Inc. has found a niche and continues to build its strong business. It has taken many years of focus to arrive at its successes.

Author: I see the use of alternate and abstract suit forms rather than mannequins in your flagship store. Is there a reason for it?

Joe: We wanted the displays to look soft, not too stiff. Clothing by Hugo Boss and Armani has an unstructured look, soft shoulders and fabrics—we wanted to focus on that. Our style of alternate mannequins and forms enables our VM to drape fabric in a soft way.

Author: There is a large amount of open space in your store, more so than in other men's stores. Some directors like congestion, believing clutter stimulates sales. In your clothing area, there are very wide aisles, perhaps three times as wide as the norm. How do you justify it?

Joe: By trial and error. We had it tighter and more congested. We decided to give the customer more room, and provide more space for the sales associate to work. This allowed more privacy and a relaxed atmosphere for both.

We didn't want to overpower or intimidate our customers. Open space, adequate seating, and an entertainment bar has become a strategy for store design and fixture placement.

Author: Men traditionally prefer shopping after work and on weekends. How do you attract customers at other times?

Joe: We schedule estate and financial planning seminars in the store. Business men as a group, such as a specific ad agency or law firm, are invited to in-store cocktail parties where new fashion trends and dressing hints are discussed. The cocktail parties provide our customers with an hour to relax after work, to socialize, learn about clothing, and focus on Bigsby & Kruthers.

We stage fashion shows and fine art exhibits. Since the historic Maxwell Street market is closing, we are planning an exhibit of early photographs of it.

Author: You have a vast collection of very notable fine art throughout the store. How do your customers feel about it?

Joe: Our customers love fine art. It's a part of their lifestyle. We will acquire more paintings and rotate them in our stores, providing an international, sophisticated, relaxed look. Fine art is such an important background for our merchandise, better than other props such as ribbons and flowers. Customers and sales associates love to talk about it, and on occasion we might sell a piece. Our customers like it, and that's important.

Author: How do you manage signs?

Joe: Signs should never interfere with the merchandise, displays, or interiors. We do not show price on our signs because we want the sales associate to explain the price, its relevance to the construction, designer, and fabric. Merchandise descriptions are important and are printed. We have a large store directory out front that is integrated architecturally. We will kick off a new season by displaying banners out front heralding the event. Other creative-looking banners are used to focus on specific designers and their looks, hung in-store in high traffic areas. They do not interfere with the clothing or the room design. The material, color, and design of banners conforms to our interiors more than traditional signs.

Author: Who are your target customers and what do they buy? Do they buy fashion-forward, occasional suiting, or a complete wardrobe? Your store projects a total look of style skewed to the businessman.

Joe: We are in the suit business. Our customers are creative individuals who are generally entrepreneurial—owning creative businesses such as ad agencies and architectural firms and publishing, graphics, and marketing businesses. They don't seem to be locked into corporate dress patterns and dress creatively. Every retail experience—buying, displays, atmosphere, promotions, events, and ads—is geared to the businessman. Their base income is about $35,000 and up, and they vary in age. We have been in business for some time, retaining our customers who have grown older. Their sons, our new customers, have less income. Therefore, we offer clothing in a variety of price categories.

When we buy European clothing, we buy very classic fabrics and avant-garde fabrics for our domestic suits. This base creates a very good business look that provides our customer with confidence when wearing our clothing.

Author: Do you feel that you project the correct store appearance and image?

Joe: We are very aware of our place in the market. We change our image, constantly providing comfortable, easy-fitting clothing. When I see changes, we address them. Change is our mentor.

Image is nurtured and communicated by our ads and marketing. Our sales associates are important—how they look, how they sound and communicate provides an image about our store. For example, when we installed a big-screen projection TV, our juice bar, the fine art and comfortable atmosphere, it all clicked. We noticed an upturn in sales and traffic.

Author: This updated, relaxed look really comes across. How many display associates do you have?

Joe: Twelve.

Author: Do you have display studios and storage space?

Joe: Yes. It's in a warehouse. The staff design props and make, assemble, and rehab them. We build props and buy them. Our studio has all the design materials, tools, and construction equipment necessary to create our displays. We have computer-driven sign machines.

Our VM covers shows and markets to keep up with new trends. He buys props from display vendors and commissions some designs from Niedermaier and other manufacturers.

We own 35 tie stores around the country called "The Knot Shop." They require a tremendous amount of presentation and display maintenance. There is constant change in both the windows and the fixtures.

Author: How often do you change your displays at Bigsby & Kruthers?

Joe: Every two weeks.

CASE STUDY: "NAMELESS" VERSUS "THE OTHER"

A large Midwestern department store chain, in business for over 110 years, targeted an upscale segment of the market. We will call the store "Nameless." Its main competitor (we will call it "Other") had captured most of the **middle-class** business by catering to its social needs. Each store understood and maintained its market segment and enjoyed continued moderate increases in sales.

Nameless was reorganized by a new California team in the late 1970s. Its market research showed that more of the region's customers were middle class than upscale. To increase sales and gain market share, the new management at Nameless aggressively targeted that middle-class shopper without understanding the middle class's preference for the competitor, Other.

As change at Nameless proceeded, its upscale customers saw the store's appearance begin to deteriorate. Sale-dump tables appeared in the aisles, large bold banners heralded "Super Savings," and price promotional advertisements appeared. The upper-end customers soon abandoned Nameless because their social needs were no longer being met. The Nameless management team had sacrificed its carriage trade or upper-end customer. Customers saw a confused appearance and image that could not completely satisfy all of the needs for any market. Nameless could not penetrate its desired middle-class market. Buyers at Nameless started to say, "We can't sell a thing anymore unless it's on sale."

After six years the California team at Nameless was terminated, leaving surviving management with a confused idea about its remaining target market. Customers sensed this, and sales at Nameless declined further. Reestablishing the store's lost image will take years. Recently an upscale Midwestern retail giant bought the Nameless chain and is trying hard to regain a positive upscale image. Other continued to do business with its established market, never losing market share.

CASE STUDY: HALLE'S

I traveled to a suburb of a city in Northern Ohio to look at a new chain store whose base was Cleveland. The interior was all glass, reflective metals, flashing lights, and loud disco music. The look certainly fit the era and was well designed. But as I looked around, I saw middle-aged shoppers, suburbanites dressed in Harris tweeds, Glen plaids, and casual "country" clothes. Customers seemed to cower under the store's visual barrage. Sales were poor—the result of executing a good idea in the wrong place with the wrong target market. This store could have been a jewel in New York City, Los Angeles, or Chicago.

DISCUSSION QUESTIONS

1. Is Sears projecting the correct image for its customers?

2. Should a Saks Fifth Avenue type of image be used in a Sears display window? Describe the customers' possible reaction, and the impact it would have on sales.

3. It takes years to build a retail image. How quickly can poor marketing strategies reverse it?

4. Explain why merchandising and presentation plans must agree to create the right image.

5. Explain how you would satisfy your customers' social needs.

6. What is the promotional role in image creation?

7. Explain how store design can establish image.

8. Why is image important?

9. Who is involved in image creation?

CHAPTER PROJECT

Project Objective: To identify a specific retailer's image.

Project Instructions:

1. Visit one successful retailer and determine its target market. Determine what appearance or image the retailer has created to satisfy its customers' needs. The local chamber of commerce or small business administration can help you locate successful retailers. Also, act on your fashion sense to locate some.

2. Visit a failing retailer and determine what image/appearance has failed to satisfy its customers' needs.

3. Write a two-page paper expressing your opinion of the image and appearance of both stores (right or wrong) and indicate how each can improve. (Note: Including simple sketches will enhance your paper and improve your grade.)

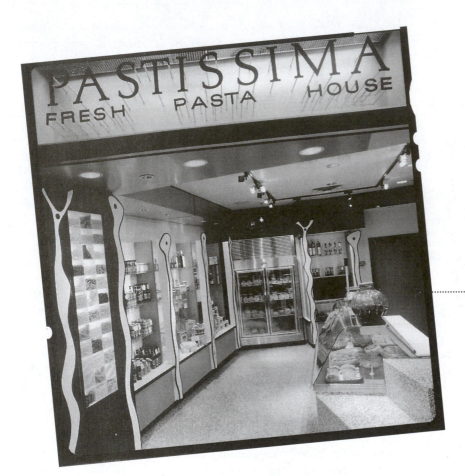

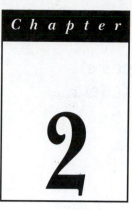

Stores

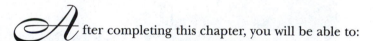

*A*fter completing this chapter, you will be able to:

1. Recognize many types of retailers.

2. Understand the display needs of each type of retailer.

3. Discuss the kind of merchandise each retailer sells.

4. Understand the presentation style of convenience stores.

5. Explain how upper-end fashion stores present merchandise.

6. Understand mass merchandise presentation.

7. Describe how location affects store design.

Types of Retailers

Many different kinds of stores in different locations appeal to consumers' varying social and emotional needs. Some customers shop upper end at Neiman-Marcus for ego satisfaction, while others are more comfortable budget shopping at Wal-Mart. Neiman-Marcus and Wal-Mart obviously attract customers of different income levels and social classes. However, wealth and class may not go together. Some wealthy consumers prefer shopping at JC Penney for everyday apparel and at Saks Fifth Avenue for special-occasion apparel.

A store must match its interior decor and presentation to its customers' wants and needs. Getting it wrong can repel customers and spell financial failure. See Figure 2–1.

Customers' preferences determine a store's location. Despite parking hassles, some shoppers prefer the large selections available at big downtown

FIGURE 2–1

Store design must match interior decor and presentation with target customers. (Courtesy of Kubala Washatko Architects, Inc., Cedarburg, WI, store, and Goldi at Bloomingdale's Chicago, IL. Photo: Mark Heffran.)

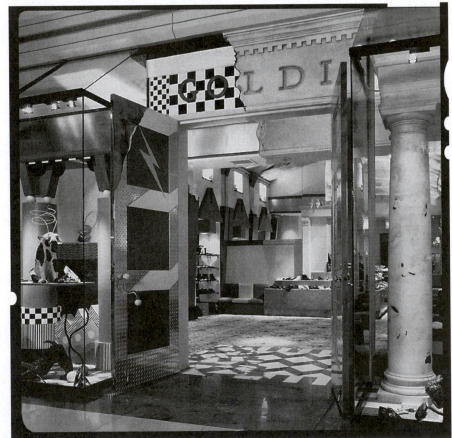

department stores. Others prefer convenience stores because they like fast, in-and-out shopping and easy parking.

Stores are in strip malls and regional malls, on neighborhood streets, or in downtown centers. Each type of store has its own display style based on satisfying its customers' social, physiological, and psychological needs.

Store decor and presentation should match location. Some city stores have a sophisticated look (Saks Fifth Avenue); some **country stores** have a casual look. Stores on Chicago's Michigan Avenue will use interior color palettes and decorative materials that differ from stores in Beverly Hills.

The benefits of a product can determine when and where a customer will shop. Some customers will buy any brand as long as it is easily accessible (Walgreen's, a midwest drugstore chain). Others compare products and prices and prefer to choose from large assortments (Target, a midwest discount store chain owned by Dayton Hudson). Many customers shop for prestige, searching for recognizable labels, brand recognition, and products that have definite high-fashion ties. Fashion-conscious customers shop earlier in the season than maintenance shoppers or shoppers who buy only when the need arises. As a result, Wal-Mart presents new seasonal fashion apparel later than Saks.

Successful retailers are aware of and satisfy shoppers' expectations in decor and presentation. All VMs must know their products well and know their target customers' wants and needs. Disappointing a customer is negative retailing.

DEPARTMENT STORES

Because of their size, department stores offer all classes of merchandise, from home furnishings to moderate and high-fashion apparel. There are large selections of merchandise in each class with varying prices and assorted brand names. In the trade, department stores are known as the "shopping store group." The department store's floor plan, **fixture arrangement** and design, interior decor, and presentation should all appeal to this "shopping type" customer. The **atmosphere** in department stores tends to be complex and intricate because the merchandise presentation must represent a large variety of categories, prices, and styles. See Figure 2–2.

Most department stores focus on the middle-class customer. Economic trends show that the middle-class consumer is disappearing and that perhaps a polarized society will emerge. In 1992, successful stores were those at the lower end, such as Wal-Mart and K-Mart, and those at the upper end, such as Neiman-Marcus and Cartier. Each end's image and shopping environment targeted a different clientele.

FIGURE 2–2

Home store merchandise, a popular classification, is presented at Younkers in a clear, well-designed, and organized manner. (Courtesy of Schaffer Associates, Inc., Oakbrook Terrace, IL store. Younkers, Omaha, NE. Photo: Bob Briskey.)

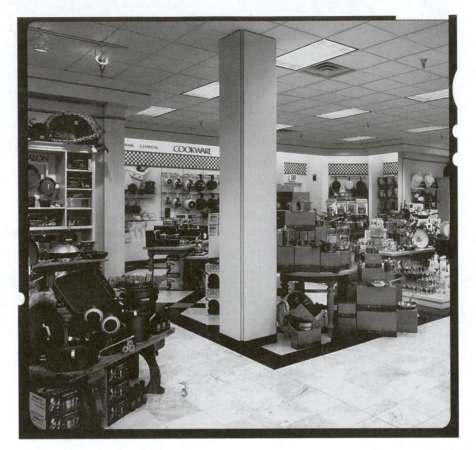

Although economic trends are unpredictable, as the manager, the VM should consider key economic indicators to provide the design leadership needed to prevent department stores from failing. When the economy is negative for retail groups, greater focus and effort should be practiced in advertising, VM, and promotions.

Department stores are controlled by central management from the flagship store, not from the outlying units, called **branch stores**. Department stores can be huge national **chain stores** (Sears) or regional chain stores (Florida's Burdine's). Their selling **price points** range from mid to high level. The stores can be mass retail and general merchandise chains. Sears, for example, is the largest general merchandise chain and sells lower- to middle-price points just under Wal-Mart. Many nationally known department stores are part of conglomerates. For example, Marshall Field's is a division of its parent, Dayton Hudson.

SPECIALTY STORES

Specialty stores may be national chains, such as the upper-end Saks Fifth Avenue, or small regional chains, such as Chicago's Mark Shale. Together these stores constitute a huge retail force. They specialize in narrow classes of merchandise in terms of product, price, brand names, fashion, style, gender, and age. They do not attempt to be all things to all people. They are small by design and do not stock huge varieties and quantities of merchandise. Their goal is to present singular items instead of a vast array of assorted goods.

UPPER-END STORES

Upper-end stores such as Neiman-Marcus, Tiffany, F. A. O. Schwartz, and Henri Bendel carry high-priced merchandise and target the discriminating customer, a tiny and rarified market. These stores aim to create a snobbish atmosphere to appeal to affluent shoppers. They ignore the middle- or lower-end shopper who would probably feel out of place or be offended by high price points. The VM should maintain and develop a look for these stores to match the customer base.

APPAREL CHAINS

Specialty apparel chains include, among hundreds of others, The Limited, Lerner's, Oak Tree, and Chess King. These stores are managed from a central headquarters and are generally located in regional malls. (See next section.) They have a narrow specialty, being restricted in terms of age, gender, price, and style. These stores are designed to help the consumer locate wanted items.

BOUTIQUES

Stores that specialize in handcrafted, one-of-a-kind, high-priced items are called boutiques. **Boutiques** are found everywhere. Their merchandise ranges from designer clothes by Armani to gourmet food, cookware, fashion jewelry, accessories, and leather goods. A boutique's interior may resemble a gallery, or it may be wonderfully cozy and filled with handcrafted art items and apparel.

DISCOUNT STORES

Discount stores are often located in strip malls. (See next section.) Their large assortments of merchandise almost equal those found in department stores and general merchandise chains. Their pricing is competitive, their atmosphere is no-frills, and their prepackaged and ready-to-go merchandise is presented so that customers can readily find what they are looking for. Discount store customers are impulse buyers and love bulk buys.

Locations of Retailers

MALLS

Numerous **regional malls** with dozens of themes are designed to specialize in a variety of fashion and price images. Most are safe places to shop. To avoid shoppers' boredom, the direction of the aisles changes about every sixty feet. The lighting, decor, background music, temperature, and botanical arrangements of regional malls are designed to please the broadest customer base. In a sense, malls are like an encapsulated Main Street, U.S.A. The stores are selected for commonalities or a similar customer base and compete in subtle ways.

Malls provide a universally accepted environment. Presentation styles and techniques of stores generally repeat and echo one another, satisfying the social and psychological needs of their clientele. Groupings of similar retailers, are by plan, enabling customers to experience one-stop shopping. In addition, window displays or presentations up front in see-through mall stores are similar; all of the stores in each class have similar formula presentations.

Most apparel stores show three or four garments adequately on mannequins or abstract **apparel forms**. Store managers, whose task it is to present the merchandise, frequently crowd windows with too many items or with unrelated products. Crowding makes establishing a theme difficult and results in a **confused look**. These stores skimp on funds to buy props that might help create a theme, and they do not budget for a VM staff to produce displays.

Retailers build mall traffic and increase store sales when their staffs create exciting, fashionable windows with special focuses. Customers spend considerable time in malls, so they should be exposed to striking display windows. Shopping environments are important to these customers. Stores with limited budgets should focus on presenting merchandise clearly and simply. Props are not always necessary. If props are needed, however, use items that help tell the story clearly, such as a beach ball from the toy department with a swimwear display from the sportswear department or wine books from the book department with a wine display from the liquor department. This is often called cross merchandising. No display is more spectacular up front in fashion stores than well-dressed and accessorized mannequins in current fashions.

Except for the anchor stores (see the following section), most mall stores are small, with only about 1,300 to 2,000 square feet. They are staffed on the average with three or four full-time associates who perform all of the store's tasks, including display. Corporate VM vice presidents (VM-VPs) provide presentation leadership, management, and control for the entire chain. Regional VMs report to the corporate VM-VP. The regional VMs travel from store to store providing display direction. They frequently use **plannograms** and floor plans to assist in communicating about and directing location of merchandise, fixtures, presentation, and display styles.

When price is their only specialty, retailers hype sales and promotion in their windows in a variety of ways. They frequently use endless kinds of signage and an overabundance of merchandise. This, in turn, often forces customers to make many choices for which they are unprepared. Clutter puts off customers.

ANCHOR STORES

Mall **anchor stores** of assorted sizes, namely chain department or chain general merchandise stores, maintain in-store VMs who are equipped to create wonderful windows. In anchor stores, budgets are adequate for staffing, buying props, and producing displays, and space is provided for VM workrooms.

Although window displays inside malls receive a lot of attention, parking lot display windows are often neglected and uninspiring. As a result, parking lot displays inadequately project the store's image. The VM's efforts are often misdirected into piling up and presenting in-store merchandise. Many stores neglect the wonderful marketing tool that a window presentation offers. In addition to showcasing merchandise, store display windows are frequently designed to allow the customer to see the store's interior. Displays backed by interior clutter look anemic. Often customers cannot see beyond the first ten feet of glass anyway. Many stores look closed as a result of clutter in the window and poor lighting.

OPEN REGIONAL MALLS

Stores grouped by style in open regional malls may vary more than those in closed malls with a common roof. Common specialties enable many retailers to attract specific audiences. Groups of price shoppers are attracted to malls where stores feature promotions. On the other hand, fashion-forward customers are attracted to high-end fashion malls, such as Oakbrook Mall near Chicago. Windows with traditional proscenia and lighting are the norm and have the potential for being exciting and creative. Some display windows are filled with clutter while others stylishly present merchandise. Anchor stores in open regional malls generally employ permanent VM staff, have adequate budgets and workspace, and are able to maintain exciting relevant presentations.

STRIP MALLS

Customers are provided easy access in **strip malls**. Low rents attract the national discount chains that anchor them. Many local merchants group with the discount chains for shopping convenience. **Supermarkets** and service units such as Price Chopper in the Northeast and Safeway on the West Coast are also often included. Some stores have windows displaying large assortments of merchandise (Walgreen's), while others use their display windows only for promotional and sale signs (supermarkets).

DOWNTOWN CITY CENTERS

Downtown locations draw a diverse range of customers. Flagship department stores are usually located downtown. The main floor of downtown centers enables retailers to have classic display windows. Many of these retail centers have experienced a rebirth because bored suburbanites have moved back to the city and the singles market has grown. Inner-city renewal in Cleveland, Ohio, and Pittsburgh, Pennsylvania, are examples of city rebirth attracting and retaining updated retailers.

INNER-CITY STORES

Large inner-city department and specialty stores provide adequate budgets and staff to create wonderful presentations. Often these stores are showcases for their products. City activities, including entertainment, clusters of restaurants, trendy bars, galleries, theaters, and elegant stores, attract downtown window shoppers and tourists long after closing hours. This is a perfect audience for fabulous display windows.

Presentation in Different Types of Retail Stores

PRESENTATION IN CONVENIENCE STORES

Convenience stores attract customers who refuse to spend much time shopping and customers who need staple, impulse, or emergency items as in White Hen Pantry located in the Midwest. As a result, products in convenience stores must be displayed in highly visible groups that are located easily and are placed at appropriate heights. Fixtures should be arranged in clean **grids** with uncluttered aisles. Highly decorative, haphazard fixturing creates clutter. Neutral colors provide excellent backgrounds for displaying products. Display is more important than merely creating stylish moods.

Merchandise signs in convenience stores must be readable and to the point. Vague presentation or signage discourage customers. Clear, direct lighting is a must for excellent visibility.

Most often situated in accessible strip malls, convenience stores should accommodate customers with a fast in-and-out, a clean uncluttered entry, and easy, adequate parking. Convenience store display windows are not intended for the browsing customer. Therefore, they should be designed to accommodate promotional sign sheets of at least 22 inches x 28 inches for products that need maximum exposure.

Price is usually not a factor for the convenience-store customer, so many convenience stores do not carry products traditionally sought by price-comparison shoppers (White Hen Pantry). For example, convenience stores usually do not carry apparel that is specially selected by color, texture, and pattern, although they do often sell hosiery, inexpensive jewelry, bandannas, and sunglasses. Food, magazines, and simple health-care items are also stocked. These products require fixturing that is easily maintained and cleaned.

The majority of the presentation budget in a convenience store is for signage and fixture replacement. Presentation should support convenience shopping styles and behavior.

PRESENTATION IN SPECIALTY STORES

Specialty stores require different presentation styles, depending on their locations and specialties. Because these stores specialize, their products should be presented with clarity. See Figure 2–3.

Specialty fashion stores may become fashion leaders with windows that shadow current international fashions or **luxe** versions of streetwear. The appearance of specialty store interiors is important because fashion customers are aware of current home fashions and interior-design trends.

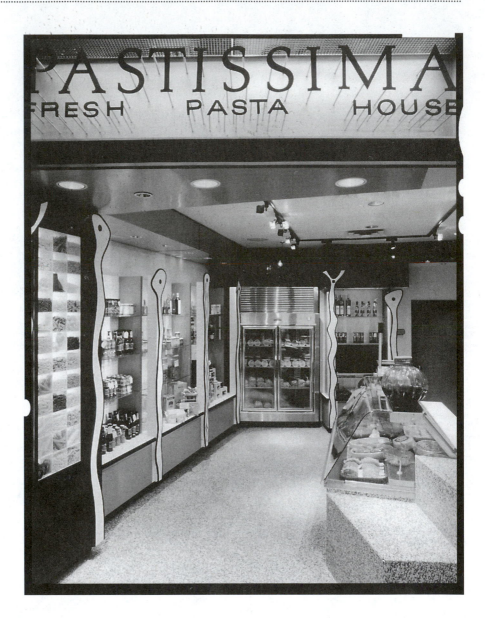

FIGURE 2–3

Specialty stores should present their merchandise in a unique way, matching their specialty. (Courtesy of Hirschberg Design, CA.)

They expect the walls to be painted in the hottest fashion colors as seen in the magazine *Southern Interiors* and the presentations to be in vogue, matching the latest apparel. The coupling of merchandise and presentation produces specific moods that satisfy a consumer's expectations and create the perfect harmony. The right combination of merchandising and presentation generates additional store **traffic** and sales.

Other specialty stores satisfy utility needs only. These **discount special-ty stores** focus less on high fashion and more on price and specialty classi-fications such as apparel, accessories, hard goods, such as merchandise sold in the home furnishing department, food, and home goods.

PRESENTATION IN DEPARTMENT STORES

Since the late 1970s, some department stores have become more ori-ented to self-service. In an effort to curb costs, many elegant department stores such as Macy's, Lord and Taylor, and Marshall Field's, have forgone sales service. As a result, these elegant stores require a VM and staff to care-fully present all merchandise in the most glamorous manner possible. The task for the VM, merchandisers, and store designers is to make the store as self-service oriented as possible, yet maintain an exclusive look. Self-service demands that fixtures are arranged on the floor in orderly rows from left to right and front to back to create an arrangement that looks like a grid. Displaying merchandise by class and color with clear signage enhances this orderly presentation.

Fixtures have evolved to help retailers achieve maximum merchandise exposure. Although the merchandise in high-end, self-service stores is placed similarly to merchandise in discount merchandise stores, the fix-tures, interior decor, and surfaces in high-end stores are luxurious. Many high-end department stores that practice self-service may want to produce luxe, glamorous looks, but the cold and impersonal sterile look that self-service often creates may result in creating a negative shopping environ-ment, and losing valued customers.

UPPER-END DEPARTMENT STORES. Although many elegant department stores have less sales help, other upper-end department stores provide adequate sales help, allowing their VMs to present merchandise in lifestyle groups with elegant mixes and styles. These stores tend to be fash-ionable and their VMs tend to become trendsetters. Because these stores fit the "shopping store" classification that encourages customers to stay and shop, as opposed to the "destination store" label that appeals to customers who are shopping for specific items only, the VM's task is to present excit-ing windows and marvelous interior displays with exciting fashion mer-chandise propped with trendy decorative elements and themes. Sales asso-ciates are required to help the customer choose merchandise and then close the sale. See Figure 2–4.

FIGURE 2–4

Upper-end department stores

provide the VM with substantial

budgets and staff to present their

exciting merchandise.

(Courtesy of Schafer Associates,

Inc., Oakbrook Terrace, IL store.

Younkers, Omaha, NE.

Photo: Bob Briskey.)

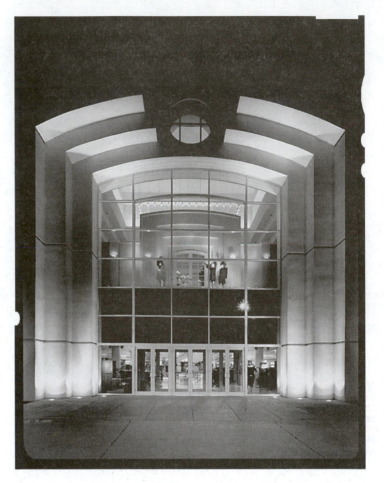

Upper-end department stores tend to know their target customers well and use every marketing technique to satisfy their customers' needs and wants. Customers with ego needs shop for prestige products and like to shop at upper-end retailers who present one or two garments interestingly instead of at retailers who present large quantities of the same merchandise en masse as pure self-service **units**.

MERCHANDISE GROUPS.   In all stores, great care is given to the location of merchandise groups. Floor plans assist the staff in selecting space for the groups. To group merchandise, VMs first refer to the architectural drawings of the building and draw a floor plan (scaled at 1/4 inch to 1 foot). They then sketch in each merchandise class on the plan. Later, the plan is refined by focusing on detail and on the location of merchandise subclassifications. The VMs select a general area for women's apparel, areas for better dresses, an area for sportswear "A" and "B," and so on.

Because women's apparel represents over 50 percent of the department store's sales volume, it should have adequate space and be situated in high-traffic areas—namely near escalators, main traffic aisles, and parking-lot entrances.

Apparel, accessories, cosmetics, and shoes are considered main floor classifications. Slow movers, on the other hand, including furniture, bedding, and home store classifications, are positioned in secondary locations on other floors. Better results are obtained if the space is studied to determine the sales per square foot. To determine the sales per square foot for each group, divide the sales for each group into the square feet for each group. Then compare the results between groups. Women's sportswear might produce $250 per square foot, while some home store classifications might yield only $75. Determine which group needs more or less space for its business and whether it needs high-traffic exposure.

The life cycle of a fashion or product determines whether it should be placed in the department's front or middle section. New product launches that sell well need aisle space for high-traffic exposure, visibility, and impact, and perhaps may even be placed on a clothing form or mannequin. As products reach a fashion cycle's plateau, valuable promotion space may not be necessary. In the final fashion cycle, products are reduced for clearance. Because they do not need high promotional locations, they are moved to the rear of the department and hung en masse on large rounders and hang bars. Throughout the cycle, the VM must make the merchandise irresistible, fascinating, and easy to locate. In short, the VM must make the merchandise saleable.

DEPARTMENT STORE STAFF.   The department store groups provide abundant budgets for presentation purposes, buying needs, prop production, decorative element purchases, and support of an array of VM activities. In addition, adequate space is provided for the VM's studio and workroom to execute displays. The staff (management, designers, trimmers, support groups, and consultants) that report to the corporate VM-VP are trained to carry out the complex store presentation requirements.

The VM spends much time coordinating display activities with store groups, including merchandising staff such as buyers, the fashion group, the advertising department, the special events department, the marketing group, and support staff.

The VM and staff alone cannot accomplish all the presentation activities that enhance sales. To achieve this goal, they must work with other store groups as a team.

Communicating with buyers helps a VM decide which special props to buy to enhance new purchases. It also helps the VM determine the arrival time of the purchases and when to present them. Buyers who select vendors, budget, buy, add price, manage markup and markdown, request promotion and ads, order signs, order checks, and pay invoices, know about their purchases six months in advance, which enables the VM (while at the market) to buy supportive props and special fixtures to house the new products. VMs who are involved in store planning must allocate additional space for new shops or for the expansion required by the new merchandise groups. As mentioned earlier, VMs create floor plans drawn to scale to guide the associates in merchandise location.

A VM's association with the fashion group helps determine fashion display **tie-ins** for the upcoming seasonal merchandise. The fashion group provides the latest fashion news and information which enables the VM to focus on new apparel, fashion colors, silhouette, texture, and other details. The interior colors and props should echo these new fashion apparel trends.

The advertising department provides the VM with schedules of the season's advertisements so that tie-in displays can be created. Advertising schedules help the VM plan sign production and the time to buy display props to support advertising campaigns.

The special events department informs the VM about the arrival of guest designers and celebrities and about the possibilities of creating special displays that will herald their coming. Special city and community tie-ins are coordinated through special events.

The marketing group helps the VM determine special display styles necessary for the store's target customer and helps determine retail activities that will be visually pleasant. Marketing identifies expectations of specific groups, which empowers the VM to satisfy those expectations through presentation.

The support staff in department and specialty stores (such as personnel, payroll, accounts payable, receiving, transportation, finance) is quite large and ready to assist the VM in budgeting, accounts payable, receivables, shipping, storage, tailoring, housekeeping, maintenance, security, and human resources.

PRESENTATION IN MASS RETAIL STORES

Mass retailers have many presentation activities in common with department stores, general department stores, and discount chain stores.

The most common activity is product presentation that generates sales in a selling environment to meet the needs and wants of target customers. Mass retail is the largest retail group because its targets are middle- and lower-income consumers.

The mass retail store may stock a large quantity of bulk merchandise, piled high in orderly grid arrangements in boxes with high visibility. In contrast, the department store, with the exception of the home store, presents a lesser volume of merchandise.

In discount stores, one sample product is displayed out of the box adjacent to the stacks of boxed merchandise. Clearly readable merchandise signs identify the classifications and indicate price and other relevant product features. Presenting loss leaders is important to lure customers to specific store locations.

On the other hand, department stores present fewer groups of products with merchandise signs, supportive accessory groups, and props. Department stores have less of a utility look than mass retailers and instead emphasize glamour and style. Although department stores tend more and more towards self-service, the look is not strongly emphasized. Self-service in many department stores generates customer confusion as to whether to pick the product up and look for a point of sale (POS) or to wait for sales help. Management knows that customer service creates additional sales and often designates capital for expenses other than sales staff.

Mass retailers use simple lighting techniques less often to create atmosphere than to prevent accidents, make signs and box flaps readable, and illuminate merchandise for inspection by shoppers.

Mass retailers also use more clothing forms than mannequins. They use an array of merchandise, self-service floor fixtures, and countertop displayers. Showcases, fixtures, shelving units, displayers, and decorative elements in mass retail stores are spartan and are built for durability, low cost, flexibility, and minimal maintenance.

Plannograms and floor plans help the staff locate, arrange, and present merchandise. The plans are designed and drafted in 1/2 or 1/4 scale by corporate VMs in central offices. In-house VMs guide the store associates in executing these plans.

The **floor plan** is a tool to help the planner visualize the entire store and determine appropriate locations for merchandise. Sensible merchandise locations are based on adjacencies. Placing women's accessories next to apparel is effective, for example, but putting men's underwear next to better dresses is not.

Many mass retailers use a VM team that moves from store to store in a region to "blitz" each store. A "blitz" is a group activity that prepares floor changes that create order, proper sales environments for the store's merchandise, and presentation of new arrivals.

The corporate chain of command and staff in a mass retail store is similar to that of a department store (outlined previously), but emphasis on the job varies. For example, a department store system might place less emphasis on regional VMs than mass retailers. This determination is based on how each retailer conducts business.

PRESENTATION IN FOOD STORES

Supermarkets rely on self-service. They present 30,000 products with optimum visibility on fixtures that are cleaned and maintained easily in stores averaging 31,000 square feet. Unique mechanical requirements of the fixtures, such as cooling, freezing, warming, moisturizing, cooking, humidity control, and sanitizing, increase their cost.

Interior decor is installed on the ceilings of supermarkets because the floors are crowded with merchandise and customer activity. For the most part, supermarket decor is created by fashion **cornices**, colorful banners, light sculptures, decorative canopies, and **stylized** location signs. See Figure 2–5.

Store planning handles presentation and the staff manages presentation and signage. The supermarket's retail staff and outside vendors execute presentation guided by plannograms, memos, and floor plans. Supermarkets are constantly experiencing growth, remodeling, and fixture maintenance. These activities fully occupy store planning. New stores require the constant supervision of architects and installers who may not be employed by the retailer.

The supermarket's shelved, self-service fixtures are arranged in grids from the store's front to its back. Similar products are grouped together to help customers find them. All products should be placed within the customer's sight line. Items positioned too low or too high are out of the customer's view and sell slowly. Customers do not want to spend excessive amounts of time trying to locate a product in several different locations.

Checkout counters at the supermarket entrance force the customer to enter the store in a specific direction. Produce is often the first product that the customer sees in a supermarket. Fresh, artfully arranged produce presented on well-designed food furniture is refreshing. Following produce in the first aisle are the impulse items such as deli cheeses, luncheon meats, and breads. This arrangement enables convenience shoppers to select impulse items and leave the store quickly.

Meats and milk are placed at the back of the store, drawing customers to the back aisle in the hope that they will pick up items on the way. Promotional items are placed adjacent to the meat on the back aisle. Frozen foods, a lower customer priority, are in the last aisle. This design is based on impulse buying.

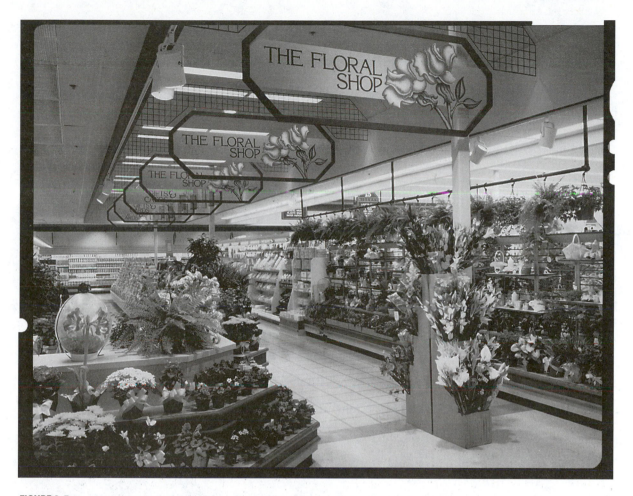

FIGURE 2–5

Interior decor in the form of banners is often at ceiling level because mass merchandise is on the floor. (Courtesy of Off The Wall Company, Telford, PA.)

End caps at the end of the long aisles are for highly promotional, super-savings items. End caps enable the supermarket staff to create maximum visibility for products pulled from stock. The merchandise is often a loss leader, a brand name priced far below market value.

As consumers change their diets, their food interests change. Meats may not be on the back aisle as the draw they once were, for example. Old locations and products might be replaced by new, hot merchandise classifications.

Supermarket associates are experimenting with cross merchandising, such as presenting wines with cheeses and pasta with Italian breads. Placing like items together creates additional impulse buying. At the supermarket Food Market Institute (FMI) trade show, an array of new counters, shelving units, and food furniture is shown to demonstrate new marketing directions. Retailers who resist change are likely to fail.

The supermarket makes an excellent lab where the VM learns about customer promotional and needs satisfaction, and presents the best example for a self-service atmosphere. A walk through a supermarket enables VM students to inspect the impact of good packaging and merchandise groupings. However, many supermarkets need to improve merchandise signage by imposing uniformity. Too many handwritten signs of assorted styles and colors are confusing.

Newspaper advertisements are excellent sales tools for grocers. The supermarket staff should ensure that advertised items are visible so that customers do not have to search for advertised products. Warm earth colors and neutrals highlighted with jewel tones make a great interior background for groceries.

DISCUSSION QUESTIONS

1. Why could economic predictions affect your VM career?

2. Why should store atmosphere satisfy consumers' psychological needs?

3. Discuss specialty stores and their display needs, types, and customers.

4. Describe the atmosphere discount chains need for successful selling.

5. Describe what customers anticipate when shopping.

6. Name some local and national stores that are fashion-forward and stylish.

CHAPTER PROJECT

Project Objective: Locating merchandise on the floor.

Project Instructions: (Choose One)
1. Draw a rough floor plan of the main floor of a branch unit of a local department store. Block all of the departments that are considered main floor departments and focus on providing adequate space in

traffic areas that fit the importance of the classification. Also consider correct merchandise adjacencies. Perhaps a local store will provide a general floor plan to be used as a model.

2. Draw a rough plannogram for a mall specialty store selling moderate juniors' apparel. Draw a rough plan for presenting sweaters and skirts in reds, yellows, and neutrals on a wall with waterfall face-outs, which are slant bars fastened to a wall or a T stand for presenting apparel with the garment's face to the customer.

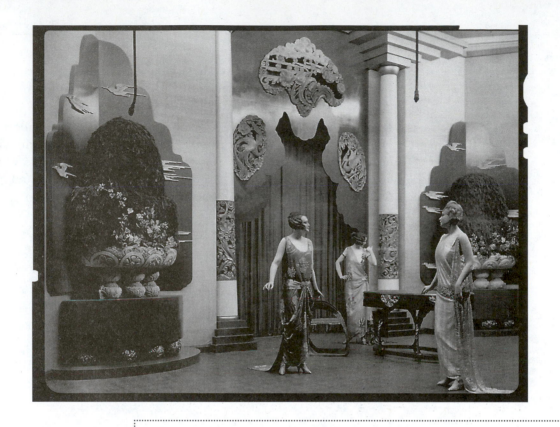

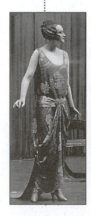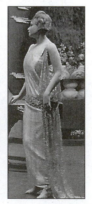

Fashion Merchandise Presentation— 1900-1992

*A*fter completing this chapter, you will be able to:

1. Identify at least eight VM superstars and describe their display styles.

2. Describe fashion and display development in New York City.

3. Describe Marshall Field's display history.

4. Describe Bloomingdale's display history.

5. Describe Macy's display history.

6. Name show people, socialites, and theater people who have influenced display style.

7. Understand how display has evolved from the early country store to the 1970s.

The American General Store — 1860s–1960s

In the early 1900s, every small town had a general store. These were usually one-room stores fronted by large windows to let in light and to display a wide assortment of merchandise. A potbellied stove usually dominated the store's central area, and the post office was at the rear. Generally, a door in the back, marked "Private," led to the store owner's living quarters.

Near the stove was the shoe department, with enough chairs for the area to double as a local meeting place. During the summer, the chairs were moved to the large shaded porch for gossip and talk about horses, hounds, crops, drinking, gambling, and so forth. See Figure 3–1.

Running a general store involved barter, trade, and retail. Trader-type general stores were centers for men who brought in produce to exchange for supplies and apparel. As a rule, traders sold any needed item that could not be made at home. Along one wall of the store were fixtures for presenting assorted groceries: meats, flour, sugar, spices, cookies, coffee, tea, and tobacco. Nearby were barrels of assorted dried beans and peas. **Textiles** and sewing notions were organized in simple fixtures along another wall

FIGURE 3–1

In country stores, the potbellied stove was the center for selling and conversation. Some of these stores remain in rural communities.

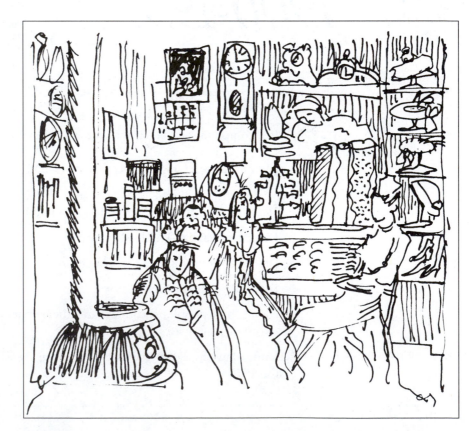

next to men's, women's, and children's apparel. Near the front of the store were household items, as well as featured and specialty goods.

At the turn of the century, most apparel was made at home. The few available **ready-to-wear** garments were quite simple in construction, style, and fabric. Shirtwaist and princess silhouettes were the extent of the women's collection. These pieces remotely resembled the current fashion of the day, and were stocked until no one wanted them anymore. Ready-to-wear hung from hooks, gas lights, and other simple fixtures. The requirement for most apparel and textile fixtures in general stores was to provide

FIGURE 3–2

Old European-style stores were along lower Manhattan in the early 1800s. Assortments of merchandise were displayed on the street out front.

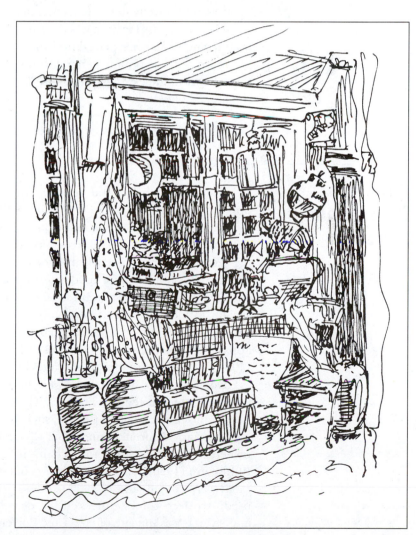

adequate shelving for the merchandise, which was neatly folded in some presentational manner. Display windows were unsophisticated—every inch of space was crowded with a wide assortment of unrelated merchandise. Store owners, wanting to show one or two of everything in the store, created enormous clutter.

Around the 1930s, modern fixtures were added, more for practical purposes than for fashion reasons. From the 1950s on, apparel was presented on basic, inexpensive rounders, rolling rods, hat and apparel forms, and **T stands**. The general store's other fixtures consisted of crates, barrels, packing boxes, and simple tables. Long wooden counters fronted the merchandise displayed on the walls. Perishables were placed in closed glass cases. Smaller cases displayed valuable items such as cigarette lighters, jewelry, watches, and novelty items. Each merchandise category was presented and classified neatly. Its location was determined by traffic and sales volume. All fast-moving items were placed up front so they were highly visible.

Many of these remote general stores were still operating successfully in tiny villages in the Central South and Midwest as late as the 1960s. Now, few remain. See Figure 3–2.

American Department Stores

Unlike the small, rural general stores, large department stores were opening in metropolitan areas to provide broad categories of merchandise in the 1860s. Much more sophisticated than the rural general stores, the department stores emphasized fashion. Because ready-to-wear was becoming acceptable and French fashions were famous, department stores became the showcases for modern design and fashion in the 1900s. Their customers were fashion-trend leaders who were both fashionable and socially influential. Department stores designed by leading architects provided environments that attracted customers who bought Parisian designer apparel and accessories by Worth (1900), Mainboucher (1920), and Poiret (1930), as well as other high-end merchandise. See Figure 3–3.

Designer dress departments were decorated lavishly with period furniture (seventeenth-century French). The garments were presented exquisitely against a backdrop of **fine art**, such as sculpture by Brancusi and paintings by Marie Laurencin and Marc Chagall. Other departments were furnished in **art deco** style with chairs by Dominique and Jacques Emile Ruhlmann (1930). The art deco doors of Gloria Swanson's New York apartment were copied, and in 1926 textiles and wallpaper by Raoul Dufy were used. Art deco colors enhanced the decade of elegance in design, dress, and style. It was the age of jazz, Cole Porter, and "City Chic."

In the 1920s, VM designer displays were influenced by the Paris Art Deco Exhibition, Scott Fitzgerald, T. S. Eliot, and Sophie Tucker in London singing "Something Spanish in Your Eyes." It was an eternal mad dash for the display team to be first on the street to present windows based on this glitzy, motion-picture-kind-of-world lifestyle. The press reported fashion news based on the social scene and exhibited drawings by Cecil Beaton, Man Ray, and Meserole. Windows along Fifth Avenue in New York City and State Street in Chicago reflected the era's sophistication. Jean Patou's tennis wear was shown and Noel Coward talked about The Lido.

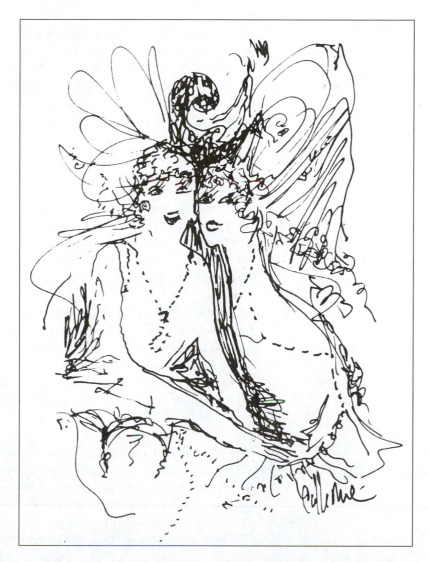

FIGURE 3–3

Celebrities of the 1920s and their lifestyles influenced store design and window displays.

At the same time, despite all the opulence, the plain-Jane budget floors in department stores still existed. Bargain prices suited the blue-collar workers who came in droves by streetcar to buy fifty-cent shirtwaist dresses advertised in the Sunday papers by Marshall Field's and Macy's. The budget floor fixtures were simple and practical because hordes of shoppers would descend on the stores on Monday mornings, knocking things over to get at the hundreds of specially priced dresses. Usually only four **silhouettes** and five colors were presented on the acre-sized budget floors.

MARSHALL FIELD'S—"GIVE THE LADY WHAT SHE WANTS"

In 1881, Field, Lleiter & Co. became Marshall Field & Co. and moved into its new building. Its old store burned down in 1879. By 1914, the retailer occupied a full block and thirteen floors.

By 1934, Marshall Field's flagship store on Chicago's State Street was a full-line department store, including a Store for Men in a twenty-story annex. These two stores, including the Basement Store or budget floor, housed more than 200 selling sections. The main building, faced with marble, terra cotta, and gray granite, contained thirteen floors and three basements, with sixty-seven acres of selling space. The workrooms and studios in the main building produced apparel, accessories, food, and home furnishings and created new exclusive products from original designs. See Figure 3–4.

Furniture departments on the eighth floor included the New Modern and Traditional Town Apartments. A series of model rooms displayed the latest in 1930s interior decoration. The Chintz House, a large room with chintz curtains on the ninth floor, displayed hundreds of colorful patterns on rolls.

The store's sixty-five huge display windows were known the world over for their uniqueness and beauty. If placed end to end, these display windows would have measured a full one-quarter of a mile. On the thirteenth floor were studios for both interior and window display designers. Carpenter and paint shops employed an army of tradesmen and apprentices who executed displays of any design or period with exquisite style and workmanship. Elaborate 1930s windows made of rare woods and exotic materials were created depicting period French rooms (eighteenth century and art deco) to showcase designer apparel.

Nothing fake was used. After each display was used, the display director, Arthur Fraser, sent all props to Holden Court, a central loading and dock alley, where they were destroyed. He did not want them reused or copied in an ugly manner. Customers of the era have remarked that, "Walking through the store was like experiencing a fine gallery." Fraser

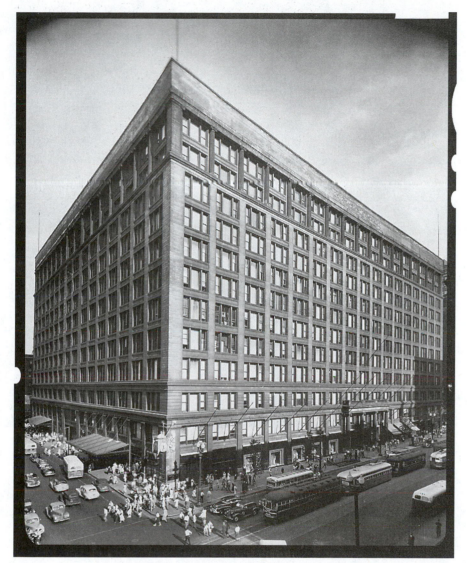

FIGURE 3–4

The architect combined several buildings at Randolph and State Streets to complete the finished department store. The display studios are on the top floor. (Courtesy of Marshall Field's, Chicago.)

designed all of the windows with provocative vision. Neither buyers nor merchandising staff interfered with their objections or buying trends. Despite current Parisian fashion colors, if Fraser wanted to present scarlet, then scarlet it was. See Figure 3–5.

Many 1960s and 1970s VMs, such as Barbara Darcy and Candy Pratts at Bloomingdale's (1970), Bob Currie of Bendel's (1975), and Gene Moore at Tiffany's (1971), displayed Fraser's same creative courage and vision.

FIGURE 3–5

In the 1920s, at Marshall Field's in Chicago, Arthur Fraser created spectacular windows. An army of European craftsmen constructed and installed these complex and detailed windows. (Courtesy of Marshall Field's, Chicago.)

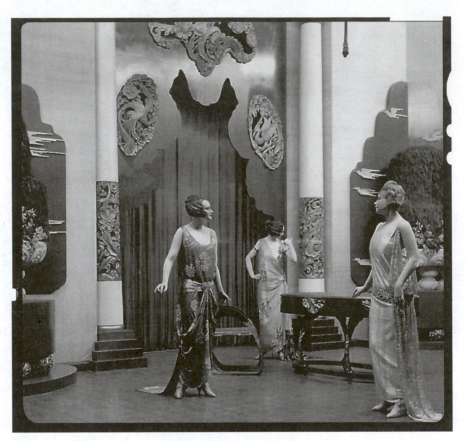

At Marshall Field's, Mrs. Wilson (as she was always called) was elected to create fashionable interior displays because Fraser was totally occupied with creating models and installing his windows. Mrs. Wilson hung fabrics, lugged around antique props, and was the first to use a mannequin in the fur salon or in the store's interior. Her new responsibility created her desire to develop the store's interior artistically. Mrs. Wilson's system (interior display) is now in place in major department stores. She also created special events, such as guest chefs, fashion shows, and expositions of fine gems and art, and experimented with impulse buying and association buying by grouping articles associated by use in one display.

Marshall Field's budgeted millions of dollars annually to create new displays and to buy fixtures for the creation of new shops to house new products, such as the Egyptian Gallery, the Contemporary Sculpture Salon, and the Wedgewood Room. The steady stream of new store fixtures continually enhanced the merchandise. Styles that 1920s customers expected to see in their own townhouses trimmed the store: modern art (1905), cubism (1912), and art deco (1920). As in all stores, Christmas was an unlimited creative and resourceful effort, often consuming as much as 70 percent of the store's annual display funds.

MACY'S —"FROM DIAMONDS TO RASPBERRIES"

The first Macy's trademark occurred in 1860, when Macy's sold hoop-skirts to the seamstress and dressmaker trade. Ready-to-wear had not quite developed. The Red Star fashion symbol emerged from that label.

In 1901, architects and contractors finished the new Herald Square store in Manhattan on 34th Street. It covered one block and became an instant fashion showcase. World designers, fashions, and home furnishings were presented in the store's stylish interiors. The main aisle was trimmed with fresh flowers or unique seasonal plantings in giant Grecian urns and itself became a symbol.

Macy's Christmas windows were the talk of New York and were well reviewed in the national and fashion presses. Parents and children stood in the cold to peer into Macy's windows at the Christmas fantasies. Families traveled great distances to Christmas shop and see these marvelous windows. Gimbel's—Macy's perennial rival for the best look, price, advertising, promotion, and merchandise—feuded with Macy's in the New York press. It was all a strategic plant by Miss Fitz-Gibbon, Gimbel's clever promotional head. Price shading began at a time when even prices were the norm. Macy's created $1.98, $4.98, and $6.98. Now these price strategies are called psychological pricing.

The Nation's Fashion Center Emerges

In New York, the Lane Bryant store was born when the city opened its first subway. Lane Bryant moved to 1489 Fifth Avenue between 119th and 120th Streets. It was originally called a bridal shop because of its large trousseau collection. The sign was misspelled "Bridle." The display fixtures were simple, and large, French-style apparel collections hung from just about everything in the shop.

In the 1900s, some of New York's most exclusive and fashionable clubs, hotels, and retailers anchored themselves at 34th Street and Fifth Avenue. Well-dressed pedestrians walked past an array of architectural styles:

elegant, signless, and very modern 1900s display windows. Visitors came to see these modern theatrical displays that were known worldwide.

The city's great art, theater, opera, fashion press, and elegant lifestyle influenced display creators. Theda Bara was doing Egyptian in 1917, as was every fashionable display window. In addition, Erté's Curtain, the Hindu Tale, and the Folies Bergère of 1922 were parroted. Mannequins dressed in Mainboucher gowns portrayed elite social activities in a setting of fine art.

Altman's was the first sophisticated store opposite the Empire State Building, having moved there from Third Avenue near Tenth Street in the early 1900s. Joining Altman's in this fashionable district were Oppenheim Collins (1907), McCreery's (1913), and Best & Co. (1910). Tiffany's, at 409 Fifth Avenue, occupied a palazzo-style building designed by McKim, Mead & White, the firm that also designed Gorham at 36th Street. Fifth Avenue became the country's leading fashion center as other retailers such as Russek's and Lord & Taylor moved to the district.

In the early 1900s, Saks Fifth Avenue, 49th to 50th Street, was the first of the larger stores on the upper avenue. Bergdorf-Goodman and Bonwit Teller became Saks's neighbors. Fifth Avenue emerged as a window shopper's dream. The best VM designers presented a unique showcase of current fashion, design, and style. The store interiors reflected exotic glamour.

Over on East 60th, Bloomingdale's embarked upon a colossal program to expand by acquiring neighboring properties. Acquisition in 1887 and 1890 filled in the 60th Street gap, and the store expanded along Third and Lexington over the next twelve years. By 1927, the entire block was Bloomingdale's. Its 1,240 linear feet of display windows presented the first and newest merchandise. In 1931 the totally new Lexington Avenue store was completed. The special events and promotional departments planned local philanthropic events and rare exhibits from around the world.

New Yorkers and out-of-towners have always loved to **window shop**. The best-dressed people in the 1920s promenaded along Fifth Avenue to and from clubs and world-class hotels. The new Waldorf's Thirty-Third Street corridor was lavish. The town's social dynasty dined in the Palm Room and everyone else came to see—and be seen. Formal wear was de rigueur—Vionnet's swirling satins, Patou's straighter satins, and Chanel's laces were worn with robe-like wraps by Patou, Vionnet, and Lanvin. This was a perfect setting for the new group of fashion customers.

THE 1940s TO THE 1970s

In the late 1930s, a new age of glamour emerged. Hair and makeup were softer looking, and VMs began to adjust to glamour on new terms. In

1939, Salvador Dali created knock-dead windows at Bonwit's. Jasper Johns and Robert Rauschenberg (Tiffany's), industrial designer Raymond Lowey (Field's), and pop artist Andy Warhol all created window displays at some time during their careers.

At Bloomingdale's in 1947, an exhibit called Woman of Fashion launched American fashion designers Claire McCardell, Adele Simpson, Pauline Trigere, Davidow, and millinery designers John Fredericks and Sally Victor into the world of fashion. The highlight model rooms by Granville (1952) and Barbara D'Arcy (1957) focused on the store's leadership in home fashions.

In February 1950, Edward Von Castelberg created an upbeat, avant-garde window, as seen in *Glamour*, of disembodied hands, feet, and driftwood to showcase the "New Look." VMs of the next two decades produced elegant thematic windows across the country with pleasant props echoing the look of the 1950s and 1960s. Flowers from Colonial, New York, a display company, revival art objects, and many screened panels from Neidermaier Displays, Chicago, created the fashion background. At the New York VM markets, the word was, "Unless it's hearts and flowers, and screened foamcore panels, you are artless."

In 1976, Candy Pratts created psychodrama windows of chaotic surrealism, such as "That's Entertainment and Fright-Agatha Christy," in which mannequins were calm but sort of strewn about with broken items and toppled-over furniture. It was called the unorganized look and presented an exciting showcase for the chic 1970s apparel designers Takado Kenzo, Jean-Paul Gaultier, Miguel Cruz, Versace, and Sonia Rykiel. The ability of displays to please and displease was apparent.

An array of notable designers and celebrities appeared for Bloomingdale's special events. Jack Lindsay and Joe Bellesi created new looks for cosmetics. Leading Paris designers opened boutiques and franchises within the store. The new men's stores "B Way" and "Board Room" blazed all light, **neon**, chrome, glass, and flash.

Bloomingdale's designer shopping bags created a collector's craze, and with each season—whether spring, winter, or fall—their impact was an unforgettable experience. The store became a showcase of newness, freshness, and superior design.

In the mid 1970s at Charles Jourdan, a store that sells expensive shoes and accessories, a toilet bowl sat in the window with pairs of exotic shoes alongside it. Crowds always assembled in front of New Wave windows.

Robert Currie at Bendel's created exotic, surreal windows that always looked both controlled and spontaneous. He stylishly grouped masked mannequins wearing late-day and designer sports with the unexpected, such as trash bags or lost-and-found items.

At Tiffany's in the 1970s, Gene Moore created minimal art windows. Simple objects became the props for million-dollar jewelry and diamonds by the yard. At Bonwit's, from 1945 to 1961, Moore immersed himself in all areas of fashion. Fine art was also a great influence. His windows reflected the style of his favorite great artists and usually eclipsed others on the avenue.

Superstars such as Robert Benzio at Saks Fifth Avenue (1977), Maggie Spring at Charles Jourdan (1976), and Victor Hugo at Halston (1976) created elegant, sophisticated theatre-of-the-absurd windows whose manner was psychodrama.

THE 1980s

"Hi Tech," a look inspired by art deco design motifs, was surgically clean. Its Spartan background created an uncluttered look for merchandise. The simplified design was inexpensive and less complex to install than highly decorative looks. Later, post modern, an architectural look, dominated interiors and display design. Pale sweet colors, lots of clouds, and heavily textured surfaces prevailed. Decorative textures such as faux marble splatter, a sponge stencil technique employed in every imaginable way, was used to enhance Greek columns and decorative panels.

DISCUSSION QUESTIONS

1. Describe the country general store in a few words.
2. Describe the presentation style of the 1920s.
3. Who was the great Marshall Field's display director, and what work made him world renown?
4. When did Bloomingdale's become a fashion store?
5. Who were Candy Pratts, Bob Currie, and Victor Hugo? Describe their display styles.
6. Describe the presentation style of the l950s and 1960s.
7. In 1917, what was Egyptian?
8. Who were the women of "47"?
9. When was the Lane Bryant store started?
10. Where were the first group of fashion stores located on New York's Fifth Avenue?

CHAPTER PROJECT

Project Objective: To acquaint students with fashion history and to use the school library for fashion research.

Project Instructions: (Choose One)

1. Using the school library to research in magazines, books, and periodicals, locate three photos for each of the fashions of the 1920s, 1930s, and 1940s described in this chapter.
2. Describe 1920s lifestyles as they related to theater, art, and show business.
3. Describe at least two fashion designers, two celebrities, and two show-people who helped create the look of the era of the 1920s and 1930s, and explain how their styles influenced window display and store design.

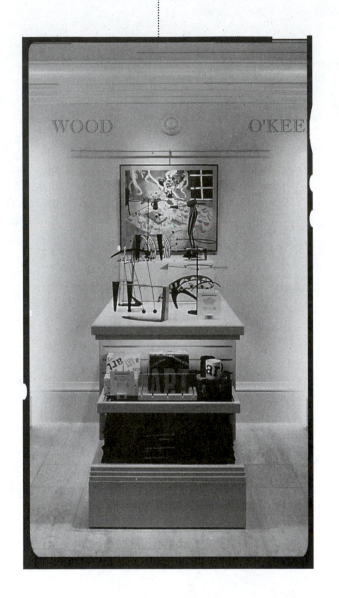

Design Composition

After completing this chapter, you will be able to:

1. Understand design laws and principles.

2. Use design to communicate.

3. Recognize basic design principles.

4. Understand the great variety of design.

5. Tailor design to fit your store's customers and merchandise.

6. Create specific design themes.

7. Appreciate the customer's search for utility and beauty.

Visual merchandising is a commercial art form that enables a retail sales associate to work in all art media to communicate a VM idea. Using some aspect of display design, an associate can communicate information such as price, promotion, **style**, newness, use, trends, stock quantities, vendor, **mood**, and lifestyle to the customer. See Figure. 4–1A.

The VM's or retail associate's design solutions should conform to the retailer's specific selling techniques and marketing concepts (mentioned in Chapters 1 and 2) to establish complete **harmony** between merchandising and **display**. See Figure 4–1B. For example, Post-Modern-inspired displays would be jarringly out of place in a country store. You may recall having seen store displays that are totally unrelated to the merchandise's quality, style, fashion, and price. As a shopper, you probably found this disconcerting.

A well-designed window stops the customer. Many designers use the spatial proportions created by the ancient Greeks named the "Golden Mean," which divides space into 3 x 5 dimensions. This simple method helps the nonartistic associate organize a design plan that looks great.

Creating interest by placing the product in the optical center of the display is pleasing visually and enables the customer to focus on the product. The optical center is the center of the display from left to right and the average visual height of a standing customer, about five feet.

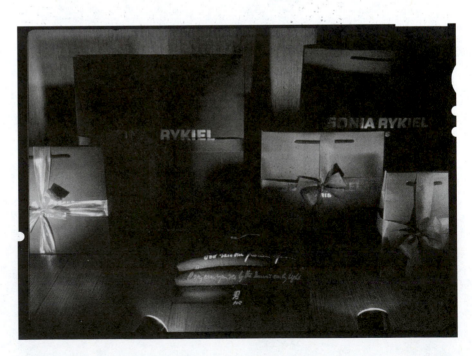

FIGURE 4–1A

Design can be used to communicate with the customer. (Courtesy of Sonia Rykiel, Paris.)

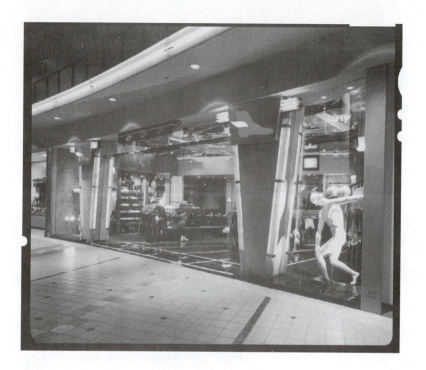

White space, the empty space surrounding the display, isolates the display. A clean border of surrounding blank space tends to force the customer to focus on one item in the display. It also separates the display items from the surrounding mass of merchandise. These few easy-to-originate methods should help an associate get started creating design solutions.

Two Composition Methods

MARKETING DESIGN

The first compositional method a VM should consider during the design process is marketing design. Where, when, and how a display is created should be based on marketing principles. The display's location, the kinds of fixturing, and floor density (number of fixtures) are based on customers' expectations, the season, and customers' shopping habits. Marketing criteria can provide solid reasons for a design plan.

Marketing studies provide data about selling strategies which determines how the selling floor is designed to meet the customer's needs. The practical reason for the design determines its artistic character.

Important merchandise should occupy most of the display space. Merchandise assortments may be shown in ways that point out their depths and breaths. Such assortments should be shown with a theme such as Italian Fair, Super-Star Designer, colors, or **brand name**, or by an activity to project a feeling of group unity. See Figure 4–2.

BASIC DESIGN

The second compositional method a VM should consider embodies basic design ideas. Planning fixture placement, merchandise, and displays

FIGURE 4–2

Present merchandise by theme for the strongest impact. (Courtesy of Hirshberg Design Group, Inc., Toronto, Ontario.)

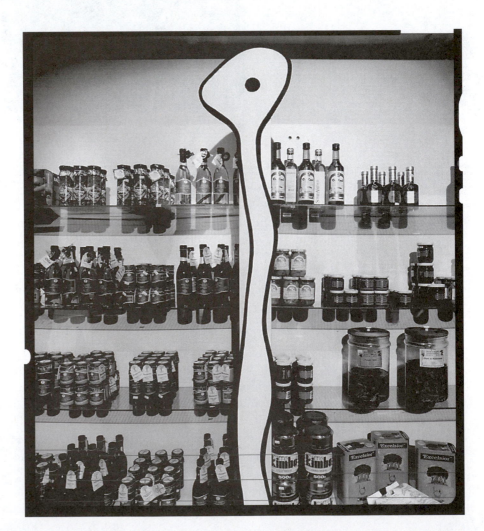

involves volume because design is three-dimensional. Walls, floors, and ceilings create depth and width. This process creates the aesthetically correct buying atmosphere. The designer creates an aesthetic buying atmosphere by executing the following principles: drafting, sketching, color, planning, textural composites, design composition, and pattern planning. To this end, the designer can take great liberties with design to better convey feelings or to achieve a more intellectual approach to a merchandising philosophy.

OTHER TECHNIQUES

Other compositional techniques include using a progression of small items to lead the eye to a mannequin or placing **elements of display** close together to emphasize unity. Mannequins often look better if placed so they are seen from the 3/4 side rather than from the full front. Props and accessories should be shown as subordinates to create focus on the central object. Presenting uneven numbers of items is also preferable. For example, three objects are easier to arrange and create a triangle effect of unity.

ADAPTATING NATURAL FORMS.   Using a flower as a design motif in craft designs and textile wallpapers for instance is adapting a natural form. When a designer's design departs from the basic flower and makes it unrecognizable, the flower becomes an abstraction. In either form, the flower is an attractive decorative element.

ARTISTIC DESIGN DISCIPLINE.   Displays are created for specific selling reasons. The store's merchandising philosophy determines those reasons. In addition, displays should be based on customer behavior and the store's selling techniques.

Basic Design Methods

The basic design methods are balance, beauty, composition line, color, and texture.

BALANCE

There are two forms of compositional balance. The first is **formal balance**, as when attractions are arranged equally on either side of an axis. Formal balance creates a somewhat static mood. The second form of composition balance is occult balance, as when attractions of varying sizes, values, and distances are arranged around an axis to create a dynamic mood. These design methods help to organize the **composition**.

BEAUTY

Intelligent humans require beauty in addition to function. In fact, the human mind craves beauty. Human behavior can measure beauty.

NEEDS.   Any design is based on a need. Customers have many wants and **needs** to be satisfied. A busy display layout says little. Less busy displays say more. Refer to Chapters 1 and 2 for additional information on displays.

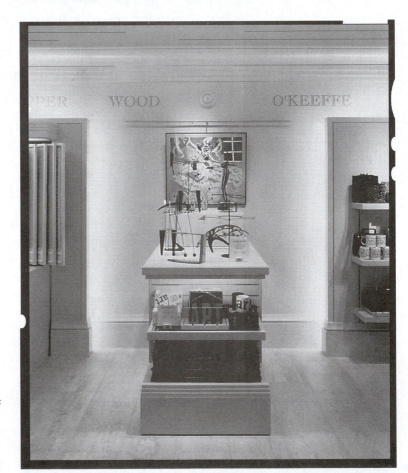

FIGURE 4–3

Customers want beauty in

addition to functionality.

The human mind craves

beauty. (Courtesy of Charles

Sparks + Company,

Westchester, IL.)

BEAUTY IN PURPOSE

As mentioned earlier, customers want beauty in addition to functionality. The human mind craves beauty and consciously or unconsciously looks for it. The VM's use of graceful lines, pleasing colors, and appealingly arranged merchandise adds aesthetics to the consumer's environment. See Figure 4–3.

BEAUTY IN LINES

Lines are classified as straight, crooked, and curved, and have endless combinations, such as wide and narrow, dark and light, or multicolored. The straight, vertical line essential in building structure has a simple, pure beauty. Lines can recreate the contour of an object or can be applied to the form's surface as decoration. See Figure 4–4.

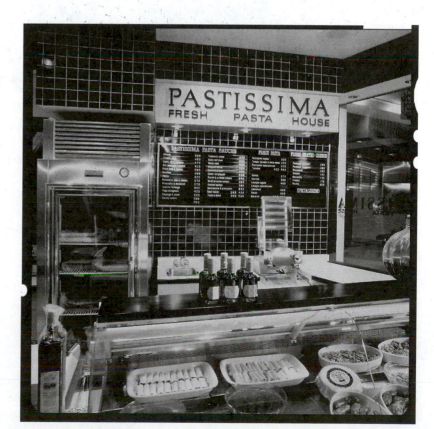

FIGURE 4–4

The straight vertical lines in building structures have a simple pure beauty. (Courtesy of Hirschberg Design Group, Inc., Toronto, Ontario.)

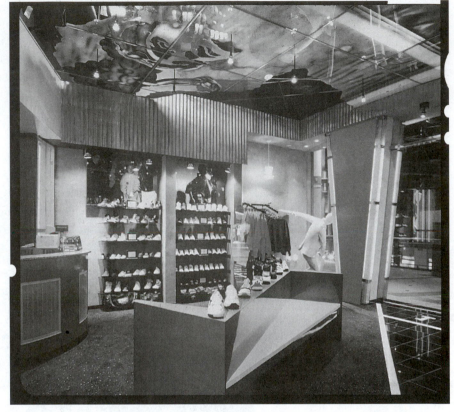

FIGURE 4–5

To be successful, the store's interior must meet the target customer's psychological needs. (Courtesy of Interior Design 101 Ltd., Chicago, IL.)

BUYING ATMOSPHERE.   The design of the store interior and presentation can stimulate sales if the design meets the target customer's psychological needs. Professor Harold Proshansky of the City University of New York (CUNY) suggests, "People, places, and the behavior of people have relationships with places. It is called 'Behavioral Mapping.'" See Figure 4–5.

SUBCONSCIOUS CREATIVE VISION.   All human beings have a subconscious vision of creativity based on an accumulation of personal experiences.

TACTILE NEEDS.   Retailers who allow customers to touch their merchandise satisfy the customers' great tactile needs. The soft look of lily pads and clouds provide a look associated with soft comforters and bed linens. Customers moved by the beauty of a product love to touch it.

COMPOSITION LINE

Compositional **line** is the visual line created by placing merchandise and props in a **progression** to form a display. An "S line" is created when merchandise is placed to form an *S*. In this display the eye follows the objects in progression around the *S*. The letters *C* and *Z* are other popular compositional line configurations. **Vertical lines** create impressions of strength, permanence, and stability. The layout pattern for a men's ski display may utilize vertical lines to suggest strength, for example. **Horizontal lines** create feelings of dignity, calm, and order. See Figure 4–6.

FIGURE 4–6

Compositional line can move

your eye into a display.

(Courtesy of Marshall Field's,

Chicago, IL.)

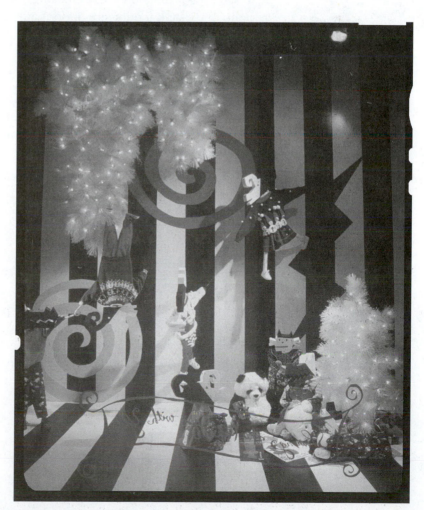

OTHER LINES.   All objects are identified by contour and surface lines. For example, a fish is identified by contour and surface lines that make up scales, fins, and eyes. Silhouette lines identify the fish's shape. These lines identify the subject and theme of a design. A stylized fish in bright colors on a sign could identify a deli's fish market for example. Stylization makes the deli sign more noticeable. Unique colors make the sign more visible.

Creating Attention

Attention is created in a display by a focal point, beauty, originality, a clear message, and a purpose. Diagonal lines are active and create attention. Pulling elements apart creates tension. Preposterous positioning, such as standing mannequins on the ceiling, is an attention getter. Bright colors, light, music, and motion are obvious attention creators.

FEATURE MERCHANDISE

The most important merchandise in a display should be arranged to create a focal point or center of attention. Focal merchandise should always be highlighted using compositional techniques.

FOCAL POINT.   The focal point is created to eliminate the monotony of a group of equal elements and to focus on an item or a group of merchandise.

Creating Displays

Creating a display requires the same artistic design methods as floor planning. Although a display and a floor plan are each developed according to the concepts that govern design, such as balance, **rhythm**, and **symmetry**, the materials chosen to execute each is different. Active sportswear might require rugged props to complete the display composition, while late-day apparel may require props that mirror entirely different images. See Figure 4–7.

SELECTING DISPLAY MATERIAL

Visual merchandisers select materials and fixtures and place them based on their artistic flair, style, talent, taste, and understanding of

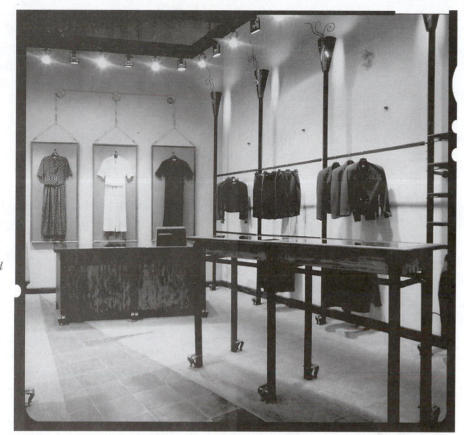

FIGURE 4–7

Each class of merchandise and each display location requires a different design solution. (Courtesy of Donald Bell Design Consultants, Inc., Toronto, Ontario.)

quality, along with the need to provide a visually exciting shopping atmosphere for the customer. The subconscious creative vision mentioned earlier stimulates the designer and is grounded in the retailer's merchandising goals. Two VMs may not create the same composition in the same location with the same display materials and the same merchandise.

Design Solutions

Each class of merchandise and display location requires a different design solution. A display of *high-fashion* merchandise may use art objects or photographs as props. Another display may require rustic colors, lots of geometric patterns, homespun textures, country furniture, and decorative home accessories. A furniture display at Burdine's, Florida, might be bright and colorful and another at Bloomingdale's, New York, might be sedate.

A freestanding display requires a design that can be seen from all sides, while a design in a closed window must be seen only from the front. Some merchandise classifications, such as furniture, may require a specific display mood, while a classification such as apparel may require another. Each display should be considered a new design challenge.

Solutions that govern design have been formulated by humanity. They are largely *adaptations* of natural forms: snowflakes, flowers, animals, and human anatomy to name a few. People have learned to see and feel these solutions and have adapted them to human needs. When a designer using these solutions produces an excellent design, a work of art results. Designers and their audiences understand these design principles. These principals become a method of universal communication and the resulting display is understood universally—an exciting display can be appreciated and understood wherever it appears.

The Purpose of Design

Designers serve six important purposes: (1) to create designs that serve a definite need; (2) to make merchandise more attractive; (3) to capture a viewers' attention; (4) to organize materials making them readily comprehensible; (5) to place the viewer in harmony with the materials; and (6) to give the viewer new experiences. See Figure 4–8.

A garment on a hanger may not look attractive to the customer, but an attractive display can make the garments come alive and look appealing, thereby satisfying the customer's aesthetic need. The purpose of a display should be to announce something definitively. Every portion of the design and arrangement should be used to make the display easily seen and understood.

The questions, "Does this display fulfill its purpose?", "Does the display satisfy a customer's emotional and aesthetic needs?", and "Does this display generate sales?" should dominate the creative process.

LINE DEFINES FORM.   Form is the structural shape of an object. It includes the object and the space in which the object exists. After a sculptor shapes a human form, lines drawn on the sculpted surface define face and hair. The form of a blanket is woven, and on it the textile printer or weaver adds line in a million ways to create surface interest.

Contour lines help us to identify a tree. Many smaller vertical lines on the trunk identify bark, lacy lines identify the branches and leaves, and circular lines identify the trunk's thickness. Many lines suggesting trees surrounding a tree suggest a grove. These lines of a tree blur the

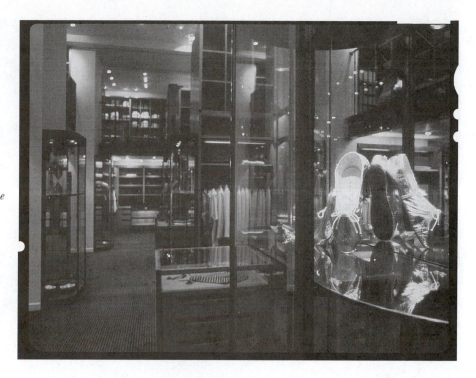

FIGURE 4–8

Merchandise must be made more attractive by the boutique environment. The merchandise and the interior must be harmonious in style and design. (Courtesy of Sonia Rykiel, Paris.)

image and create the look of a forest. Some degree of **contrast**, such as a dark tree against a white background, helps us see objects clearly. Too much white background, however, could overpower the tree. Linear patterns can be applied to create definition on a prop or in an entire display.

Lines have distinct characteristics. The line that defines a floral country chintz is different from that of a contemporary flower print, for example. The thickness of the line, how it repeats, and how it outlines its subject suggests variety of period and style.

Lines can also be used to connect shapes. The positions of a shoe and a handbag in a display cause the eye to follow one object to another and create a compositional line. See Figure 4–9.

Imaginary compositional lines are important because they keep the eye involved in and constantly moving throughout the display. These imaginary lines can keep the eye moving in fast or slow rhythms, in and out, and they prevent the eye from leaving the display.

Some **curved lines** can define the contours of jewelry. Others, such as waves on a lake, create endless, beautiful motion. A crooked line in a crazy quilt is everchanging in a lovely way. Study these elements to determine the means of creating beauty.

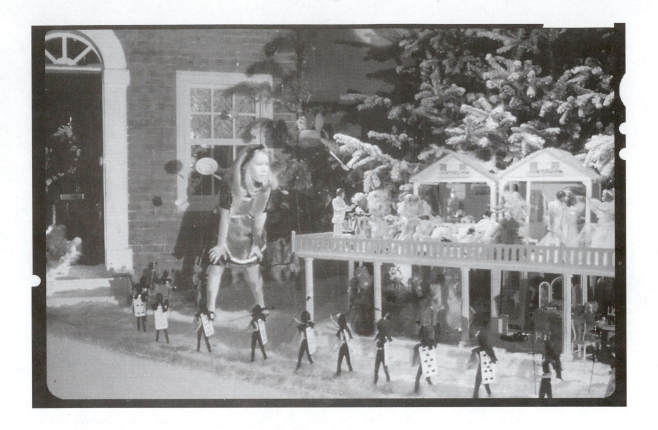

FIGURE 4–9

Placing items one

following another

creates a compositional

line. (Courtesy of

BEAUTY IN VOLUME

Three-dimensional form (roundness or squareness) is emphasized by light, shadow, color, and texture. Assembling merchandise with all of these dimensional characteristics creates a display. See Figure 4–10.

A display is made up of a collection of harmonious parts. It may be shallow with all of its parts close together or very deep with all of its parts spread apart. Controlling these values enables a designer to fit the display into an environment, which is another form. To achieve **perspective** in a display, arrange the merchandise according to traditional perspective lines.

Lines that repeat vertically create static balance. Lines that repeat on an angle create action. Horizontal or curved lines create a relaxed image like the horizon.

FORM CAN ESTABLISH MOOD.   The form of a perfume container suggests a delicate mood, while the form of a country blanket suggests a rugged mood. Flat, horizontal forms suggest a quiet summer's day.

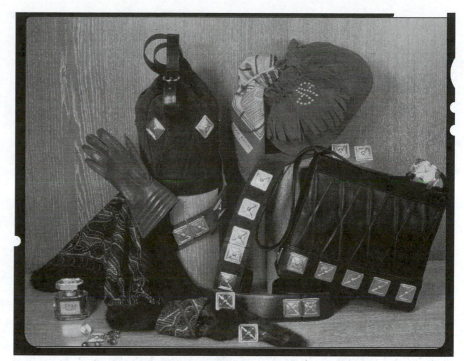

FIGURE 4–10

A display is made up of a collection of harmonious parts. All of the dimensional characteristics create a display. (Courtesy of Patou, Paris.)

Objects may be identified by form. A designer's task is to find commonalities between objects while creating a composition. Putting objects together that belong together enables a designer to focus on and emphasize an aesthetic point.

FORM CAN IDENTIFY OBJECTS.   The round shape of a plate suggests china. When creating a china display, a designer may assemble and combine round items common to the plate that match the plate's color and texture. This technique emphasizes the plate's roundness. On the other hand, a designer displaying 170 pieces of china might consider emphasizing a cube, because the overall bulk forms a cube.

Most often a store's fixtures, platforms, and showcases compose a basic cube made of straight lines and flat planes that are adjacent and produce hard line forms. When the lines and planes meet they form a cube. Like the plate, you might want to emphasize that point in your display. See Figure 4–11.

In stores, basic design is determined by how shapes combine in certain rhythms, balance, contrast, or unity. To create a good design, rely on judgment and good taste, good **proportions**, and harmonious shapes. Color, texture, and line combinations create the mood of the design.

FIGURE 4–11

The store's fixtures, platforms,

and showcases are composed

of a basic cube, straight lines,

and flat planes. (Courtesy of

Interior Design 101 Ltd.,

Chicago, IL.)

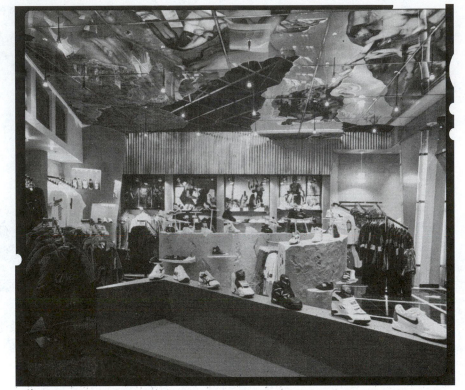

Linking sizes and surrounding shapes alters the design and also changes the mood. Visual scale is relative. For example, a dinner plate is larger than a fork, but, through juxtaposition, the plate may look smaller. Product character changes based on how the product is ornamented and how it is lit. Materials, such as reflective glass, soft wood, or rough gray stone, can be used to establish additional character.

Oranges, limes, melons, balloons, globes, pearls, and berries are spherical. Pine trees, flowers, funnels, flower containers, and ice cream cones are conical. Tree trunks, arms, legs, torsos, tubes, pipes, and tanks are cylindrical. Houses, boxes, televisions, and furniture are cubes. Cubes, spheres, and cylinders appear more frequently than cones. The human body is a complex combination consisting of all manner of forms.

BEAUTY IN TEXTURE

Texture is a design element that deals with the sense of touch. Although tactile values may also be seen, thus creating visual mood, they are appreciated more when they are touched. Retailers who enable the customer to feel the product satisfy the customer's tactile needs. The textures created by the building materials used in store architecture provide satisfaction.

Displays, interior trim, decor, and fixtures are additional textural sources to which customers react. Textural themes may be controlled, created, or changed by color, line, **value**, and material.

A **display theme** created by the natural textures of thatch, plaster, and stone may enhance apparel that looks handcrafted. Structural glass, stainless steel, and synthetics enhance sophisticated, metropolitan-looking apparel.

Texture is associated with historical periods. An eighteenth-century highboy has an unmistakable Georgian texture. In contrast, sleek, steely textures pervade all forms of the modern period. Fast cars are best made with colors and steel that reinforce the idea of speed. The designs of sleek steel buildings, geometric shapes, and 1930s modern Zephyr railroad coaches are based on art deco style.

The textural theme of a display should be in character with the color and form of the merchandise. The textural theme of a store should relate to the psychological needs of its target customer.

BEAUTY IN ENHANCEMENT

Putting things together that belong together is an art. Color and shape must be considered carefully when combining merchandise to match subordinate display props. Strong messages are created when all elements in a display support each other. They may be harmonious, or they may be selected for contrast value.

Contrasting items should have one design feature, such as color, texture, theme, balance, use, or form, in common. A theme of harmony or a theme of contrast establishes an eye-catching display. Harmony or contrast should dominate to avoid sending confusing double messages.

For example, the apparel used to develop a presentation, may have many colors, textures, and forms. To reduce confusion, organize the items by color, texture, use, style, or any other common feature. To develop continuity, emphasize the most common feature within the group. In a display of tweeds and penny loafers, for example, a sophisticated and refined silk scarf or a delicate, suave lace blouse put together in an awkward manner will seem out of place.

When displaying merchandise, the props and accessories should have a commonality, such as matching lifestyles, textures, or colors. The creation should provide a clear image and be uncluttered by different elements.

Displaying woolens with barn boards emphasizes their rough textures. Combining flattering groups of colors, props, and merchandise creates visual pleasure.

BEAUTY IN COMPOSITION

In creating a design, keep in mind that conventional forms that create realistic effects are not wanted. Instead, extract only beautiful lines, colors, and forms from nature and adapt them for decorative purposes. Because a display cannot replicate a real situation, strive to create impressions.

Replicating a swimming pool to present swimwear in a display would be overkill. Only a few symbols are needed to establish a point. A beach ball, towels, a paper sun, or a beach umbrella would do the trick in this case. The selective eye, with a knowledge of history, tradition, lifestyles, and culture, helps the designer choose appropriate, understandable display symbols.

Most merchandise has been inspired, created, and shaped by a designer whose designs are based on universal design principles. Identify the best of these design principles and repeat them in a display composition. Repetition may establish continuity in a display. Any design element used again and again establishes a pattern. This repetition leads to harmony and focus.

BALANCE.   As discussed earlier, formal or static balance, which creates the mood of equilibrium, results when elements are arranged equally right to left. Formal balance creates a flowing look of dynamic rhythm. Informal balance, which creates an active mood, results when elements that do not frequently repeat each other are placed together. *Radial balance* (formal) creates an organized mood and is characterized by a bull's eye or wheel arrangement.

EMPHASIS.   Creating the proper sense of importance to the specific parts of a display makes the merchandise dominate. **Emphasis** relieves monotony, simplifies the display, and produces a unified look.

Generally, the large items in a display are the focal points and are the featured merchandise. In contrast, the smaller, surrounding items, support the large items. These smaller items may be merchandise accessories or props that create an accent or are in secondary positions.

LANDSCAPE SUBJECTS.   Arranging elements to complete a subject, such as placing color masses of distant sky, trees, and fields in the midrange of a display and flowers in the foreground, constitutes a map for a **landscape**. Vertical lines in a landscape suggest stability while horizontal lines suggest rest. In contrast, oblique lines suggest unrest and curved lines suggest movement. The landscape may be expressed by **realism**, abstraction, or any other style. The subject may form a background or entirely make up the landscape display.

ARCHITECTURAL SUBJECTS.   Architectural subjects are decorative and add nicely to a display. Drawings or photographs in any artistic style of buildings make excellent backgrounds.

Try to establish a compositional theme. Whether it is a landscape, cityscape, or other subject, research the theme and choose the best symbols to communicate the message and enhance the displays.

DISCUSSION QUESTIONS

1. Describe surface interest and how it applies to a composition.
2. What are tactile needs and how do retailers satisfy them?
3. How is a focal point developed and why is it needed?
4. What is a buying atmosphere?
5. What is an artistic discipline?
6. What are merchandising goals and how do they apply to display design?
7. Why use a developed theme for a display?

CHAPTER PROJECT

Project Objective: To create a display using architecture or landscape props.

Project Instructions: (Choose One)
1. Create an apparel window or tabletop display with a landscape backdrop.
2. Create a men's apparel display using a city theme.
3. Create an apparel display with a landscape theme.

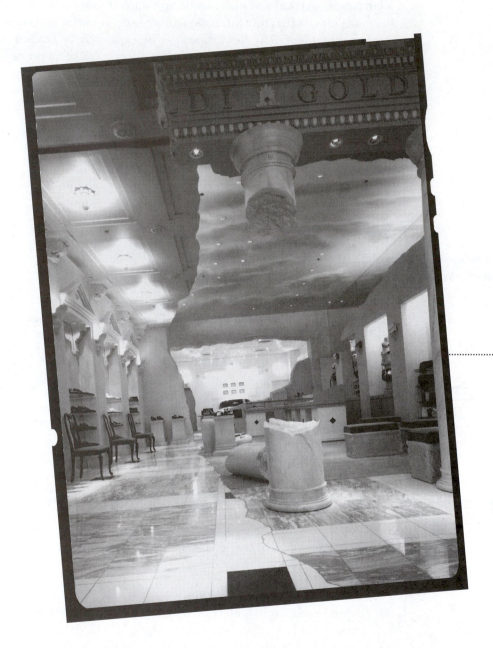

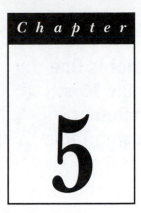

Color

*A*fter completing this chapter, you will be able to:

1. Understand how color is seen through light.

2. Identify the basics of color composition.

3. Describe the five color families.

4. Arrange merchandise on the selling floor by color.

5. Recognize dominant and accent colors.

6. Name who does color forecasting and explain how it is done.

7. Color match.

Color Is One of the Most Important Design Tools

Color is the first thing a customer notices. It is one of the most important design tools to communicate style and mood in store displays. In addition, it is an important consideration for customers when selecting merchandise. Customers generally select apparel and home-fashion items based on current color trends. Exciting colors are eye-catching and make a store come alive. Customers react immediately to trendy colors and to the color themes of displays. Retailers who understand and apply the power of color in selling benefit from increased sales.

Initially customers may be aware of current color trends through international fashion news. These trends are reinforced storewide by promotional color themes, advertising, and displays. Repeating a color fashion theme throughout the store reinforces the customer's awareness of the color message. Several ways to repeat color patterns and build the display theme include presenting collections of merchandise using color, banners, menus, tablecloths, flower arrangements, signs, highlight areas, handouts, and fixtures. See Figure 5–1.

In addition to being an important consideration for the customer, color is an important consideration for the VM in creating displays and in presenting collections of merchandise on the selling floor. The merchandising by color strategy keeps many retailers ahead of their competition. Because busy customers spend only a few seconds looking at displays in search of fashion and color ideas, they must be able to understand a fashion color message quickly. If all of the red skirts are hung in one area of the selling floor and all of the blue blouses are hung in another, discovery is easier for the busy customer.

Developing a display based on color results naturally following a basic merchandising system. Exciting displays are dominated by one color, known as the **dominant color**. Choose one color family for a display and make it dominate by at least 80 percent. Too many colors in equal amounts confuse the customer and weaken the presentation. As the theme builds, remember that the more a color repeats, the more significant it becomes. Designers should not be afraid of frequent color repeats or of excessive color use.

The "rainbow color system" is helpful when color planning the selling floor. Begin the arrangement by using dark colors on all fixtures and continue to the right of the selling floor with light colors. The reverse of this plan is also acceptable. Many stores begin with light colors on their fixtures rather than dark ones. Whichever plan is used, be consistent throughout the store. Refer to an illustration of a rainbow in nature and use it to guide your plan: go from dark blue to blue, dark green to green, and so on. See Figure 5–2.

FIGURE 5–1

The neutral color family dominates this presentation. The apparel, display surround, and props are all the same color family. Other colors combine to make one complete look. Determine the percent of dominance of the neutrals. (Courtesy of Sonia Rykiel, Saint Germain, Paris.)

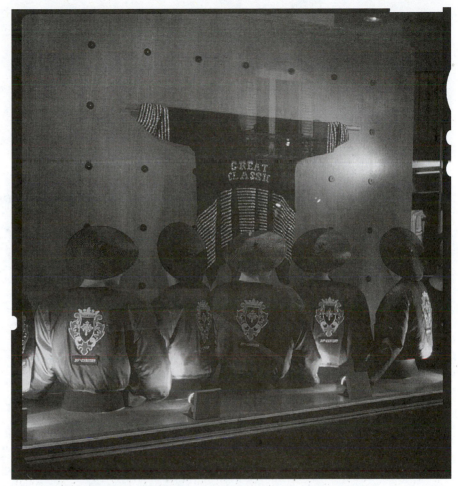

On waterfalls and face-out arms, hang dark colors to the back, light colors in the front, and mid colors in between. This creates an even color transition from front to back. **Waterfalls** are slanting arms with fixed knobs that hold five or eight garments. These garments are attached to a floor fixture such as a T stand or quad or they are mounted on slat board walls. **Face outs** are straight or slanted arms that present garments in a frontal manner. They can be mounted on a floor fixture or on a slat board wall. On cubes or shelves, place light colors near the top and dark colors toward the bottom. On **rounders** begin color arranging at one point and continue the rainbow scheme back to the beginning color at that point.

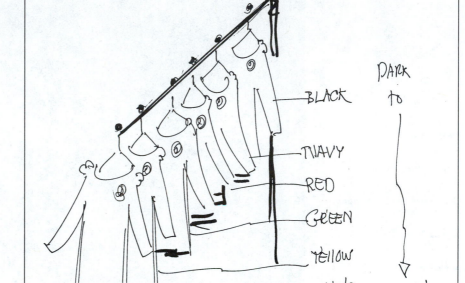

FIGURE 5–2

Hanging the same garment in color order is called the "rainbow color system." This helps the customer locate an item and helps the associate present it.

A Mini Color Glossary

It is important to understand the color vocabulary when using color or when learning and communicating about color. The following definitions will help you understand color principles and theory.

ANALOGOUS PALETTE

An **analogous palette** is an assemblage of three adjoining hues from the color wheel (see the Color Wheel section in this chapter). The mood of the palette, whether dark or light, creates sophistication and close order. Some analogous palettes create a mood of tranquility.

APPROACHING COLORS

Approaching colors are dark colors that can make an object look nearer. They are also known as **near colors**. Large objects painted with dark colors always look a bit smaller. Endless variations on this theme allow you to change the look of an interior space. Some walls look better if they appear closer. Warm colors are near colors and cool colors are distant.

ASSEMBLAGE

An assemblage is a collection of colors that create a design. Designers are always working in terms of assemblage as they develop apparel coordinates and matching **accessories.** All of the elements in a display are an assemblage of fashion colors. Fashion designers base each collection on an assemblage of compatible colors. Focusing on color as a key presentation style creates customer demand for mix-and-match. Customers love to build coordinates and collections. Designers employ this theory when designing a garment. Sportswear designs are not based on one item, but rather on a collection of skirts, blouses, slacks, shorts, and accessories in one color or color family.

CHROMATIC VALUE OR CHROMA

Chromatic value refers to the degree of intensity of a color. Bright red is intense. Its degree of brilliance is called a **chroma**. Compared to other colors, red has a medium chroma. Yellow is the most brilliant color, with the least saturation and the palest chroma. Apparel and decorative colors most often have a medium to low chroma.

COMPLEMENTARY COLORS

Complementary colors are the colors opposite each other on the color wheel. Red complements green. Yellow complements blue. Using opposite colors can sometimes be disagreeable, however. Rather than combine red and green, try combining pink and mint, which are variations of red and green. Soft blue and yellow ice are more agreeable and less clashing than are bright blue and bright yellow.

COMPLEMENTARY PALETTE

A **complementary palette** uses complementary colors as both dominant colors and accents. Using green opposite red on the color wheel intensifies redness. Opposing colors combined in equal intensities can create discord, however.

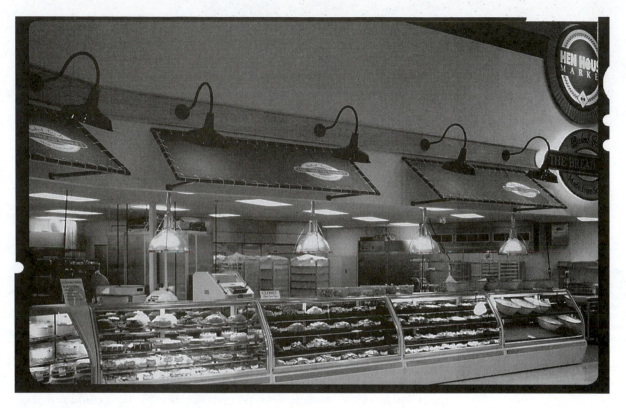

FIGURE 5–3A

Dark green enhances the dominant neutral family here, creating a pleasant effect. The colors enhance each other to create a color arrangement.

(Courtesy of Off The Wall Designs, Telfor, PA.)

ENHANCING COLOR

An **enhancing color** is any color that flatters or makes a second color look better by making the second color look richer, prettier, lovelier, or more glamorous. White enhances red because it does not compete with it. Other colors that enhance red by not clashing or competing with it include varieties of orange, yellow, magenta, black, and purple. Pink and the other variants of red enhance red by focusing on its redness. Green, a color opposite red, can clash with red and is therefore nonenhancing. See Figures 5–3A and 5–3B.

FINISH

The degree of gloss or shine in paint is called **finish**. A matte finish has virtually no shine while a high-gloss finish has a lot of shine. A semigloss finish falls somewhere in between the two. Faux or fake finishes such as stippling, sponging, feathering, and graining add drama to spartan materials and are associated with specific decorative periods.

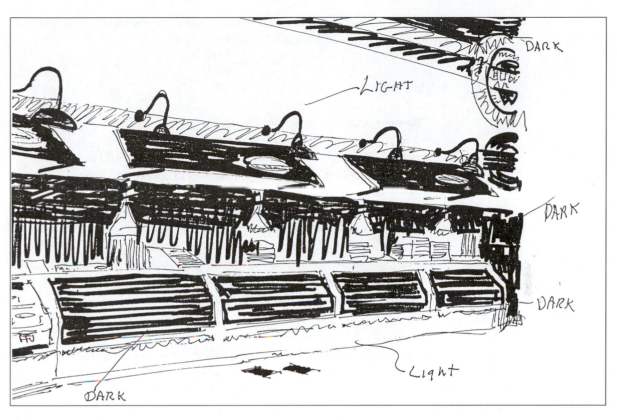

FIGURE 5–3B

Dark green balances

the lightness and

darkness in this design.

Lightness and darkness

add stimulation.

HUE

Hue refers to a color itself and to a color's basic intensity or value. When you imagine red in all of its forms from dark to light you are imagining hue. The three basic hues are called primary colors (see the following Primary Colors section). They are red, yellow, and blue. These colors are considered basic because they are pure and not produced by mixing other colors. Secondary colors (see the following Secondary Colors section) are produced by mixing the primary colors in equal amounts. For example, red and yellow produce orange, red and blue produce violet or purple, and yellow and blue produce green. Do not assume that secondary colors are not important in developing strong themes, however. The term "secondary" is a scientific description only. Secondary colors may also assume major importance in a composition.

ONE-HUE PALETTE. As its name implies, a **one-hue palette** uses only one hue. Contrast is developed by varying tonal value (dark and light).

This monochromatic color assemblage creates a harmonious look and is a favorite of fashion and textile designers.

PIGMENT

Pigment is a substance that produces a characteristic color. Paint is prepared with pigments manufactured from chemicals for color fastness and longevity. A few pigments include carmine, a strong, brilliant red which comes from cochineal insects; cobalt blue, a bright blue which mixes well with other colors and comes from a silver-white metallic element occurring in compounds; chrome yellow, which ranges from shades of lemon to deep orange and comes from chromates of lead, barium, or zinc; cadmium red, a strong reddish color with a strong, slow-drying film, which comes from cadmium sulfide and cadmium selenide; and earth green, a grayish pigment lacking in tinting strength and permanence, which comes from iron silicate and is called "terra verde" by fine artists.

FIGURE 5–4

Red, blue, and yellow are

the primary colors.

A color wheel is an orderly

arrangement of color.

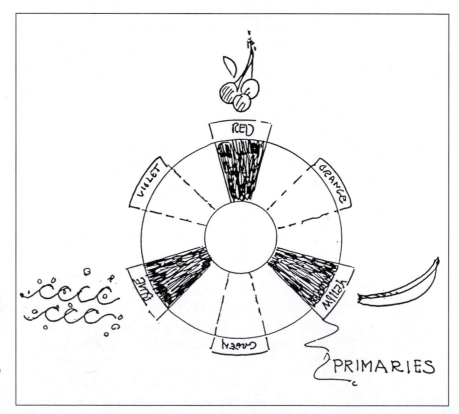

PRIMARY COLORS

As mentioned earlier, red, blue, and yellow are the **primary colors** or primaries. They are not obtained by mixing other colors. See Figure 5–4.

SECONDARY COLORS

As discussed previously, **secondary colors** are produced by combining any two primary colors. Red and yellow produce orange. Yellow and blue produce green. Red and blue produce purple. These blends are often more subtle than primary colors. See Figure 5–5.

TERTIARY COLORS

Tertiary colors are produced by mixing secondary colors and primary colors in equal amounts. The results are red-orange, yellow-orange, yellow-green, blue-green, blue-purple, and red-purple. See Figure 5–6.

FIGURE 5–5

Violet, green, and orange are secondary colors that are produced by combining equal parts of red, blue, and yellow.

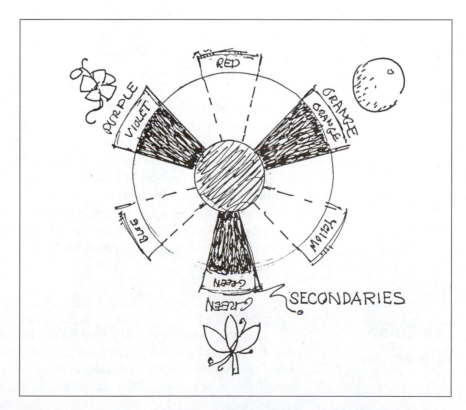

FIGURE 5–6

Tertiary colors are produced

by mixing primary colors

and secondary colors in

equal amounts. Green, a

secondary color, when mixed

with yellow, a primary color,

produces lemon.

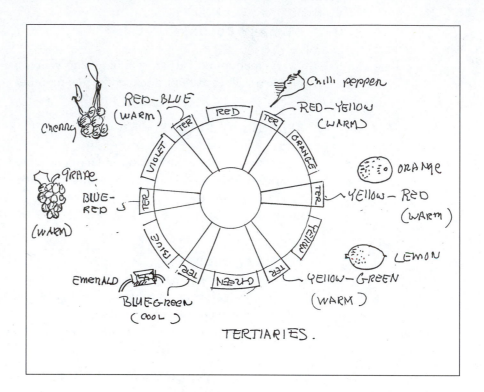

TONAL VALUE

Tonal value is a color's lightness or darkness. Light colors are often called **tints** or **pastels**. Dark colors are called shades or grayed colors. Pink (a tint or a pastel) is a light tonal value of red and burgundy (a shade or a grayed color) is a dark variety of red. Tone and value are produced when the original color is mixed with black or white. White pigment mixed with a color lightens the color and produces a tint. Black pigment mixed with a color darkens the color and produces a shade. Another way to gray a color is to mix it with its complement on the color wheel. Mixing blue and yellow pigments produces a grayed color, for example.

The Color Wheel

The basic **color wheel** is designed for reference and to help identify colors. A typical color wheel might show the red family at the top and all the other colors within the spectrum clockwise in order. **Chromatic distribution** is established by arranging hue on the wheel. See Figure 5–7.

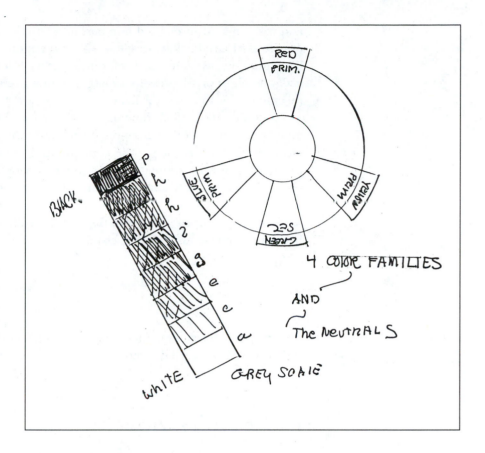

FIGURE 5–7

A basic color wheel plus

a gray scale helps visualize

and plan color.

The color wheel is the result of theory. The color families are the result of practice. Some color families are not illustrated clearly on the wheel. The neutral family, which includes beige, brown, black, white, and slate, must be visualized in terms of how designers use it. Practice thinking about the neutrals to appreciate their tonal value. They appear insignificant on the wheel but are a strong marketing utility.

Colors that do not appear on the basic wheel change often but through practice you will learn their common names such as taupe, rose pink, turquoise, and Wedgewood, or the painter's pigment names such as Van Dyke brown, sienna, and ochre to name just a few.

COMMERCIAL COLOR SYSTEMS

Albert Munsell and Wilhelm Ostwald created commercial color systems. Instead of using common or romantic names for colors, such as taupe and rose pink, Munsell used numbers and letters. In this system red is #5, orange is #15, red is R, and yellow is Y. As mentioned earlier, yellow is very light and reflective. On a scale of tonal value, yellow is #1 and charcoal gray is #5. A yellow or #1 dress looks larger than a dress in #5 because #5 is a receding color that absorbs light.

Ostwald (1852–1932) developed a systematized color-harmony plan by mixing primary colors in harmony throughout the entire range of colors. His charts, which are in a cone configuration, relate each primary color through ranges of white to black and compare achromatic colors. In Ostwald's system each color is identified by a number and a letter.

The apparel industry has its own groups of fashion colors. Each fall the same dark red appears. In 1989, this red was called burgundy. In 1990, it became deep rose and in 1991, claret.

The Five Color Families

Designers have always planned schemes using five **color families:** red, yellow, green, blue, and neutral. Let us look at each of these families in more detail.

THE RED COLOR FAMILY

When designers understand the subtle characteristics of each color family, they can create compositions with speed and skill. The red color family is considered **warm color** and natural color family. It has two variations: warm and cool. Warm reds (mixed with yellow) can be intensely hot. Cool reds are mixed with blue. Violet, a blue-red, is perfect when a red that is less hot is wanted.

Red is a conspicuous, signal color that becomes fragile, soft, and subdued in its pastel form (pink). The mood of late-day red is mellow, while its early-morning version is fragile. Bright reds are synonymous with action. Consider these possibilities when color planning. See Figures 5–8A and 5–8B.

Both warm colors and **cool colors** of bright intensity clash because their makeups are opposite. The warm and cool variations of red clash, and their differences create contrasting moods. They do not enhance each other. In harmonious compositions only one color dominates. One way to combine clashing colors is to vary their intensities or values. Think in terms of green (cool) clashing with red (warm). If both colors are pastel tints, they cease to clash, as in combinations of pink and mint.

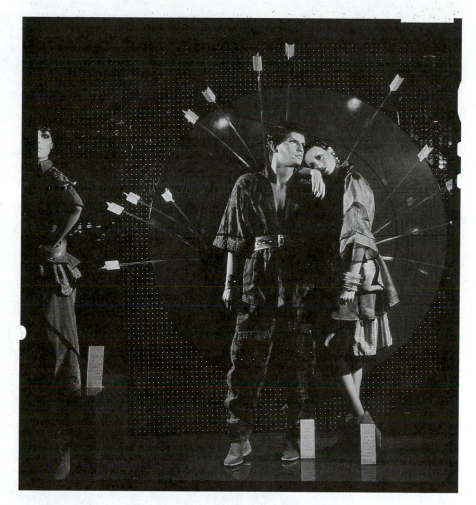

FIGURE 5–8A

Red is a strong visual force.

Close up, its impact is great.

Viewed from afar, its impact

is less. (Courtesy of Adel

Rootstein, Inc., London.)

When mixing pigments for clarity and intensity, mix only cool pigments with cool pigments or warm pigments with warm pigments. If you mix a red-blue pigment with a red-yellow pigment, the resulting color will be grayed and its brightness will be subdued. Blue and yellow are complements and produce gray when combined. On the other hand, this combination might be the best way to produce a grayed red. Red may also be grayed by mixing it with black or green, which dilutes color clarity.

Reds, like other color families, are affected by texture. Red shaggy wool is robust looking. Red silk looks refined and red glass looks shiny and sophisticated. Using the same red, a designer can change mood with texture. See Figure 5–9.

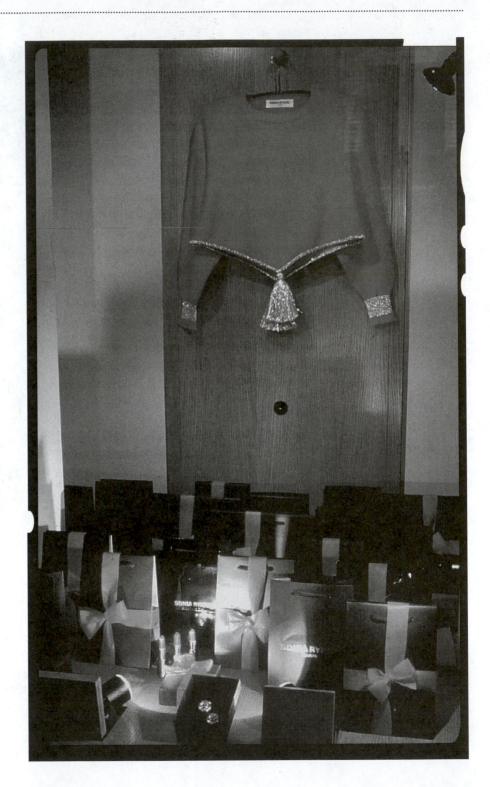

FIGURE 5–8B

Red is a signal, a

conspicuous color. It

flatters skin tones.

(Courtesy of Sonia Rykiel,

Saint Germain, Paris.)

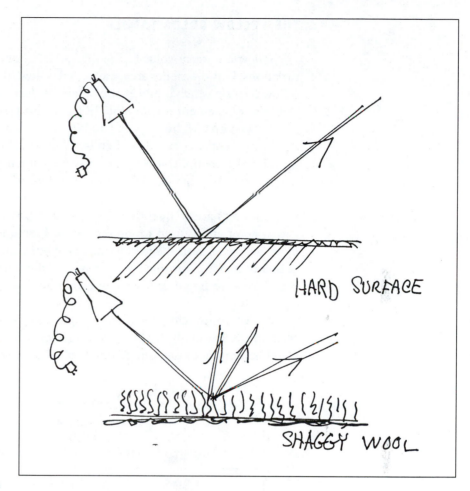

FIGURE 5–9

Surface texture changes color force. Red looks sophisticated on a resilient, reflective surface and looks robust on a shaggy wool.

To achieve a pure color, work with it until no other color is in its make-up. In the case of red, no trace of yellow or blue could remain.

Red is a romantic color, as suggested by a red rose or candlelight. It enhances wood and most skin colors. Mahogany contains traces of the red family and yellow-red is found in maple, oak, and walnut.

RED
(Warm Color Family)

Warm Variety (Orange)	Cool Variety (Violet)
YELLOW	BLUE

THE YELLOW COLOR FAMILY

Yellow is a warm color family that is rich, light, and fresh in all of its variations. Its two varieties are a warm, red-yellow (flame) and a cool, green-yellow (celery) which reminds one of lettuce, fern, and new willow sprouts. Yellow's complement is cool blue. In its grayest form, yellow remains light and looks crisp and fresh when combined with white. Yellow flatters many skin colors, enhances food, and enlivens wood colors.

Like the neutral colors, yellow may be painted on large areas to create low impact. As a pastel, it does not interfere with the foreground, merchandise, or displays. Yellow-orange is strong and is excellent as a signal. Caution areas are frequently painted school bus yellow. Yellow is also an action color and is used to identify active sportswear. In its dark, late-day form, yellow suggests the mellow moods of burnished copper and gold, the patina of antique furniture and brass, and the warmth of fire. The morning yellows are fragile and sensitive, while midday yellows are clean, clear, and bright.

As just mentioned, blue is the complement of yellow. However, intense blue and yellow clash. If you wish to mix these colors, make them pastel. Combinations of orange sherbet and soft blue are excellent.

YELLOW
(Warm Color Family)

Warm Variety (Orange)	Cool Variety (Lemon)
RED	GREEN

THE GREEN COLOR FAMILY

Green is basically a cool color family. Its two varieties are warm and cool. Yellow-green (avocado) is warm, while blue-green (forest) is cool. A #3 in value on the Munsell numbering system, green is midway in intensity.

Yellow-green is a natural color associated with garden greens, while a cool blue-green is considered man-made or artificial. Although red is green's complementary color, blue-greens do not enhance warm color families. For some, green is a difficult color to wear and it does not enhance the majority of wood colors. Yellow-green is usually the choice of apparel designers because its warmth is both wearable and flattering. See Figure 5–10.

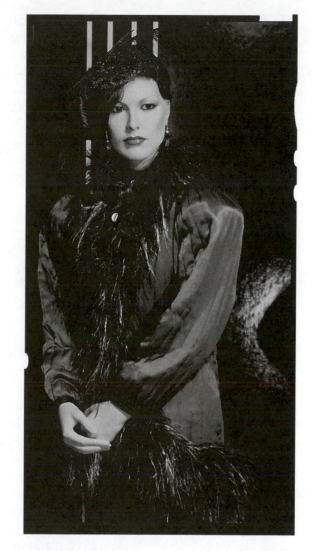

FIGURE 5–10

Few people can wear the

chilliest, emerald blue-green.

Fashion designers prefer to

develop neutral-colored lines

because they are wearable.

(Courtesy of Greneker, CA.)

Blue-green is such a cool family that it is used in packaging to symbolize refreshing, thirst-quenching drinks. Green always symbolizes the freshness of summer. Pastel green is a summer apparel color, while dark green is a favorite for fall. Yellow-green characterizes vegetables and is a good accent color for food presentation. Because green symbolizes grass, it makes a wonderful floor color when creating a summer landscape. It is not always necessary to use traditional colors in displays, however. Twentieth-century fine artists painted grass pink with great success.

GREEN
(Cool Color Family)

Warm Variety (Celery)	Cool Variety (Emerald)
YELLOW	BLUE

THE BLUE COLOR FAMILY

Blue is a cool color family. Blue is the color of iced water and creates a chilling effect. Like other colors, blue has both warm and cool varieties. Its cool variety is green-blue (turquoise) and its warm variety is red-blue (violet). Blue is a dark, recessive color and absorbs a great deal of light. It is a #4 in value, which means it is darker than green. Because dark colors absorb more light, additional light is needed for a display containing blues.

Blue is classified by some color theorists as artificial because it is not an earth color, although it does appear naturally in the sky and sea. Generally, blue is associated with sophistication, royalty, and worldliness. It does not enhance many wood or skin colors, however, and it is difficult to wear because it makes some skin colors look pale or anemic. Orange is its clashing opposite. See Figure 5–11.

Blue looks diffused in a nubby wool carpet, but it is sophisticated and classy on a lacquered box and light and airy in an atmospheric blue silk scarf. Blue-green is a fashionable resort apparel color. People in equatorial countries love to use cool blue and lots of white in their home interiors and in their garments. On the other hand, dark red-blue is used more in northern climates. It is very visible on white, and it is an excellent substitute for black letters when printing signs. The colors navy and blue jean indigo are red-blue varieties.

BLUE
(Cool Color Family)

Warm Variety (Violet)	Cool Variety (Aqua)
RED	GREEN

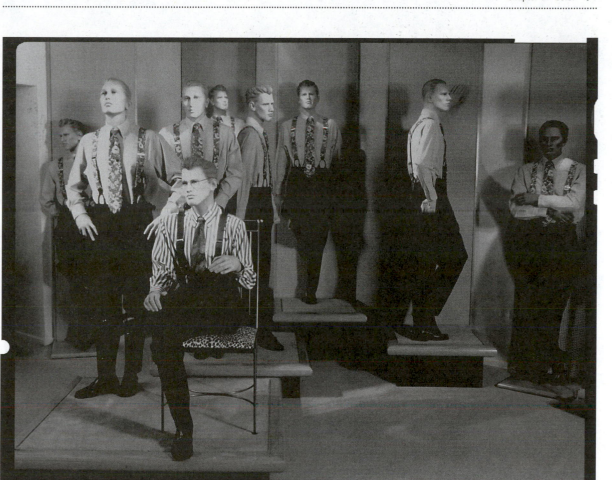

FIGURE 5–11

THE NEUTRAL COLOR FAMILY

Beige, black, buff, white, mushroom, and sand are generic names for some of the colors in the **neutral color** family. They do not impact strongly because they send weak color messages. Neutral items have a strong textural look because the object's surface has little color to focus on. See Figure 5–12.

It is impossible to think about the neutrals without thinking about the textural quality of fur, glass, metal, shaggy wool, and frosty silk. Excitement can be created by combining opposite textures such as rough wood and smooth metal. A tranquil mood can be created by combining similar textures such as velvet, glass, and silk. To help create a strong textural mood, use the neutral color family.

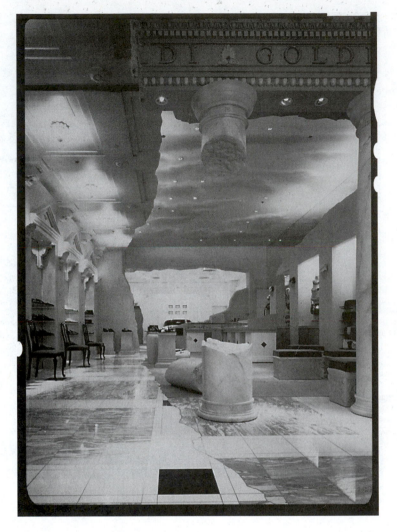

FIGURE 5–12

Although blue is a conspicuous

color, its small contribution

(20 percent) does not make it

dominate here. The neutrals

affect the textural look.

(Courtesy of Kubula Washatko

Architects, Inc., Cedarburg, WI

store. Goldi Shoes. Photo: Mark

Heffron, Milwaukee, WI.)

The neutrals do not demand or dictate color. Therefore, they are enhanced by all of the color families. There are two varieties of neutrals: warm and cool. The warm makeup is red and yellow (sand) while the cool variety is blue and green (slate).

For the past several decades, neutrals have been the biggest color fashion news and a favorite with clients. The neutral family is foremost in an apparel buyer's mind when ordering at market. Collections will always be developed with the neutrals as a base. Customers like the neutrals because they are so wearable. Correspondingly, buyers do not want to buy large quantities of skin-tone clashing bright colors that will eventually become

markdowns. For these reasons, many apparel designers develop collections based on the neutrals consumers want.

Neutrals make excellent tranquil background colors for public spaces, store interiors, and workrooms. Neutrals are perfect for merchandise and do not interfere with the endless seasonal color changes. A favorite fall/winter color scheme, neutrals look perfectly natural in a winter landscape.

Huge cities look neutral all year because they have little vegetation to establish the season's mood. The profusion of building materials, such as wood, glass, stone, and concrete, have influenced the look of city interiors, and make the neutral family a perfect choice.

NEUTRALS
(Warm and Cool Family)

Warm Variety (Sand)	Cool Variety (Slate)
RED and YELLOW	BLUE and GREEN

Color Planning for the Selling Floor

When presenting many unrelated classifications of merchandise on the selling floor, show all of the plum-colored shirts in one zone and all of the yellow bottoms in another. This system makes more sense than displaying by size or by vendor because it helps customers make related choices and thereby builds multiple sales. Customers often buy an item they see as one color in the store, only to find it is quite another color when they get home.

Apparel design within the primary market and at the retail level begins with color. Color is the first consideration of the manufacturer, the designer, and the visual merchandiser. The simplest way to plan color is to think of it in terms of color families. Many designers begin their planning based on the five distinct color families discussed previously. Apparel and home furnishings designers build entire collections around the neutral color family. Interior designers have made the neutrals dominate the market throughout the 1980s and 1990s.

Customers search out color. Color is often foremost in customer's minds when they are shopping, whether they are looking for a yellow chair, a red dress, or a blue suit. They will select some exciting, irresistible color by **impulse buying**, often adding significantly to their planned purchases.

Selling-floor presentations organized by color families help the customer locate merchandise classifications. Hang all like colors within a family together. Presenting merchandise by color families also creates an orderly look within a mix of merchandise and enables a customer to interact immediately with the merchandise.

Large assortments of mixed merchandise carried by mass merchants should be arranged by color for customers who cannot spend hours making selections. It is easy for customers to locate their favorite colors and begin selecting in this type of arrangement. On the other hand, small groups of clearance merchandise are best shown by size because the collections are broken up. Exclusive specialty stores may not be able to develop collections by color as easily as mass merchants because their stock consists of one-of-a-kind items. However, all items of similar color can be grouped to create harmonious color displays.

Some smaller chain store buyers keep the store's look in mind and select only those seasonal "hot" colors that are harmonious and coordinate well. A customer in a mall sees the impact of a one-color palette, which is very powerful. Buyers and regional managers use a plannogram to help the store associates fine-tune the placement of merchandise. A plannogram is a detailed drawing of the elevation of a fixture. It illustrates specifically where each item is to be presented on that fixture. The drawing might show blue tops on the third shelf and green tops on the tenth shelf, for example. The color placement of garments on the fixture might be determined by the store's color placement plan (rainbow color placement).

ARRANGING MERCHANDISE ON FIXTURES BY COLOR

Retailers who use plannograms to decide merchandise location by color identify their products by SKUs (pronounced "skews") or classification codes. These plans are not for individual interpretation and must be adhered to strictly to enable all of the stores in the group to maintain a uniform appearance. This control is important because chains may have hundreds of stores.

The rainbow color system is implemented when arranging merchandise by color on fixtures. Whether you are using a rounder or a quad, begin by arranging presenting dark colors to the left and progress to light colors to the right. Refer to a rainbow spectrum as you plan the position of the colors.

Merchandise presented in cubes can also be presented using the rainbow color system. Sizes in the same color are often arranged by placing small sizes on top shelves; larger sizes are placed on the bottom shelves. Begin a new row with each color change. Arrange patterns in the same way as they would be arranged on rounders or quads: place dark colors to the left and light colors to the right.

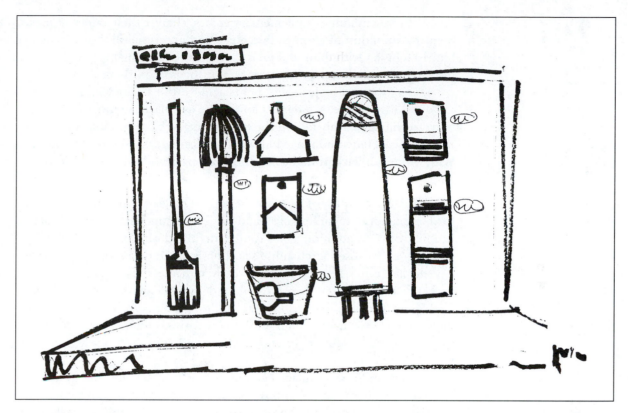

FIGURE 5–13

Plannograms are drawings given to the stores by central management to help the store associates organize merchandise on fixtures. This is a presentation of cleaning supplies in a home store.

COLOR COMPOSITION IN THE DISPLAY

A painter produces a picture by painting with pigment. A visual merchandiser produces a display by arranging merchandise and props to form color compositions based on display and design methods. The VM's color scheme is the result of arrangements produced using every item (such as merchandise or props) in the display. See Figure 5–13.

The surest way to develop a color plan is to base it on the merchandise. Evaluate the item and determine its dominant color. Repeat that color sufficiently (80 percent) in mass areas to create a dominant effect, and repeat the accent colors sufficiently (20 percent) to enhance and develop the color scheme. Consider the mood or character of the merchandise and select colors accordingly.

If all of the accent or dominant colors are assembled on the display's left, a lopsided look will result. If all the accent and dominant colors appear on the bottom of the display, a layered look will result. Therefore, all colors should be arranged evenly throughout the display.

When assembling complementary colors, change their values to make them harmonious and compatible. Reds and greens clash, but they combine well in shades of pink and mint green. If two clashing props are placed next to each other, undue attention will be focused on them.

Using balanced color value helps achieve the desired look. Balance dark and light colors. If a dark color is used as a background, a pale color in front will appear obvious. If the two colors are close in value and intensity, they will blend and make it difficult to distinguish one from the other. With white as a background color, the items in front look very obvious.

COLOR THEME.   Color has the capacity to establish a display theme for merchandise. It can establish and project all moods: happiness, gaiety, action, needs. In addition, color can be identified with price, quality, style, and image. Because merchandise selection is based on mood and lifestyle, any display can be constructed to communicate these qualities. Color evokes a theme faster than any other design element. Color planning enables an associate to develop merchandise presentations based on a thematic scheme for mannequins and display forms. Other design elements, such as texture, silhouette, and balance, enhance and strengthen the theme and mood.

For example, when black earrings are a "hot" fashion item, dress as many of the mannequins as possible with black earrings. This could be the first step in developing an accessory theme. In addition, black belts and shoes enhance the earrings and strengthen the theme. Avoid adding other colors because they dilute the impact of the focus color. Do not worry that too much of the same color will be monotonous. The silhouette, light, texture, and location of the items produce endless variations in how the color is seen.

In addition, a theme may be developed based on the color of a garment. A detail, such as gold buttons on a jacket, may provide inspiration. Reinforce the look by adding gold jewelry. Gold metallic props further enhance the look and the theme. For more impact, repeat the color from one mannequin to another and in displays from department to department. The customers will be inspired by the consistent and harmonious accessory theme.

Lifestyle represented by the garment determines the color theme for the presentation. Because active sportswear is associated with bright color blocking and late-day wear is subdued, these characteristics create a good beginning for establishing a display. See Figure 5–14.

New color ideas can come from other sources. There was a popular apparel color theme in the 1920s, and again in the 1930s. In the 1920s colors

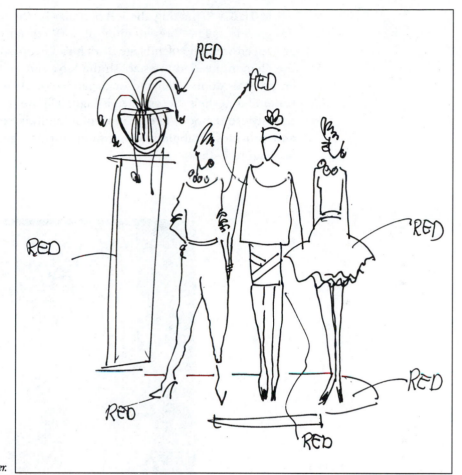

FIGURE 5–14

When creating a display, plan color repeats. All items in the display contribute color. Based on the merchandise, red is repeated sufficiently to create color dominance and color order.

were neutral, pearl flesh, metallic, lustrous colors, and whites; soft lavender, peach green, and rose were second-level colors. In the 1930s colors were brighter than the 1920s, and there were neutrals, metallics, straws, and floral colored solids. Mass merchants use some specific color families for their store interiors, while elegant specialty stores use others. Furniture presentation requires the use of one color family and a men's store requires another. The merchandise in each store requires a specific color theme to maintain the store's image. New Yorkers prefer one color and Chicagoans prefer another based on their distinct regional lifestyles, the look of their cities, and their climates. In addition, there are Southwestern regional colors and West Coast regional colors. A customer will dress for the occasion, and the style varies from New York to Los Angeles.

MOOD.   Thinking about mood may be the beginning of yet another design idea. The presentation of a Victorian-style garment may be enhanced with an assemblage of rich red props. The props might be just the element needed to establish the look and mood. As mentioned earlier, neutrals do not demand or dictate color. As a result, their moods are tranquil and their acceptance is high. The neutrals can establish a high-tech style and mood. The neutral color family is excellent for public spaces and provides a fabulous background for art, **antiques,** and collections. See Figure 5–15.

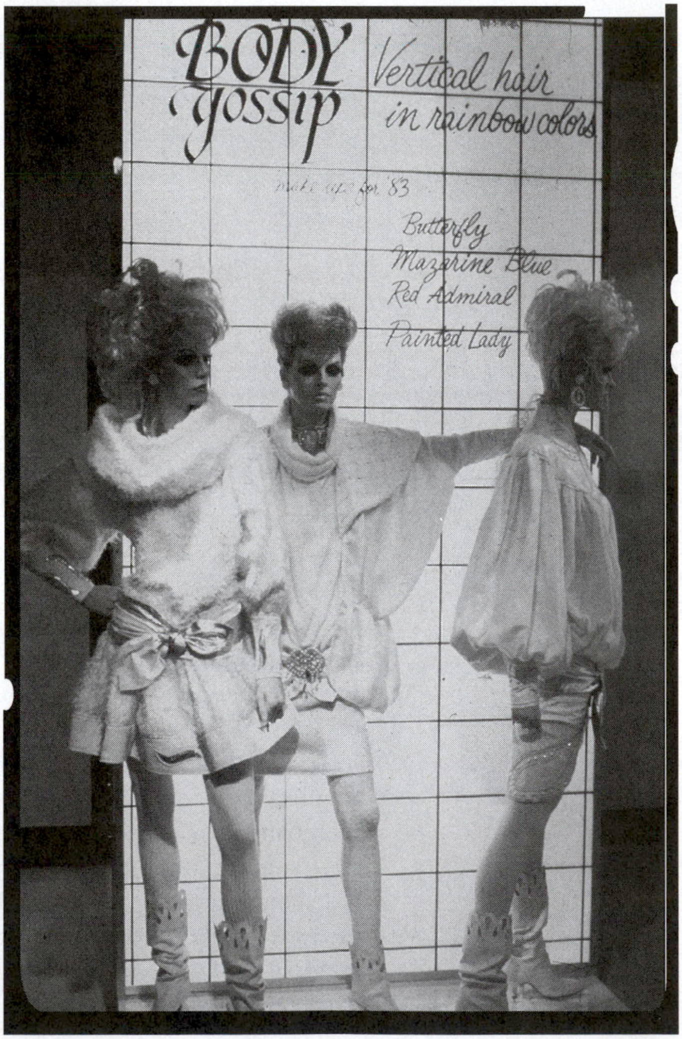

FIGURE 5–15

The color mood of this updated transitional group is expressed well by the designer's choice of winter whites. Color for the presentation was based on lifestyle. (Courtesy of Adel Rootstein, London.)

Green, on the other hand, creates a strong, cool mood, which is too strong for some public places. A combination of soft greens can provide the mood of a rich, tranquil forest. A soft mood, created by an assemblage of stuffed toys, can be enhanced with pastel colors. Warm reds enhance food and create an excellent mood for dining. Romance is associated with red, pink, rose, and violet. Sophistication is associated with blue; informality is associated with aqua.

The fashion press is constantly describing color as "shocking" or "quiet." The following are some moods created by color: white: joy; red: warmth; blue: truth; black: despair; and gold: elegance.

DOMINANT COLORS. Displays that are assembled with a busy mixed palette—equal amounts of green, red, yellow, blue, and neutrals—look unorganized. Customers reject these compositions because they are constantly looking for order and direction. When the VM assembles color with one dominant color family, the VM develops order.

Begin assembling by developing a dominant color family. Accent colors are important to embellish one's composition. Accent colors add character. It is sometimes difficult to identify the dominant color of patterned garments. Do not confuse the dominant color with the most conspicuous color. Always look for the color that contributes the largest percent of mass.

ACCENT COLORS. **Accent colors** are so named because they are found on small items and do not dominate. Accent colors are important for design development as **enhancements**, but they should make up only 10 to 15 percent of the composition and should be repeated evenly throughout. It is wrong to paint accent colors on large mass areas because they weaken the theme. Their purpose is to embellish the dominant colors and to remain secondary.

Accent colors can be chosen from any color family, including complementary colors, as long as they retain secondary importance and embellish the dominant color family in hue, value, and intensity. How the color ratio percentages (90/10, 95/5, or 85/15) are assembled determines the individuality and creativity necessary for good design.

COLOR MATCHING. The ability to match dissimilar items is easy if they are the same color. An assortment of garments and accessories of different designs and textures look matched if they have the same color. Vinyl and velvet, which are texturally different, look alike when viewed from five feet away if they are the same color. Their differences become visually undistinguishable.

Props of glass, wood, stone, and paper can be blended to match merchandise by painting them the same color. Change the value of the items to create added excitement and variation.

FORECASTING.   In planning spring displays, the VM should use current colors. Color forecasting informs the retail industry about the new colors that are introduced each year, those that remain current, and others that are on their way out. Fashion and home furnishings designers want to use the most up-to-date colors for the season. VM designers must know about these colors far in advance so they can plan and buy for future storewide promotions. Merchandise and props must be based on the "hottest" colors. They cannot wait for the season's arrivals before making their color plans.

Large retailers, designers, and **manufacturers** pay for color forecasting services. Associations, fashion groups, textile producers, apparel manufacturers, home furnishings manufacturers, and **freelance** advisors are some of the professionals in the color forecasting business. When selecting color services, you might request specialized advice because professionals tend to specialize in textiles, paint, bath fixtures, apparel, cosmetics, and accessories to name a few areas.

According to Margaret Walch, director of the Color Association of the United States, "There are basic principles of color forecasting: (1) people like change; (2) there's a logical, cyclical color progression; and (3) taste will change in an orderly way." Said June Rocke at Milliken, "Color forecasting has to do with the human response to color. It's highly subjective, and a good color forecaster will know what to pay attention to. The 1980s can be thought to be colored in a pastel way. Sure enough the 1986 Cadillac was Light Driftwood, Rose Quartz, and Sun Gold."

Ed Newman of Dan River, Inc., commented, "Many colors make the natural progression through the seasons; a wine becomes purple, the purple moves to magenta, and the magenta to pink. No mystery—just logic" (Jarnow et al, 1991).

Communicating About Color

When a group of people is asked to think about red, many varieties of red come to each person's mind: intense red, pink, or rose. Because each of us thinks about color differently, VMs should communicate about color with specific fabric swatches or color chips. A VM communicates daily with many store associates about color, so try to be specific.

SUMMARY

1. Color is a mood generator that influences how customers shop and what they buy. Color is the first thing customers have in mind when they shop for apparel and home fashions. They look for fashion color ideas and news in store presentations.

2. A store's color theme can be established by the quality of the merchandise and how it is displayed. The lifestyle projected by the apparel influences the color theme of the corresponding promotions and displays.

3. A composition begins with a dominant color family and an accent color family based on a theme. The ratio is 80 to 90 percent dominant color scheme, 20 to 10 percent accent color family.

4. A color wheel is a logical, theoretical explanation of color arranged in a circle. Color is used by application, however. In practice, although the neutrals are not a dominant part of the wheel, they are important when selecting color families for store interiors and merchandise.

5. Historical periods are identified by specific popular color families.

6. Use the five color families to help organize displays: red, yellow, green, blue, and neutral.

7. Good color planning can help organize merchandise on fixtures and on the selling floor. Use the color families as an organizational guide.

8. Repeating color in displays creates focus. If a color repeats often, it becomes obvious.

9. Use fashion colors projected by color forecasters to update displays.

BUSINESS HIGHLIGHT

Color Feature:
Is Heaven Really "Linen White"?

An interview with Ken Charbonneau, color and merchandising manager at Benjamin Moore & Co., a paint manufacturer in Montvale, NJ.

Author: How do you develop color projections?

Ken: I am a member of the Color Market Association with a membership of 1,200 color stylists who are color experts in the industry. We work with manufacturers of textiles, wallpapers, and home furnishings to review the hottest-selling colors. We discuss colors that are past the peak on the fashion curve and colors that should be introduced. We make our choices based on a great deal of brainstorming and careful comparisons.

Author: How would you advise a student or new professional to research color?

Ken: Join a color group or subscribe to a color service. The Color Association of the United States, NY, the Color Marketing Group, NY, National Home Fashion Group, NY, and the Fashion Group, NY, are but a few who forecast color and provide color workshops. In addition, the color services Color Box, NY, Alison Webb, NY, Judy Owens, NY, and fashion magazine color editors provide color forecasting on a subscription basis.

Author: Do fashion and interior-design color palettes have commonalities?

Ken: Yes, we share the same vogue color palettes. But nonclassic colors have a shorter life in the fashion industry. New interior colors are introduced in commercial places. Macy's may have a display or department with a very new color, the customers soon begin to ask about it.

Author: How does lifestyle impact on color?

Ken: War, economic downturns, social change, and political events, in addition to the customer's education, all influence color choices.

Author: What are some current fashion colors?

Ken: Violet is, and it wasn't five years ago. Mauve is disappearing. Classic colors such as navy, indigo blue, and dark red are always fashionable. They experience name changes for sales stimulation. Ivory was our best seller for years. We renamed it Oriental Silk and its sales moved from twentieth to sixth place, outselling our reliable off-whites.

Author: How often do you change color palettes?

Ken: We create new color boards every two years.

Author: How do customers prioritize color when selecting merchandise?

Ken: At POP, it's the customer's first consideration.

Author: I love off-white. Is it still in demand?

Ken: I must tell you a story. I was interviewed by James Barron for his article in the *New York Times*, "Which White is the Right White?" After a long interview, I could not resist a parting word. Shaking his hand, I said, "Jim, when you go to heaven, it will be Linen White."

DISCUSSION QUESTIONS

1. How do you begin a color composition?
2. How do you establish a color theme and mood?
3. Name the five color families.
4. Why is color important to the customer?
5. Who uses color forecasting services?
6. Why create color dominance?
7. How do you develop color accents?
8. Why does the color wheel represent a theory, and how does it differ from color practice?
9. Why is color important in setting up a floor?
10. Why is color enhancement important?

CHAPTER PROJECT

Project Objective: Working as a group, develop a display using a dominant color family and two supporting accent colors.

Project Instructions: (Choose One)
1. In the school display window or on a tabletop, create a display with one color family dominating by taking 90 percent of the space and an accent color taking only 10 percent.
2. If you do not have a school display window, ask a local merchant to allow you to create the display in his or her window. Most merchants will welcome the opportunity.
3. Create a tabletop display fashion of accessories, making one color dominate by assuming 90 percent of the space. Fill the balance with accent colors.

REFERENCE

Jarnow, J. et al. 1991. *Inside the Fashion Business,* Fifth Ed. New York: Macmillan.

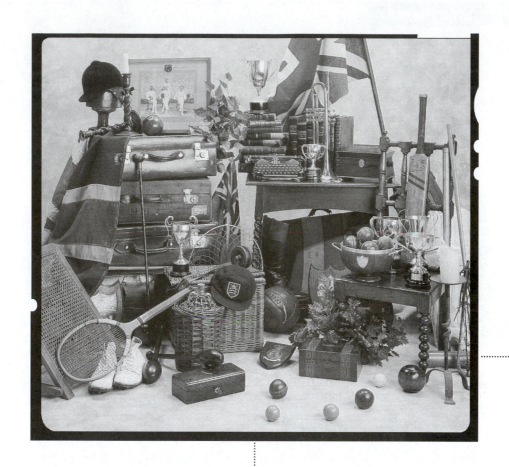

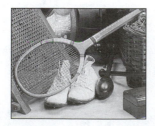 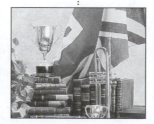 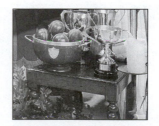

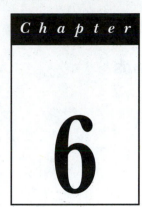

Display Props

*A*fter completing this chapter, you will be able to:

1. Appreciate the vast number of available props.

2. Describe where to locate props.

3. Identify what merchandise is used as props.

4. Explain why props are subordinate to the merchandise in a display.

5. Tell why props are used.

Props

The mood, character, and number of display props required to dazzle the public depends on the store's target market (customer), merchandise, size, and type. Upper-end department stores and large upper-end specialty stores allocate big budgets to buy, build, and rent decor. They tend to offer thematic displays and make fashion points with elaborate, stylish, and complex windows. These stores want to create the fashion experience. Their windows require either fine art and decor of exceptional quality or simple materials handled creatively to enhance their luxe designer apparel. See Figures 6–1 and 6–2.

THEMATIC DISPLAYS

Thematic displays are just what their term suggests—themes should be based on merchandise that can be displayed and promoted successfully. The theme should be determined by the style, price, and quantity of merchandise on hand, as well as on the merchandise's easy identification with a specific topic. For example, the topic or theme could be "A Garden at Macy's" or "Donna Karan at Barney's." Most displays are based on a topic.

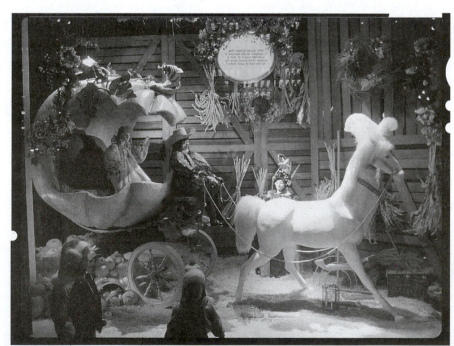

FIGURE 6–1

Giant retailers provide large budgets to create complex thematic displays. (Courtesy of Marshall Field's, Chicago, IL.)

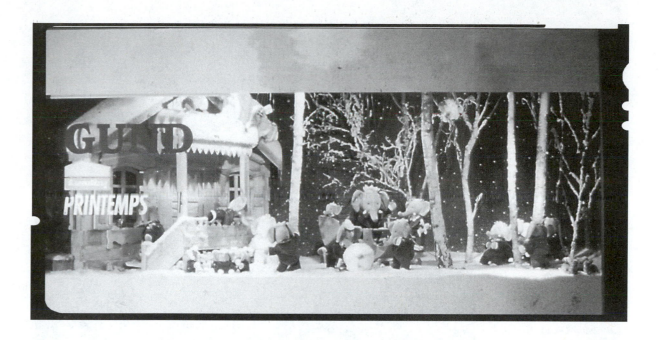

FIGURE 6–2

Decor of exceptional

quality is used to create

this stylish display.

(Courtesy of Printemps,

Display highlights are in focus display areas, with tie-in promotions, events, and advertising. Marshall Field's has had Italian and French promotions; Saks has used the theater for inspiration. Their "A Little Night Music" was a successful theme with which New Yorkers could readily identify. Topical and trendy thematic displays have the added advantage of drawing free press and other publicity.

The experienced VM knows how to balance props and merchandise for importance and impact. All items other than the merchandise in a display are props. Merchandise from other divisions that support the look and theme can become props, however. This is called cross merchandising. Furniture used as a display backdrop is both merchandise and a prop, for example. The housewares, department, food-wine, china-glass, art, fabric, furniture, accessory, and drapery departments are all wonderful sources for props. Ladders give merchandise a lift and frying pans make the look hot.

Props must be subordinate to the merchandise. They should complement and enhance the merchandise, but they should never upstage it. Merchandise must be highlighted and placed in front and central to the display because the merchandise must capture the customer's focus. Props should never clutter a display. They should always relate to the display or the merchandising theme. A strong, clear message must be sent to the customer.

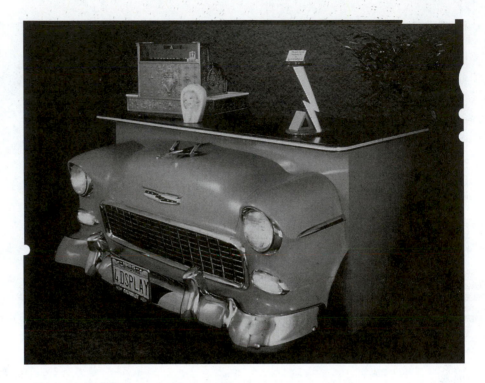

FIGURE 6–3

Creative VMs experiment

in the race to showcase the

newest look. (Courtesy of

Continental Design Group,

Sacramento, CA.)

TRENDY PROPS

In most metropolitan centers, upper-end stores face fashionable avenues. Their VM staffs are expected to be the first to present the newest look in the most creative way. To be first to do so is a never-ending race. See Figure 6–3.

The VM staff at fashion-forward stores always know where to locate art, antiques, and other materials to use as props to support their fashion themes. Their superstar status depends on trendy backgrounds and "in vogue" props for each new season and each new style. See Figures 6–4 and 6–5.

In the 1970s, one could pick up a **consumer's** fashion **publication** and often see fashion shots with camels and the desert as backgrounds. Display houses were soon producing hundreds of foamcore pyramids and palm trees to use in display windows. The VMs also used stylish movies, interior-design trends, and television to create "now windows." In the mid 1980s, scrubbed Irish pine tables and cabinets were hot display items. At first, only a few trendy stores used them. Later they were used everywhere. Many vendors sold the Irish tables at the New York display shows but soon, true to the fashion bell curve, they were on their way out. Any fashion item that is big today will be passé tomorrow.

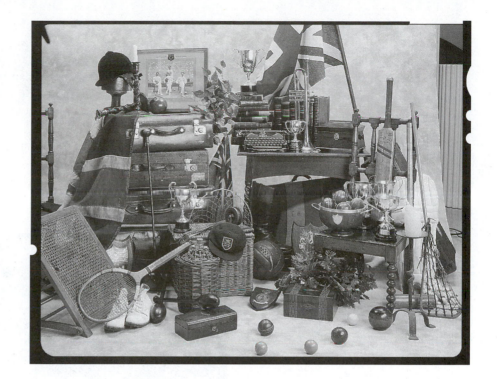

FIGURE 6–4

Antiques are trendy props

that are always in vogue.

They fit every merchandise

classification. (Courtesy

of London Antiques,

Costa Mesa, CA.)

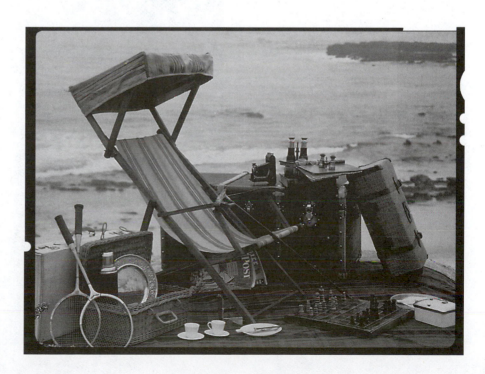

FIGURE 6–5

Shopping for props is easier

when the vendor stocks the

most exciting antiques.

(Courtesy of London

Antiques, Costa Mesa, CA.)

A WORLD EXPERIENCE

To determine display themes, one can look to London, Paris, Tokyo, Florence, New York, and Chicago for fashion declarations, namely art exhibitions, social happenings, and political events. Gene Moore, display director at Tiffany's in the early 1980s, often used newspaper clippings as background decor for his display windows. Bob Currie, display director at Henri Bendel, New York, in the 1970s used pop-culture items to enhance his fashion themes.

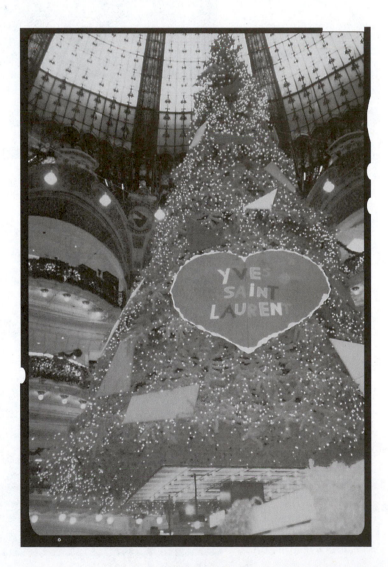

FIGURE 6–6

Christmas display

theme. Yves Saint

Laurent focuses on an

international event.

(Courtesy of Printemps,

Paris, France.)

Whether the decor you choose is an architectural element or a **frieze**, it must be current and it must be understood by your customer. Above all, it must enhance the merchandise. Window decor is so trendy that customers are willing to buy props. Many of the best fashion-forward customers copy display decor and ideas to use in their homes. See Figure 6–6.

FORMULA TYPE WINDOWS

Sales associates at small regional and national specialty shops create **formula type displays**, which consist of one prop, one to three mannequins, one platform, and three overhead spotlights. Budget and staff constraints at these stores demand the simplest displays. The store manager may install the window with props shipped from corporate display using installation instructions. The regional display associate or team might assist the sales associates with installing the display.

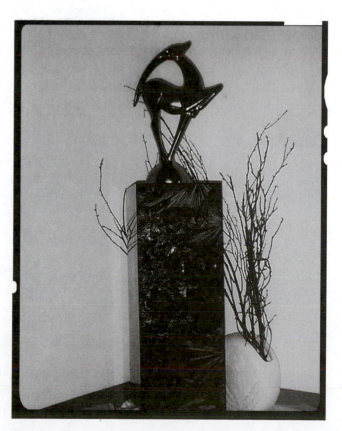

FIGURE 6–7

Display vendors create thematic groups of props enabling the VM to buy only the column or all of the props in the group. This group would be excellent to prop art deco looks. (Courtesy of Continental Design Group, Sacramento, CA.)

The regional team is usually overbooked, which affords little time for installing more than the simplest display. At your local mall you will probably find endless variations of formula windows. A few mall stores present merchandise creatively, however, and take the time to select and present unique decor provocatively. See Figure 6–7.

DECORATIVE SYMBOLISM

Realism in a display window is disturbing for most people. These windows are theatrically located, proportioned, designed, and lighted. In addition, the **mannequins** are not realistically proportioned. They are taller than average and have large, stylized hands and large feet. Their bodies are designed to enhance specific fashion silhouettes. They have higher waistlines for an empire look and much longer legs for miniskirts, for example. For these reasons, creating real-life backgrounds for these mannequins is absurd. Simple decor, such as a panel with a huge blowup of the Sear's Tower and metro colors, may be all that is needed to create the look of a city for a small store. A beach towel may suffice to prop a swimsuit window. On the other hand, sophisticated national chains such as Saks may require more detailed, complex windows.

Choosing Props

When choosing props for a display, think of the obvious relationships between the decor, theme, fashion, and event. Make many compositional notes or sketches of the intended display and choose one. Then edit the concept by eliminating superfluous items. Select only those props that look as if they belong without detracting from your subject. Some props are difficult to find, make, and install. Do not waste time trying to create the impossible.

DIFFICULT PROPS

When planning to make the prop, consider every detail of its fabrication, structure, material, installation, and handling before proceeding. Remember, window temperatures can reach extremes and melt plastics or freeze water. Think about electrical sources for lighting. If you want to hang a prop, check for sturdy ceiling hooks and grids.

One fashion store decorated its beautiful Christmas trees with real fruit. On his daily window check, the store's VM was surprised to find a gooey melted mess of dripping fruit. Intensely hot spotlights had ruined the beautiful, elegant trees he had spent hours meticulously creating. Mistakes can be costly. Consider the gigantic task of redoing all of those trees and all of those windows during the hectic Christmas season.

Designer paints do not react well to hot sunlight streaming into a display window. Many glues melt with changing temperatures. Because of heat, cardboards warp in just a few days. Fabrics and wood expand and shift due to heat and vibrations caused by exterior traffic.

ANTIQUES AND REPRODUCTIONS

Antiques and reproductions have always been the grandames of props. Their interest and value are riveting, and pieces from any period can be chosen to match merchandise. High-tech pieces establish a look that suddenly wanes. Antiques, however, remain elegant decorations. Forty-year-old items are now considered collectible or antique.

Furniture, household items, architectural fragments, friezes, glass, china, textiles, costumes, and interior fragments provide endless materials to prop displays. Every retailer uses antiques from time to time as display background, props, or fixtures on which to show merchandise.

ART OBJECTS

Paintings and fine art have graced display windows since the beginning. Fine art, the first choice, has been a leader over decorative art, but the relationship of the two art types has always been close and they are used interchangeably. Paintings, drawings, and sculpture can establish and enhance mood for any period or style. The social value, as well as the decorative impact, of art is understood by our society.

ARTIFICIAL GRASS AND SNOW

Unfinished display windows and showcase floors should be covered, preferably with something that can be integrated into the display. Artificial snow or grass provides interesting floor cover for displays and mannequin platforms. Additionally, bark, cork, sawdust, oatmeal, grain, and just about any material that matches the display's color, texture, or theme can be used for this purpose.

FLOWERS, CANE, AND BAMBOO

Flowers, whether fresh, dried, silk, or paper, are available in huge varieties and make excellent decor. Select from large tropical blooms to diminutive garden buds for showcases, display windows, or interior store decor. Choose flowers to fit the season. Flowers can be grown, purchased, picked in a field, or made from exciting **Italian papers**. Decorate the selling floor with inexpensive branches in baskets or fasten the flowers above a light cornice to decorate a back wall. Flowers are eye-catching in natural colors and look upscale when sprayed an exotic, electric color to match a display theme. A stock of varied branches and flowers can provide instant display material. See Figure 6–8.

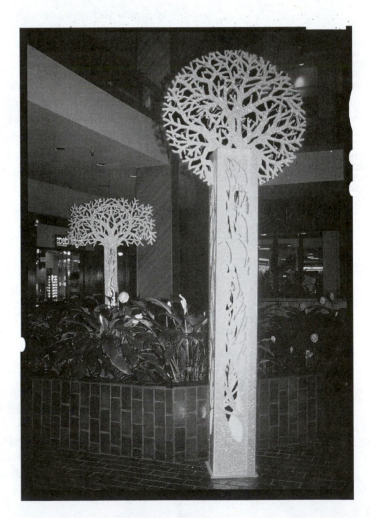

FIGURE 6–8

A stylized tree standing in a mall court adds interest and decorative impact. (Courtesy of R & K International, Jersey City, NJ.)

Cane and bamboo poles add interest to the garment displayed on them. Bamboo poles are exciting when massed by the dozens in oversized urns with textiles flying from them. Bamboo is also interesting when placed on the floor in geometric patterns or when tied in bundles as background pieces. For centuries Japanese flower designers have arranged them beautifully and effectively.

RIBBONS, BRAIDS, AND BOWS

Ribbons and braids in the colors of flowers and fashions are readily available and fit any theme. See Figure 6–9.

Consider elaborate designs, colors, and widths for finishing panel borders and tablecloths. Ties for gift boxes, festoons, proscenium swags (the theater-like valance or arch surrounding the window glass), flower arrangements, and architectural friezes require special widths and should be flexible enough to bend around curves and mitered corners. Metallic fancies provide stability for large swags. Tinsel colors shimmer and glitter in the light. Scotch-plaid ribbon in almost any colors enhances pots of heather

FIGURE 6–9

Ribbon, a VM's favorite material, is available in many colors, textures, and patterns. This overscaled ribbon attracts attention. (Courtesy of R & K International, Jersey City, NJ.)

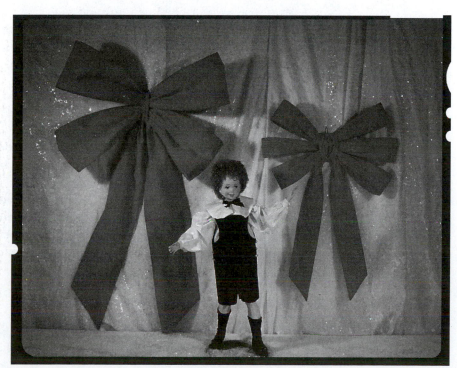

FIGURE 6–10

Patriotic bows

reaffirm a U.S.A.

theme. (Courtesy of

R & K International,

Jersey City, NJ.)

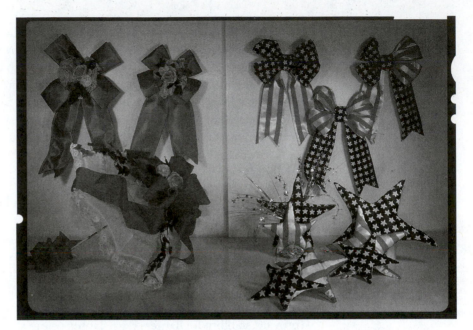

and English woolens. Use colorful, elegant ribbons of grosgrain (brocade-style weave with ribbed texture) and moiré (a watermark appearance on cotton, silk, and synthetics) patterns to trim jewelry pads and showcases. Keep an assortment of ribbons on hand to be used as art borders or box bows, or to bind and decorate a bundle of dried weeds. See Figure 6–10.

BANNERS

Felt, cotton, and silk banners can be highly decorative when screened with interesting lettering, decorative borders, and clip art announcing the store's merchandising message. To herald a special sale, use banners on floor stands to place the message next to the merchandise. For an overall store effect, however, hang banners from the ceiling. Banners are visible and effectively printed with bold colors and **typeface**. They are excellent substitutes when traditional signs and holders will not do the job.

BASKETS, BARRELS, AND BOXES

Baskets, barrels, and boxes are nontraditional fixtures that can organize and hold merchandise. Their colors and textures enhance many merchandise classifications. Their special use as props can generate a theme, such as the look of a general store. Plastic and wire crates in vivid primary colors create a high-tech look that is especially effective in high-tech food stores.

DECORATIVE SCREENS AND PANELS

Decorative screens and panels hide unsightly looks and ugly structural details and camouflage display window back walls. Highly decorative screens establish a theme and add beauty. In the 1960s, display suppliers began silk-screening foamcore with electrifying designs such as flat patterns, architectural photographs, landscapes, prints, interior sketches, and street photographs. These suppliers used nearly every subject or art form.

Foamcore is a joy to use. It is lightweight, easy to cut and shape, and simple to install. It can be painted to create murals, solid colors, and illusion finishes. It can be stapled or glued to objects, and objects are easily glued to it. It is available in varying thicknesses in sheets 4 feet x 8 feet and 4 feet x 4 feet. It also comes in an array of colors and finishes that include metallic and textured.

In time, excessive use of foamcore created the formula type display mentioned earlier, which uses three mannequins. Floor material is added and a decorative foamcore panel is installed in the background. Almost all display vendors carried a large collection of preprinted scenic foamcore panels. Many VMs now prefer to cut their own foamcore designs and paint the panels with their original themes and colors. In so doing they create striking oriental designs, barn doors, Victorian doors, superscaled art, paintings, architectural fragments, and friezes.

FLOOR COVERINGS

The floor of the display window commands about 25 percent of the display's total space. Many VMs overlook the floor's great contribution to design and the importance of its large area to the total display look. Like all of the other elements in the display, the floor should match the display's theme, color, texture, and design. Most displays are on platforms. Floors in display windows are generally elevated 12 to 18 inches. The floor's elevated sight line makes it conspicuous. Therefore, it should be treated interestingly.

If the floor finish is permanent and is carpeted or painted in a color inconsistent with the display's dominant color family, cover it to match the theme. Any material can be used to cover a floor. Cork comes in many colors and is easy to store and use for this purpose. Other floor-covering materials include gravel, sand, bark chips, raw oatmeal, grains, confetti, textiles, signs, and macaroni. Experiment with floor covering possibilities to add excitement to a display.

Inspired floors can be achieved by using textured foamcore, branches, leaves, dried flowers, or Italian paper that is cut into striking floral and petal designs. Textiles can enliven the floor when draped, stretched, shredded, knotted, woven, and used for upholstering.

To become more aware of design solutions, make many sketches that exaggerate the floor's emphasis and experiment with floor covering possibilities.

PAPER AND CARDBOARD

Seamless paper creates an instant display background. It is available in a large array of colors and widths. Art papers, construction paper, tissue paper, and matte boards are readily available and have limitless uses as showcase liners, package wraps, container covers, and flower construction. Wallpapers are interesting when applied to decorative panels. Cover a floor with paper and streamers to add excitement.

Cardboard tubes of varying diameters and lengths can be wonderful columns when spackled and painted in fantasy finishes. They are light and easy to work with. Tie them in bundles and place them horizontally on the floor in unusual patterns.

POTS AND FLORAL CONTAINERS

Grecian urns and flowerpots piled high or placed in rows of oversized clay planting boxes can add visual impact to a display. Use huge pots as pedestals to hold dress forms and merchandise or fresh plants and paper flowers. Pots and floral containers are long-lived props.

PEDESTALS

Columns, orange crates, and oil drums can be used as pedestals for mannequins, forms, and merchandise. Old porch columns are perfect for shop fabrication. Architectural fragments in assorted finishes can hold flower arrangements or add the special theatrical touch to decor that shoppers have come to expect.

TEXTILES

Draping fabric in a display or in a background can produce a fabulous romantic look. Use soft, flowing textiles in solid colors or choose interesting textures, florals, geometrics, trompe l'oeils, and scenics to create any mood to enhance any merchandise. Upholstered pads and panels are great to showcase floors or to serve as stylish props to create a period style. Fabric is a lush way to cover just about anything that needs a surface change. Felt, rayon, burlap, muslin, and chintz are used by the bolt for display pads, tablecloths, and backgrounds.

CHRISTMASTIME PROPS

The Christmas season requires the VM to use a vast assortment of props. This is when the store is more completely decorated than at any other time. Trees, wreaths, swags, ornaments, papers, lights, animations, and endless assortments of artificial pine trims and flowers are used. See Figures 6–11, 6–12, 6–13, 6–14, 6–15, and 6–16.

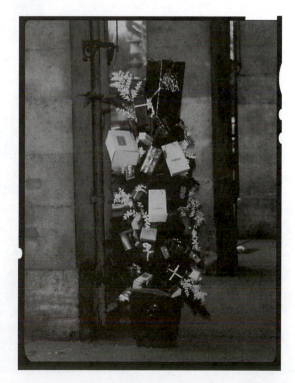

FIGURE 6–11

It is refreshing to discover a

display not in a store, but out

on the street yards from the

store. In Paris, on Rue de

Rivoli across from the Jardin

des Tuileries, stands the small

jewelry shop's tree.

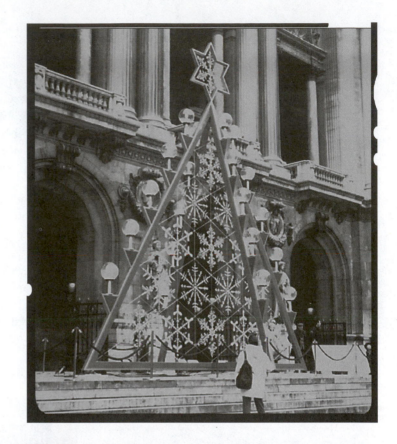

FIGURE 6–12

Christmas is a lush time when vast sums are spent on VM. In Paris, Baccarat created a giant tree on Opera's steps with crystal ornaments. A guard and a dog were posted to protect this valuable tree.

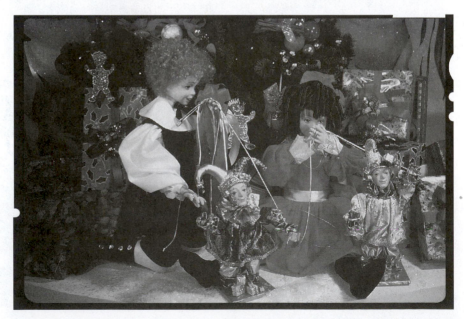

FIGURE 6–13

At Christmastime, VM and vendors create magic. Animated mechanical displays delight all shoppers. (Courtesy of R & K International, Jersey City, NJ.)

FIGURE 6–14

Extravagantly elegant Christmas displays such as this one from R & K are installed across the U.S.A. and Europe. They seldom present merchandise. (Courtesy of R & K International, Jersey

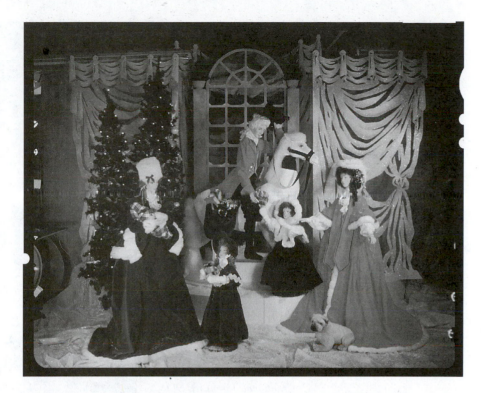

FIGURE 6–15

This is how a VM would see the display in the vendor's New York showroom. There are panels, columns, and animations. The VM could buy the package as shown or she could purchase just part of it. (Courtesy of R & K International, Jersey City, NJ.)

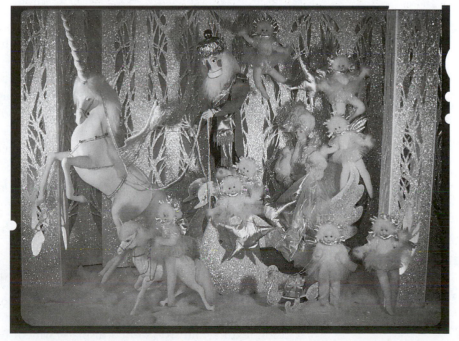

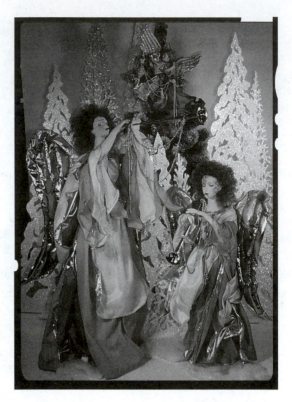

FIGURE 6–16

Sometimes Christmas trim is called "institutional." The holiday or season is celebrated without presenting merchandise. A VM would ask R & K to scale this design to fit the dimensions of the store. (Courtesy of R & K International, Jersey City, NJ.)

Decorating a store for one Christmas season can be very costly. Many VMs begin by buying a smaller amount of trim and adding to it for the next three or more years. Also, main store trim may be used later in branch stores, but this requires adequate packing and warehouse storage.

Retailers spend huge amounts for **Christmas trim** throughout their store, hoping to demonstrate their caring attitude. In the season's spirit, sales associates are motivated to sell more and, as a marketing tool, the gift-giving tradition is reinforced. Trim is placed as early as possible so that, as customers acquire more ready cash, they will be inspired to make repeat purchases. After-Christmas buying is stimulated by leaving trim up for at least one week after the holidays.

Rent, Buy, or Build?

Small, 1,300-square-feet mall, chain, or independent stores lack storage space for large prop collections. As a result, whatever props are used must be discarded. This means that inexpensive, simple props should be used.

A department store's VM can borrow the perfect shoe in the perfect color, texture, and style to fit a display garment from a stock of hundreds in the store's shoe department. In contrast, small fashion stores may not have a shoe department and may have to borrow, rent, or buy shoes. In fact, small fashion-forward stores must rent props, such as antiques, art, fashions, and housewares. If adequate budgets are not set up for shoe rental, for example, mannequins wear the same shoes for many apparel changes and styles. Often the shoes are out of season. Also, some shoes may not look good with some garments. A store lacking home furnishings, fashion accessories, an art department, and a carpentry shop to build or refurbish props must rent these corresponding display items.

In large metropolitan centers, many retailers rent merchandise to the advertising industry for use as photo shoot props. The rental charge is based on a percentage of the item's retail value. Many antique stores and art galleries also rent their merchandise for prop use.

Unlike small, independent stores, large department stores usually have huge **warehouse** areas to stock and maintain props. These large stores are equipped with carpentry shops to custom build or refurbish props and fixtures. Carpentry shops enable the VM to have anything designed and built to fit any display. In a vast store such as Marshall Field's or Macy's, the VM can borrow any merchandise from any department to use as a display prop. Art departments, antique galleries, and home furnishings departments can lend the VM huge assortments of decorative merchandise.

DISCUSSION QUESTIONS

1. Why are antiques favorite props?
2. Why do small stores use inexpensive, disposable props?
3. Why are display windows in department stores trimmed with complex decor?
4. Give three reasons why VMs frequently use foamcore.
5. What are formula type displays and how can one avoid producing them?
6. If you do not own a specific prop, where can you obtain it?
7. What time of year requires the most complete store trim?

CHAPTER PROJECT

Project Objective: Make your own prop using foamcore.

Project Instructions:
Create a tabletop or window display using foamcore as a background. Sculpt, shape, and paint solid columns, textiles, or scenics on the panels.

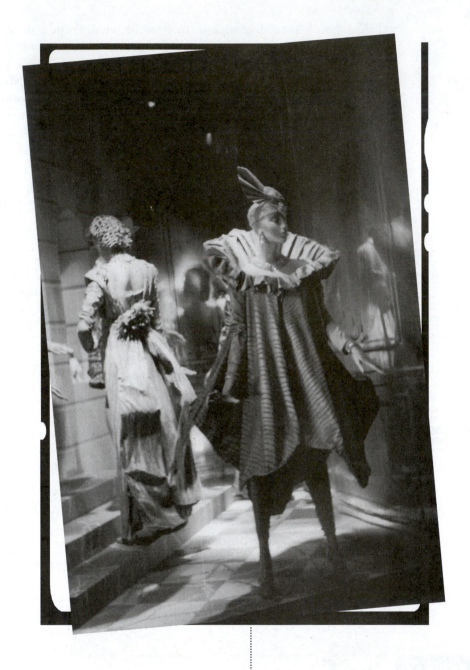

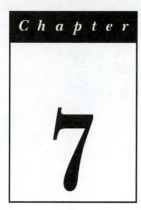

Store Lighting

*A*fter completing this chapter, you will be able to:

1. Explain basic lighting technology.

2. Describe the importance of light as a design tool.

3. Balance light and shadow effectively.

4. Identify what equipment is needed to light a display window.

5. Explain how light affects mood and color.

Seeing with Light

Good lighting is an essential part of any store. It functions to help customers see better and to enhance the merchandise and displays. Lighting should be planned to show off the merchandise, wake up the store, and add color freshness. Customers cannot see displays or merchandise without adequate lighting.

Customers see displays because of light. Customers are also aware of volume because of light. Light emphasizes or diminishes texture. Light illuminates workspaces and provides general overall visibility. The VM establishes mood-using light. The VM can create an exciting shopping environment using light to make merchandise look desirable and irresistible. See Figure 7–1.

FIGURE 7–1

Crate & Barrel's new Chicago store on Michigan Avenue is outstanding by day and a jewel at night. In addition to creating an architectural mood, light makes the merchandise and store interior clearly visible from the street. This is important because Michigan Avenue draws many window shoppers. (Courtesy of Crate & Barrel.)

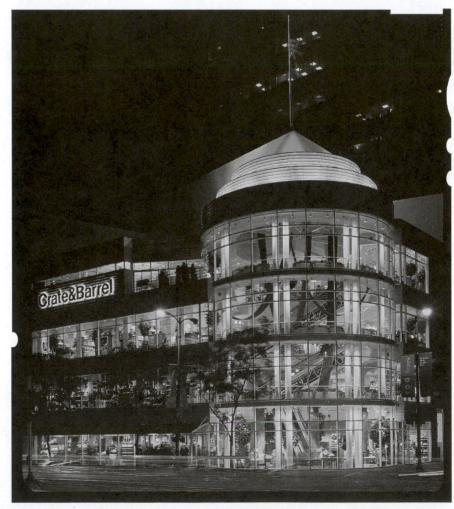

Customers see color because of light. Light determines the quality, mood, purity, and nature of color. Fine jewelry highlighted in a showcase requires different lighting from costume jewelry. Similarly, pastries in a baker's showcase look fresher with the appropriate light. The VM emphasizes the attractiveness of assorted merchandise based on texture and color and enhances this attractiveness using the appropriate light.

Light and the Customer

Customers have spent hours choosing and matching colors for their homes. Good store lighting enables them to color-match merchandise, visualize how it will combine with their home furnishings, and enjoy seeing their purchases by day or night.

Customers live with soft, natural, residential lighting. It is important to light merchandise in the same way that it appears in the customer's living environment. Residential interiors, theaters, and fine restaurants are, for the most part, illuminated with varying levels of incandescent light. Customers expect their purchases to appear at home as they did in the store. In stores lighted with fluorescent light or, in some instances, high-intensity halide (see next sections), merchandise looks textureless and cooler in color than it does at home. It is important to understand that incandescent light has the intensity and warmth favored for most residential interiors. Because customers live with this lighting, it should be the criterion for planning light in your store. Customers buying cosmetics or apparel have color foremost in their minds. Therefore, providing appropriate, well-balanced lighting is critical.

For example, the furniture department should be lighted similarly to residential interiors to enable customers to easily visualize how the furniture will fit in their homes. Table lamps are necessary both to soften and to offset the intensity of ceiling downlight (see the General Light Planning Techniques section later in this chapter) and to create a more homelike environment. Customers light their interiors softly, without glare, as do fast pizza palaces.

A Lighting Mini Glossary

BEAM SPREAD

Spotlights are reflectorized to produce a narrow, focused beam (see the following Spotlight section). They are available in several wattages with medium screw bases or with many track clip-on mountings. They are incandescent, **high-intensity discharge (HID)** (see following section), halogen, low voltage, in-line voltage track fixtures, or flex-track mounted. **Floodlights** have a wider beam spread than spotlights, which enable them to focus on many items. They are most often incandescent with screw-mounted bases. One floodlight can cover from one to fifty items. **Beam spread** allows you to light an area without adding to, or moving, the lighting equipment.

CANDLEPOWER

Candlepower is the amount of light given off in a particular direction. The light may be of soft, intermediate, or intense brightness. Candlepower has many variations.

COLORED GLASS FILTERS

Colored glass filters are available in all hues: primary, secondary, and tertiary colors. They attach easily to a spotlight fixture, swivel, or can with adapters. A color looks more intense with a matched color filter. For example, red filters make red objects appear very bright, rich, and intense.

COLORED SPOTLIGHTS AND BULBS

Colored spotlights and bulbs produce the same effect as a colored glass filter, but depending on the manufacturer, their color range is limited to a few primary colors.

CONTRAST RATIOS

Contrast ratios or brightness relationships are illustrated by footlambert tables (see following Footlambert section). The three contrast zones are: (1) the task; (2) the surface immediately surrounding the task table or bench; and (3) the general surrounding area, floors, and walls. An example of a task is reading a magazine on a table. If the magazine reflects 50 footlamberts, the tabletop should reflect 30 to 50 footlamberts and the floor should reflect between 12 to 300 footlamberts for excellent reading conditions.

COEFFICIENT OF UTILIZATION

The coefficient of utilization (CU) is the quantity of lamps and fixtures and how they perform in a given space with given reflecting surfaces. Manufacturers provide CU ratings for their lamps. These ratings determine how the lamps perform.

DIMMERS

Box-mounted **dimmers** control light to any desired intensity with a touch of a control knob or by remote control. Transformers and digital controls can increase the efficiency and decrease the operating costs of dimmers.

FLUORESCENT LAMPS

Fluorescent lamps are not color corrected, they produce little heat, and are longlasting. They intensify blue and green while making warm colors look slightly grayed. Fluorescents produce intense, shadowless light which makes textures look flat and uninteresting. Warm fluorescent lights produce light that is more intensely red and suppresses green and blue. A cool fluorescent light produces light balanced with the green and blue color families.

Many retailers buy fluorescent light systems because they are easy to install and operate. Many customers, however, avoid shopping in stores with fluorescent lights and prefer shopping in boutiques with lifestyle light. Many retailers specify low heat-generating illumination in their building contracts. About 35 to 40 percent of a store's energy costs are lighting, depending on the store's size, location, and design. Air conditioning and heating costs are either increased or decreased by lighting systems.

Savvy food chains want their merchandise to look fresh. In one food store, decorated birthday cakes looked day-glow and artificial under fluorescent lighting. In contrast, the new incandescent spotlights made cakes look natural as if they are fresh, at home, and on the table.

FOOTCANDLES

The light landing on an object is measured in footcandles, which is the light reflected from the object. Lists of minimum footcandle levels for adequate viewing are available.

FOOTLAMBERTS

Reflected light or bounce light from an object is measured in footlamberts. A store planner may bounce light off of a wall or off of an object to illuminate something else. Footlambert measurement tables are available to help designers create the brightness levels they desire in their stores. Each store requires a different level of brightness for viewing. The lighting needs for different areas of the store may be general: floor, walls, and ceiling, surround: as a surrounding activity, or focus: light focused on display or presentation area.

HIGH SODIUM VAPOR

High sodium vapor lights produce a red-yellow (orange) color and can confuse the color appearance of an object. They are high intensity and longlasting.

HALOGEN LAMPS

Halogen lamps consume less energy than standard lamps by producing 33 percent more light output. These lamps are designed to replace Parabolic Aluminized Reflector (PAR) reflector lamps. They produce a white, slightly blue light that can distort an object's natural color. High-wattage, incandescent spotlights are called PAR bulbs.

HIGH-INTENSITY DISCHARGE

The HID lamps are smaller than fluorescent lamps. They produce shadows similar to those of incandescents and enhance texture. The HIDs make colors look slightly cool. They generate less heat and last longer than conventional fluorescents.

LIGHT COVE

A light cove is a small wooden or metal trough in which fluorescent tubes are mounted. Effective premade sections may be hung over windows, doors, around an entire room, or over specific slat-wall installations.

LIGHT REFLECTION FLOOTLAMBERTS

Designers have tables that indicate the average reflectance desirable for specific installations. For example, the ceilings in offices should reflect 80 to 90 footlamberts; walls, 40 to 60; furniture, 26 to 45; office equipment, 25 to 45; and floors, 20 to 40.

LOW-VOLTAGE LANDSCAPE

Low-voltage landscape lights are 12-volt luminaries that are safe, easily installed, and require simple planning.

LUMENS

Lumens are used in all lighting calculations. One footcandle equals 1 lumen per square foot. Lamp efficiency is measured in lumens per watt. If a 100-watt bulb has 17.5 lumens per watt, the bulb produces 1,750 lumens (17.5 x 100). Another variety of 100-watt bulb may have 14.9 lumens per watt and produce 1,490 lumens.

MAINTENANCE FACTOR

Maintenance factor describes the depreciation of light created by such factors as soil, dirt buildup, and surface wear. An instrument with a maintenance factor of 100 is maintenance free. Remember the old yarn: bright, clean, and shiny.

METAL HALIDE OSRAM HQI-DE

Metal halide OSRAM HQI-DE describes a lamp in two color temperatures with an intensity strong enough to light a baseball park.

PHOTOPIC

Cone vision curve determines the daytime sensitivity of the human eye. The human eye is most sensitive to color around 550 nanometers, which is yellow-green on the spectrum. Blue affects the size opening of the pupil and the warm range "high pressure sodium" causes the pupil to open too wide for the comfort of some people, impairing vision.

RECESSED LIGHT

Recessed light is usually mounted in a ceiling can. It produces down light and wall washing. Two variations are incandescent and low-voltage halogen.

SPOTLIGHTS

Spotlights with lenses are light-directing lamps. Knowing the candle-power of a spotlight helps select the right spotlight bulbs for display windows. See Figure 7–2.

SPOTLIGHT GRID

Spotlight grids are tubular or channel steel grids mounted below the ceiling with a spotlight system. A mix of spotlights and reflector lamps can be used. See Figure 7–3.

FIGURE 7–2

Ceiling-mounted track light

systems provide the flexibility

to light a subject in countless

ways. (Courtesy of Translite

Systems, Redwood City, CA.)

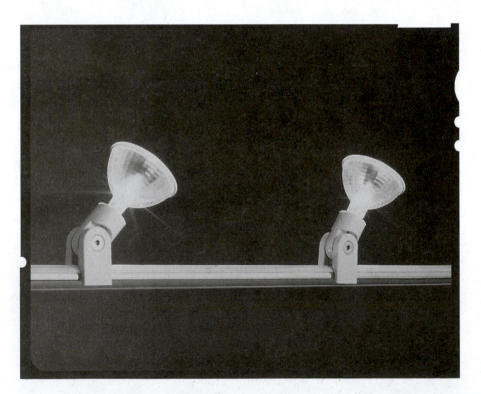

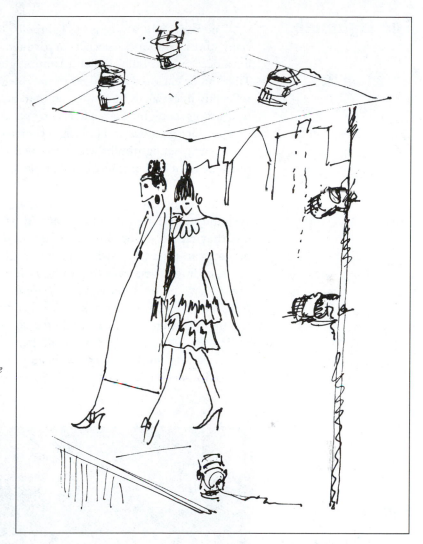

FIGURE 7–3

Suspending metal grids over displays enables you to arrange spotlights in endless patterns by clamping them with "C clamps." Each new display requires a different light arrangement.

TASK ZONES

Areas to be lighted are designated as task zones. Zone 1 includes the desk, tabletop, or bench on which the task is done. Zone 2 includes the area surrounding the area on which the task is done and should have footlamberts equal to one-third the illumination of Zone 1. Zone 3 includes the walls and floor and needs only one-fifth the illumination of Zone 1. For example, if the task reflects 50 footlamberts (Zone 1), the surrounding area should reflect 15 to 20 footlamberts (Zone 2), and the surrounding walls should reflect 10 footlamberts (Zone 3).

The Lightbulb

The basic light source is the lightbulb. The workhorse of lighting in specialty stores, boutiques, specialty department stores, and upscale stores is the incandescent lightbulb, called a lamp. Lightbulbs vary in size and wattage. They can be enclosed behind protective shields, mounted in ceilings with back-reflecting material, or fitted with lenses to produce a general nonfocused light or a strong spotlight. They can also be parts of highly decorative chandeliers that produce glamour and little light or parts of highly decorative table lamps.

Clear glass lightbulbs when grouped on a wall in a sculptural pattern produce light and are decorative. Table lamps placed on end tables in the shoe department or on countertops in the cosmetic department add a friendly, decorative light source. Floor spotlights behind a group of plants are enjoyed for their decorative quality as well as for the mood and shadows they create. Lightbulbs arranged on the ceiling in an interesting grid pattern can even lead customers in a specific direction.

A ceiling is generally dull without decorative interest, but its contribution to an interior is too significant not to be treated as a design. Light patterns that form monotonous grids on ceilings can be enlivened by changing their arrangement. Chandeliers and light sculptures add interest to a ceiling. Hanging metal, glass, wood, banners, and Plexiglas squares at different ceiling levels can create beautiful patterns when alternated with lightbulbs. See Figure 7–4.

FIGURE 7–4

Lighting is part of the magic of design, creating atmosphere and image. The ceiling at Jean-Louis Scherrer, Paris, is reflected by the walls and floor. (Courtesy of Jean-Louis Scherrer, Paris.)

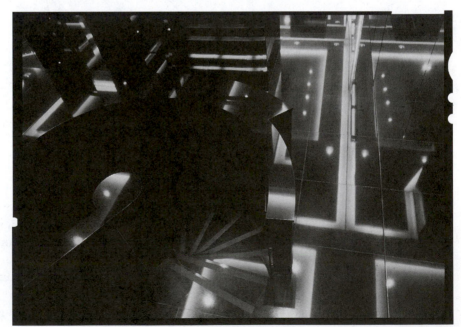

Altering the warmth of a lightbulb can emphasize a color mood. Warm red and yellow floodlight bulbs, alternated with cool green and blue bulbs, make objects look rounder and adds color to an object's shadow.

The Two Light Sources: Daylight and Electric Light

The VM must consider two light sources: natural daylight and electric light. Electric light must compensate for the lack of daylight and also balance the quality of daylight.

DAYLIGHT

Interiors chilled and cooled by early daylight can be warmed with an incandescent light. If designers rely on natural light flooding the store through an atrium or a skylight, they can expect to see different qualities of light at each time of the day. In the morning, daylight is fragile and chilly, making colors appear gray and less intense. In addition, forms and shapes look weaker and have low shadow contrast in the morning. Early daylight emphasizes the best qualities of the cool color families.

Midday light is a stronger and well-balanced light. This light makes colors look pure and intense and makes contrasting shapes and forms more visible. Late daylight is warm and **romantic**, emphasizing the warm color families. In this light, colors look dark, robust, and rich. The strong shadows that are produced emphasize strong shapes and forms that can be dramatic.

Daylight generates heat, as well as light. Therefore, draperies or shades must be installed for control. The strong glare of the setting sun should be shaded to prevent blinding customers.

ELECTRIC LIGHT

Electric light must compensate for the lack of daylight. At the end of the day, special fill light, such as spotlights to eliminate harsh unwanted shadows, might be required. Many store planners prefer excluding daylight

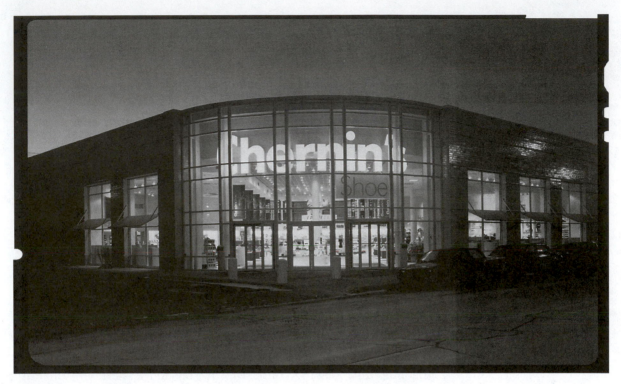

FIGURE 7–5

Although window displays here are nonexistent, lighting makes the importance of the interior, signs, and banners distinct. With minimal exterior light, customers focus their attention on the store's interiors. (Courtesy of Charles Sparks + Company, Westchester, IL.)

altogether. Windowless stores are lighted totally with electric light because it is both easy to control and it is predictable.

Many kinds of electric lamps, fixtures, and equipment are available for the designer's use. Some are portable and some are stationary; some are decorative and some are traditional. Some are simply uncommon. There are electrical systems for lighting task areas and living spaces. Electric lights are designed to light gardens, displays, theaters, streets, architecture, and store interiors. With such an array of fixtures and lamps, almost anything can be illuminated in any mood. The challenge is to light an item to enhance its best qualities. See Figure 7–5.

Neon is an attention-getting light that is more attractive than functional. Although neon produces little light, its decorative impact in a display window is tremendous. Because it does not generate a lot of light, it does not generate a lot of heat that could damage merchandise. Neon can be complex shapes and multicolored.

Creating the Right Mood with Light and Shadow

Light and shadow are combined and balanced to create depth and drama and to emphasize specific qualities of merchandise. Complex lighting techniques and equipment are required for these effects. Therefore, a sound lighting and shadowing plan should be developed. See Figure 7–6.

Begin light planning by choosing the merchandise mood. Shadows can make an item look round or flat, they can emphasize the textural quality of items such as oriental rugs, and they can provide the illusion of

FIGURE 7–6

The light in the Museum Shop is well balanced with no strong value differences. Many showcase interiors are lighted from above by ceiling spotlights. Simple, effective, and flexible track lighting and ceiling cans are used for overall light and to highlight merchandise categories. Perimeter light washes the walls and merchandise. Some showcases are lighted from inside. (Courtesy of Charles Sparks + Company, Westchester, IL.)

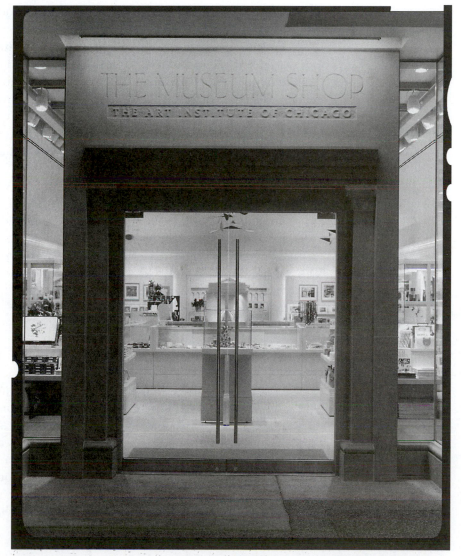

depth in display windows. The right amount of shadow on a luxurious fur emphasizes its luster, while overall general lighting makes a fur look dull and uninteresting.

Lighting the Display Window

Display windows must be lighted intensely to eliminate the sun's unwanted glare and reflections on the glass that make some stores look closed. In addition, they must be lighted intensely enough to create a greater impact than the impact of the store's imposing architecture. Imagine the Saks Fifth Avenue store in New York with weakly lit display windows, for instance. The displays would be overpowered by the store's dramatic neoclassic facade. The VM should light active windows brightly off-balancing some light to stress tension and adding strobe lights to heighten activity. It is important to focus on creating a brightly lighted window display to get the sales message to the customer quickly and powerfully. The display look must be unusually powerful to be effective.

Windows with dark, fall, light-absorbing merchandise require stronger light than windows with summer merchandise which is often pale, soft, and light reflective.

Changing the light intensity of an item that is in front of another emphasizes the silhouette and uniqueness of both objects. Some visual merchandisers create dark backgrounds and floors in their display windows to create huge contrasts between the backgrounds and the merchandise. This scheme is synonymous with theater lighting. Brightly lighted merchandise is very conspicuous. All product is very visible as it contrasts with its background.

WINDOW LIGHTING TECHNIQUES

Because display windows are somewhat isolated from the store interior, special lighting effects can be created for them, either by a back wall or by a designated area that is set apart for displays. A see-through store needs special controllable light in its designated display areas, as in the closed display window. The closed display window must also be separate from the general store lighting, however. Theater light equipment can be installed in window displays because, unlike displays on selling floors, customers will not trip over the equipment and the lights will not shine in their faces. See Figure 7–7.

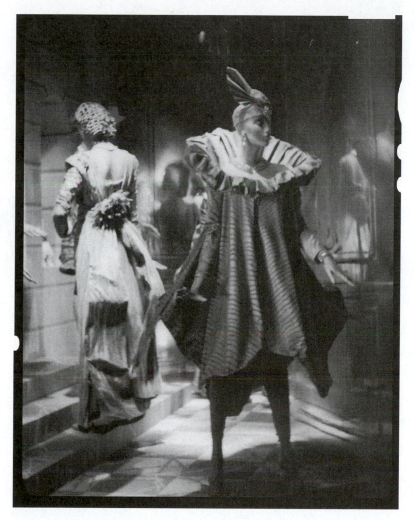

FIGURE 7–7

Great contrasts in light

and shadow create drama

and emphasize the specific

mood of the apparel in this

Paris boutique.

OVERHEAD LIGHTING

A display window should be lighted with overhead spotlights for highlight. It is called downlight. This is normally how customers see daylight in nature—light streams down from the sky. See Figure 7–8. Daylight illuminates customers' heads and shoulders.

In the display window, an overhead metal grid fastened to the ceiling enables a VM to mount multiple fixtures of varying intensities and colors from front (proscenium) to back and from side to side. The grid arrangement

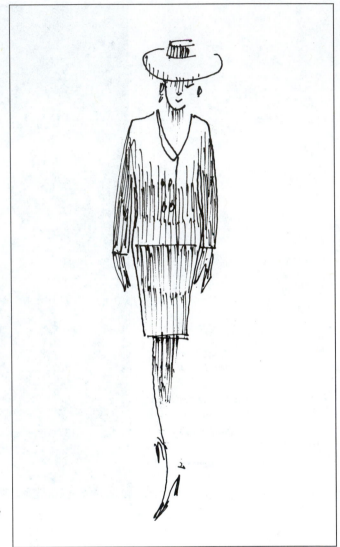

FIGURE 7–8

As light streams down from the sky, it lights the model's head and shoulders. Overhead spotlights produce the same effect.

is varied easily by making cluster patterns. Fixtures that can be "C clamped" to the grid can be moved easily. Fixtures that swivel all the way around increase flexibility. Flexibility is important because each window change requires a new lighting plan.

Arrange the brightest lights to highlight the central product (focal point). Lights of lesser intensities should highlight secondary products and supportive display materials. Arrange the remaining **secondary lights** or "fill lights," evenly from back to front and between the bright **primary lighting**.

Mix some flood lights and spotlights that vary in wattage. Mix others that have a variety of focusing beams, reflecting shields, and panels. Avoid focusing light on the wrong parts of the display, such as the window corners, or on any part of the window that is visually uninteresting unless it is part of your design plan. All of the light in the window should be balanced to look as if it comes from one source. See Figure 7–9.

The light fixtures should be hidden from the customer's view unless a hi-tech look is desired. Front, side, upper, and footlighting should be concealed by valances and footlight shields. **Backlight** fixtures (see the following Backlight section) on the floor can be tucked out of sight behind merchandise, screens, plants, or decorative items.

SIDE-FILL LIGHT. In nature, customers see bounce-reflected light coming from many directions. Bounce-reflected light lights vertical, geometric planes. Side-fill lights are needed in the display window to eliminate unwanted shadows and to create softer secondary light on each side of the display. See Figure 7–10.

FIGURE 7–9

Metal grids and towers

fastened to the ceiling or side

of the display window and

interior provide the designer

with a fast, flexible method

of changing light fixtures for

each display. (Courtesy of

Translite Systems, Redwood

City, CA.)

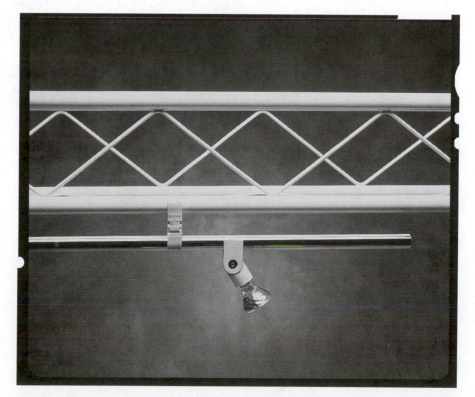

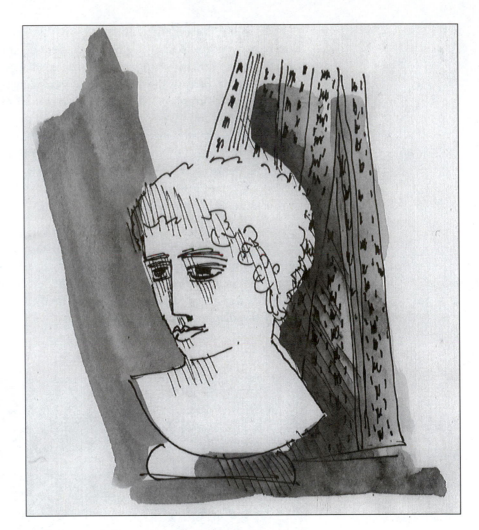

FIGURE 7–10

Using only overhead light creates many unwanted shadows. Adding a sidelight to the overhead light eliminates these shadows.

Side lighting is more effective when placed at a variety of heights from floor to ceiling between the brighter primary light sources. One side of a display can be lit more intensely than another and upper to lower light planes can create a layered look from floor to ceiling. The light fixtures should be mounted on tracks or "C clamped" to metal channels or poles to enable vertical movement.

BACKLIGHT. The back wall can be lighted to emphasize the display background, color, or contour. It can also be lighted to dramatize the volume of the window and merchandise. This is known as backlighting.

FOOTLIGHT.   Footlights on the floor at the front of the window can be positioned from left to right, in other desirable groupings, or hidden from view when possible. The main source of light in the display might come from above. Therefore, footlights can be used as fill light. A light **wash** eliminates shadows that often appear at the hem of a jacket, skirt, or bodice and under the chin. Footlights help produce a fully balanced light on a mannequin's face.

LIGHTING THE MANNEQUIN

There are numerous ways to light a mannequin's head. The number of lights used and their locations determine its roundness and mood. Using one portable spotlight and a **model's** head in a dimly lit studio, move the spotlight to different locations and observe the effects. For example, holding the light above the mannequin's head directed down highlights the mannequin's hair, shoulders, cheekbones, top upper lip, and nose. Dark shadows appear under the mannequin's forehead, nose, lower lip, and chin. See Figure 7–11.

To eliminate most of the dark unwanted shadows created by the overhead spotlight, add one spotlight to the side of the mannequin and direct it on the face. Another spotlight directed on the opposite side of the mannequin balances the face. Move the three lights forward and direct them on the mannequin's face. The face appears somewhat shadowless. Then move the three lights to the back of the mannequin's head. The mannequin's silhouette appears intense and its face diminishes in importance under the slight shadow that results.

One spotlight under the mannequin's chin directed on the face creates dark shadows under the eyes, on top of the upper lip, on top of the nose, and above the eyebrows. Move the light forward and the shadows look less severe. Add spotlights to the left and right of the mannequin's face and the shadows disappear. Add one spotlight above the head and the look will be somewhat even. Move the upper spotlight and one side light forward and the shadows will be less obvious on one side of the mannequin's face. On the other side, however, the shadows appear darker.

Next, place one light behind the head. The profile is emphasized, highlighting the contrast between the background and mannequin. Move any of the lights away and the mannequin's face appears less intense. Directing the lights onto a reflective surface and allowing them to light the face produces a soft look.

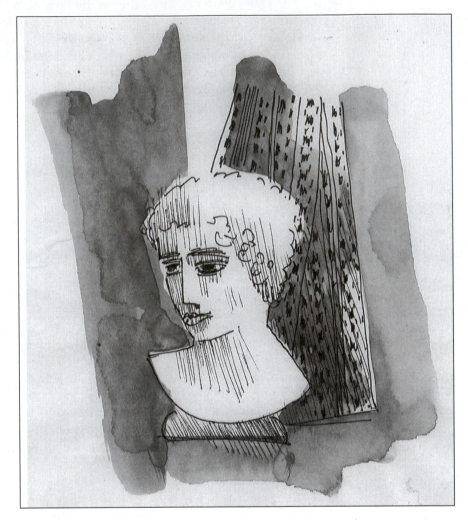

FIGURE 7–11

A spotlight held above a mannequin's head directed down highlights the mannequin's hair, shoulders, cheeks, upper lip, and nose.

Special Events

Special events and fashion shows need additional attention when planning light. Fashion shows staged in a store, a restaurant, or on the selling floor are difficult to light because equipment is limited. The cumbersome, heavy, theater light equipment and controls that can do the perfect job are huge and unsightly for permanent installation. What is more, the power sources for this equipment are often not available. A few lighting companies rent light control boards and high-intensity portable theater equipment that can be powered from somewhat standard electrical sources. Mounted on tall moveable stands, this equipment is suitable for temporary store use.

Fashion shows staged in Paris, New York, and Chicago sizzle when produced in auditoriums. A wide range of light techniques produce endless effects. The sizzle and range of bright beams to subdued lighting and the use of full color to project patterns make these shows dazzle. See Figure 7–12.

If your fashion show is staged in a department or in a restaurant and requires standard lighting, illuminate the runway with a bright light wash to separate it from its surroundings. The models' pivot locations should also be highlighted. Flowers and props should be visible but lighted with secondary lighting.

All light should be directed to eliminate shadows on the models' faces. They should also avoid beaming into customers' faces. The quality of light should fit the mood of the special event and it should separate the exhibit event from its surroundings.

FIGURE 7–12

Shows staged in auditoriums

sizzle with light produced by

complex theater light equipment.

Full color, endless mood, and

project patterns can be created.

(Courtesy of Adrienne Vittadini.)

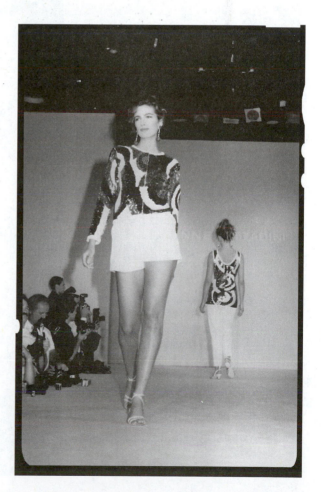

Light Planning — Light and Shadow

Combining light and shadow artfully is a key factor in creating terrific looking displays and store interiors. Developing a system to make merchandise look as desirable as possible is not a complex process. Feature displays need highlighting to set them apart visually from other assortments. See Figure 7–13.

Large merchandise assortments have specific illumination and space requirements. Secondary classifications must be illuminated less intensely than their primary counterparts. Highlighting can set sales events apart visually and can make key sale items a focus for customers. This requires some permanent electrical power source with many outlets. Multiple outlets enable the sales associates to plug in any form of light fixture.

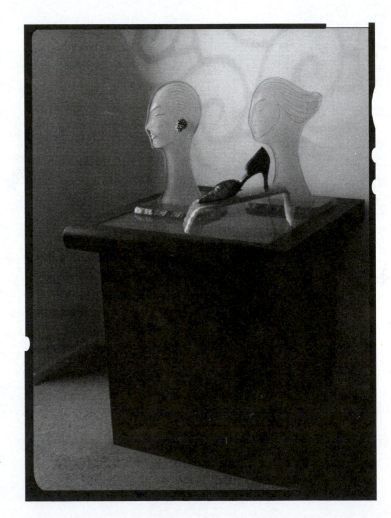

FIGURE 7–13

Feature displays create attention when lit internally. (Courtesy of E. T. Cranston, NY.)

SPECIAL LIGHTING FOR THE SELLING FLOOR

Try not to formulate one general lighting plan for the entire store because each department needs a specific lighting solution. Begin by evaluating the store design, mood, and character. Then match the light to fit its style. General lighting is needed to light traffic aisles and public spaces. Specific lighting is needing in specific areas. The shoe department might need lighting close to floor level to illuminate the customer's foot, for example. Light fixtures mounted under bench seats to direct light down to the floor is one solution to this lighting requirement. Determine the lighting needs of each department and plan solutions for them.

For impact, light mannequins and apparel forms more intensely. Although they are in specific zones that are generally highly visible, they need more highlighting to make them sizzle. Customers see quickly the merchandise on mannequins and evaluate any merchandise messages about sales, new arrivals, textiles, colors, or other important features.

Perimeter lighting is needed to illuminate signs, mirrors, cabanas, decorative walls, and perimeter merchandise. Much of this lighting is mounted permanently. However, perimeter slat-board walls with elaborate presentations of face outs, hangers, shelves, and hang rods should have a variety of lighting intensities and should be flexible enough to be moveable. The selling floor and perimeter lighting should be placed carefully for even balance. Although both types of lighting may vary in intensity, their differences should not be jarring.

Lighting All Store Types

GENERAL LIGHT PLANNING TECHNIQUES

When remodeling or planning general store lighting from scratch, draft rough floor plans using architectural lighting symbols, and use the architectural elevations and floor plans to make notes and rough sketches.

Once the lighting concept has jelled, draft a more detailed plan that specifies all light equipment and its sources. Use a checklist to make sure you have covered everything. Universal electrical symbols are straightforward and easily read. See Figure 7–14.

Overall lighting is most often produced by downlight, in which the fixtures are in the ceiling and beam light down toward the floor. The addition of uplight is necessary to balance downlight and to create desirable light and shadow. Uplight fixtures can be on the floor, fitted with spotlights washing the walls and displays, or placed to enhance architectural details. Uplight can be part of a cove molding, cornice, or back wall.

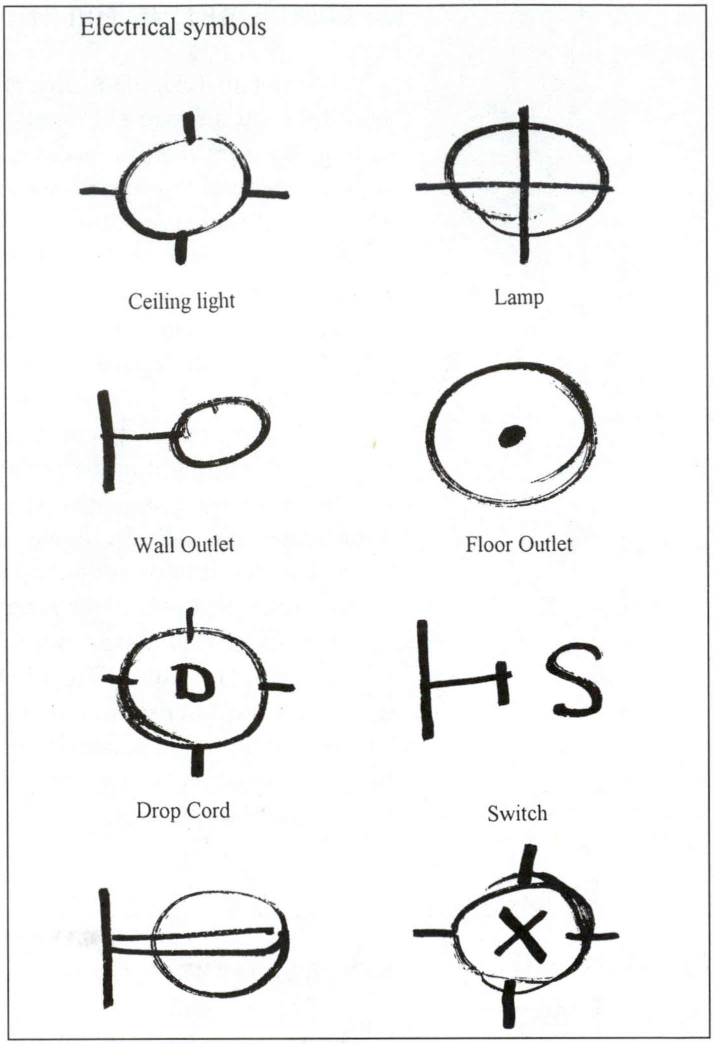

FIGURE 7–14

General overall light is produced by ceiling downlight. Perimeter light washes the walls and the merchandise. Lights under island fixtures produce uplight to balance downlight and to create focus on the merchandise. (Courtesy of Store Equipment & Design, Chicago, IL.)

Electrical symbols

Ceiling light

Lamp

Wall Outlet

Floor Outlet

Drop Cord

Switch

LIGHTING BOUTIQUES, SPECIALTY STORES, AND SPECIALTY DEPARTMENT STORES

General downlighting and uplighting in boutiques and speciality stores should vary in intensity and purpose from department to department. These types of lighting add character to the merchandise and mood to the store's architecture. Lighting columns that provide specialty light and washing walls with colored light add drama but can be added after the lighting plan is complete.

After establishing downlight and uplight, focus on lighting departments and store perimeters. Each department is a different color and texture and requires specific illumination to visually separate and enhance from the next. Walls of shelving and signs need special focus. Pin spots might focus on display forms or special face outs. A pleasant balance of light and shadow on the perimeter walls of a department cause customers to walk to see the special effects and merchandise. See Figure 7–15.

FIGURE 7–15

Mass merchandisers,

discount stores, and

supermarkets require good

visibility and longlasting,

cool-burning lamps. A good

lighting plan sets a

merchandise category apart.

Little mood is created.

(Courtesy of Store Equipment

& Design, Chicago, IL.)

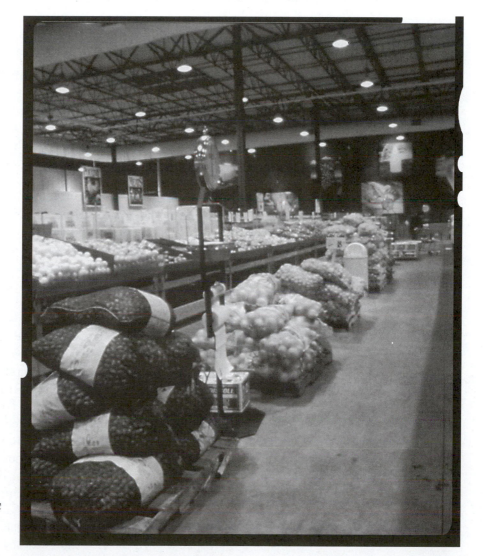

The track lighting systems necessary to successfully light feature mannequins and forms in boutiques and specialty stores should have flexible designs because varied light intensities are required to match each season's color. Also, lights should be portable for fixture relocation. Each department changes the merchandise for the two major seasons: spring/summer and fall/winter. New merchandise arrivals require relocating most of the floor fixtures. A well-designed track lighting system enables associates to mix and change a variety of appropriate spotlights with an assortment of colors and intensities. A mix of pinlights, spotlights, and floodlights might be required to highlight the new mannequin and merchandise locations.

LIGHTING MASS-MERCHANDISE STORES, DISCOUNT STORES, HYPERMARKETS, AND SUPERMARKETS

Good visibility is a criterion when lighting mass-merchandise and discount stores. The longest-lasting, coolest-burning lamp is a must. The metal halide OSRAM HQI-DE lamps discussed earlier fit this need because much of the presentation in mass-merchandise and discount stores is based on piling boxes high in groups. Bulk sales are important to these stores. The challenge is to make all boxes, box labels, signs, and their groupings very visible. See Figure 7–16.

Softer lighting should be used in apparel areas to subdue the looks of synthetic textiles and many bolder, synthetic colors. This may be achieved with low-hanging light grids and many spotlights of warm color balance. The ambient ceiling light above the grids could be dimmed to eliminate any glare that could beam down through the grid.

Less flexible lighting is necessary because a good overall ceiling system lights all of the selling space in mass-merchandise and discount stores and makes frequent, huge departmental relocations possible. Clusters of ceiling metal halide floodlights and spotlights hang on architectural steel skeletons that support the roof. Unlike in boutiques and specialty stores, however, little valuable floor space is set aside for light fixtures that could produce uplighting.

Many showcases are lighted with halogen, which consists of (a) three or four lights in a six-foot case, (b) one thin-line, continuous fluorescent tube, and (c) standard fluorescent light. All produce a chilly light. Many food colors look almost Day-Glo in cool light, however, making them slow sellers. Unfortunately, incandescent fixtures are too large and too warm for the task. Supermarkets present designers with the never-ending problem of supplying light that is warm but not too warm for food. Standard fixture lighting can be eliminated from open-fronted coolers and freezers by dropping track lighting from the ceiling, containing enough spotlights to beam down on the food.

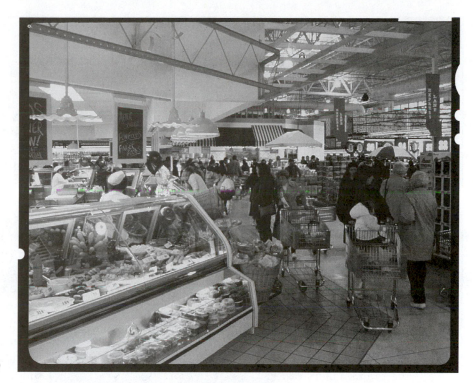

FIGURE 7–16

(Courtesy of Charles Sparks

+ Company, Westchester, IL.)

LIGHT FOR NONSELLING AREAS

Ideally, light levels in general nonselling stores are varied in task areas. Employees develop eye strain and fatigue working in the glare of high-intensity work lights. If light levels vary, the employees can move in and out of lighted areas at different intensities to rest. Eye strain is reduced and employees will work longer and with increased productivity.

Corridors, aisles, and waiting areas can be lighted with less intensity than the selling floor.

Electrical Receptacles

The quantity of electrical receptacles is frequently underplanned. Receptacles must be abundant in display windows and on the selling floor to plug in Christmas trees and wreaths, table lamps, turntables, china cupboards, neon, art, and light sculptures. Not all light in window displays or on the selling floor is supplied by spotlights and floodlights, however a good light plan will make costly additions and rewiring unnecessary. Some light is merely decorative.

Lighting Feature:
Grand Hall Gallery—The Museum Look

A Charles Sparks + Company Westchester, IL, designer created a permanent museum look for the Museum Shop of the Art Institute of Chicago in Oak Brook Center, Oak Brook, IL, which won the VM & SD (Visual Merchandising & Store Design) award in January 1992. The designer set out to replicate the look of the grand gallery of the Art Institute. The result was a designed lighting system that incorporated museum-style lamps and techniques. This lighting solution instantly registers a memory of what the museum is all about. See Figure 7–16.

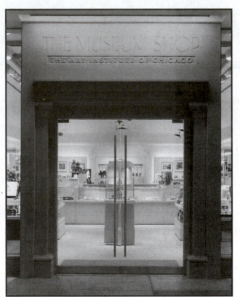

The Museum Shop is painted in only one color: Benjamin Moore #995. However, endless variations of that color are created by combining the Charles Sparks gallery-style lighting and assorted surface textures.

Sparks said, "On the pan ceiling, there are only two light sources: PAR 38 capsolite spot 91 and, for specific punch, 50-watt metal back spot, 10 degree for the appropriate aim from the 13-foot ceiling." Perimeter walls are lighted with warm fluorescent and MR16 spotlights which beam down through the glass shelves from under the canopies.

In addition to the store's general walk-around lighting, the showcases are lighted with beams from the ceiling in lieu of the standard, internal, cool showcase light. Traditional overscaled moldings, limestone facades, the floor, and the columnar entry are classic design elements combined with the museum-style lighting that has produced "The Grand Gallery Look"—a look of permanency. ◗

Note: Photo courtesy of Charles Sparks + Company, Westchester, IL.

DISCUSSION QUESTIONS

1. Why create shadows in a window display?
2. Why light the furniture department differently from the cosmetics department?
3. Why design store lighting based on the customer's lifestyle?
4. Is a customer's residential lighting a good model for a store?
5. Explain some of the problems cool "blue range" lamps create in an apparel department.
6. What are footcandles?
7. Describe footlamberts.
8. Why use flexible, moveable light tracks on the selling floor?
9. Describe how hyperMarkets (updated warehouse stores) are lit.
10. What are the light limits in enclosed selling fixtures?
11. What is downlighting?

CHAPTER PROJECT

Project Objective: Learn to use nontraditional lighting techniques through experimentation.

Project Instructions: (Choose One)
1. In your school or school bookstore display window, create a display using side lighting only. Vary the wattage and color of the spotlights to see how the merchandise and mood is affected.
2. Invite a lighting expert to speak to your class and illustrate the lecture with lighting catalogs.

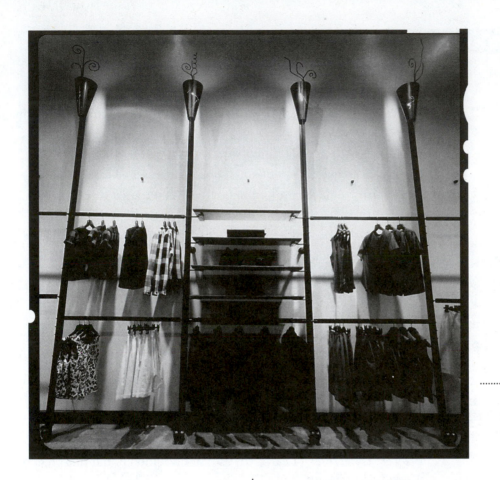

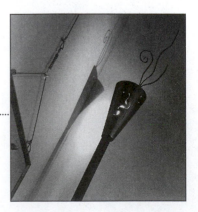

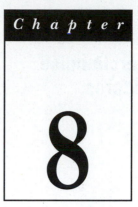

Fixtures

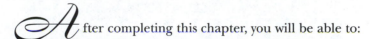

$\mathcal{A}$fter completing this chapter, you will be able to:

1. Explain why specific fixtures are chosen for specific classifications and stores.

2. Outline the basics of setting up fixtures on the apparel floor.

3. Recognize fixture planning for supermarkets.

4. Describe how sales goals influence fixture planning.

5. Tell how fixture design evolves, based on lifestyles.

Merchandise Fixtures

Merchandise fixtures are essential for presenting merchandise to the customer clearly. Their style, color, material, and design should relate to the merchandise. For example, luxe, expensive merchandise might look better when presented on fixtures made of exotic materials such as marble, slate, walnut, ebony, or brass. In contrast, active sportswear might look better when presented on fixtures painted action colors, on shelving made of basket weave, or on distressed wood. Food might look terrific in huge wicker baskets.

Many fixtures do not have the appropriate utility. Shelves might not hold all of the necessary assortments, for example. They may be too narrow or too wide to fit a specific product. Some countertop fixtures may not support items that can hang only a certain way.

Because prevailing architectural and interior styles influence the look of fixtures, designers in the hi-tech period created many fixtures with hi-tech looks. See Figures 8–1A, 8–1B, and 8–1C.

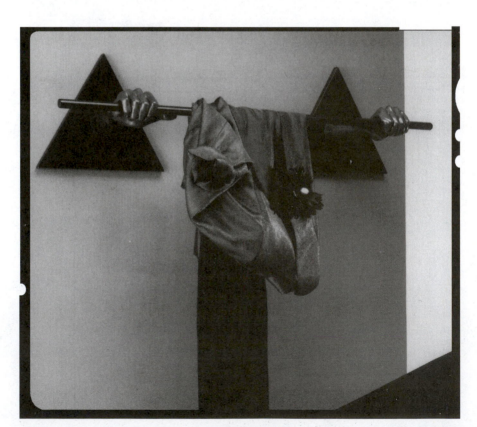

FIGURE 8–1A

Fixtures are essential for presenting merchandise in a clear manner. (Courtesy of Dan Dee Display, Chicago.)

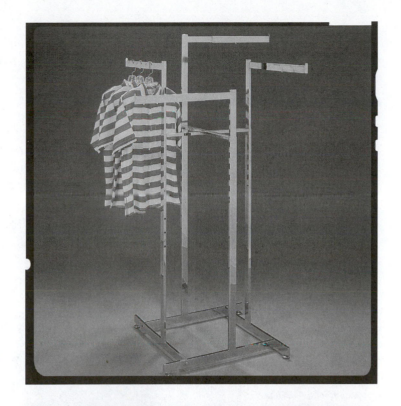

FIGURE 8–1B

Active sportswear can be presented clearly on a quad fixture, which is excellent for presenting coordinate groups. (Courtesy of Dan Dee Display, Chicago.)

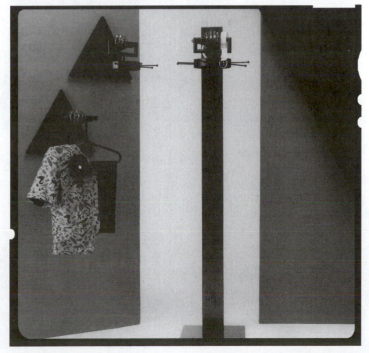

FIGURE 8–1C

Hi-tech fixtures fit hi-tech interiors. Exotic shapes may enhance expensive merchandise classifications. (Courtesy of Dan Dee Display, Chicago.)

Well-planned fixtures make it much easier for store associates to inventory and sell merchandise. An excellent plan enables associates to organize groups of merchandise that are orderly and have great visibility. With such a plan, an associate can immediately see whether stock levels are adequate after a quick look at the selling floor. If merchandise is stocked in order, such quick-count inventories are easy to do.

Customers can also locate items faster with the help of user-friendly fixtures that make products visible, allow pricing and signs to be seen, and are aesthecially pleasing. When customers locate items quickly, they have more time to shop. Additional shopping time generates multiple purchases. Impatient shoppers love orderly presentation on well-designed fixtures. Chaos drives the customers from the store. See Figures 8–2A and 8–2B.

FIGURE 8–2A

Terrific fixtures for super looks are custom made for The Candy Lab, London, Canada, by Bell Design Consultants, Inc. Donald Bell said, "The firm's approach is directed by the belief that to be successful, an environment must be enjoyable, comfortable, and, most importantly, efficient." (Courtesy of Bell Design Consultants, Inc., Toronto, Canada.)

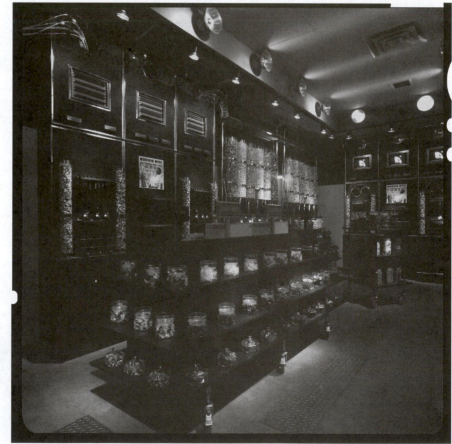

FIGURE 8–2B

Candy can be a treat as are these efficient fixtures at The Candy Lab. Donald Bell, before creating his retail-design firm, worked as a VM at Robert Simpson Co. He said, "The creative VM experience was most helpful in the process of understanding stores." (Courtesy of Bell Design Consultants, Inc., Toronto, Canada.)

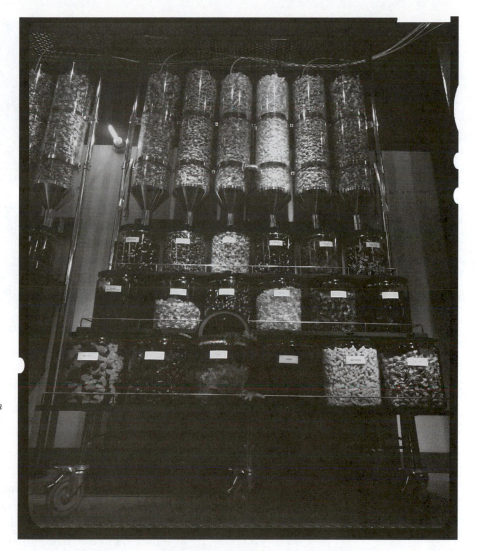

Generally, when sales are good, the cost of a medium-range fixture can be recovered after selling the merchandise presented on that fixture for two active days. Many retailers put off fixture replacement until the fixtures fall apart or become outdated. However, fixtures are the sales tool of the self-service retailer and constitute an important investment.

Managers of high-volume stores appreciate the value of fixtures and budget annually for fixture updates and replacements. In fact, large retailers maintain a small crew of staff tradespeople who repair, refinish, and update fixtures. See Figure 8–3.

FIGURE 8–3

Customers locate merchandise easier and faster when correct fixtures are organized in an excellent plan. This provides customers with additional time to select more merchandise. (Courtesy of Store Equipment & Design, Chicago.)

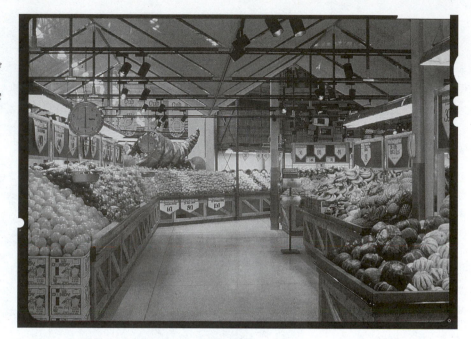

Retail and Apparel Fixtures

THE ROUNDER

Fully loaded, the rounder is designed to hold 136 garments. The tri-level rounder holds 110 garments, one garment per inch of rod. Rounders are available in several diameters as well as in a half-rounder version with a T bar, which can be adjusted up or down to accommodate long or short garments. A customer can easily walk around the fixture to locate color and size.

Tri-rounders provide more flexibility because they offer a choice of three different levels which makes it possible to present coordinates of varying lengths. Rounders are best located in the back of a department and make a good transition to the back wall. When large fixtures are up front in a department, they tend to block customer traffic throughout the store and obstruct a customer's view of the back wall.

When arranging rounders, form a grid by making straight aisles from the right to the left and from the front to the back so that customers can freely walk throughout the store. Positioning fixtures too close together creates a closed-in feeling and causes customers not to walk to the back of the department. See Figure 8–4.

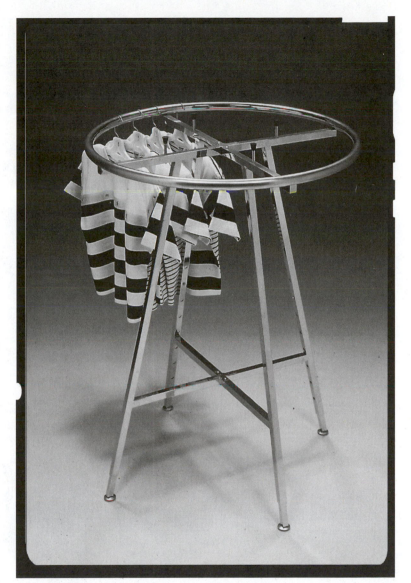

FIGURE 8–4

The small rounder is available in several sizes, is adjustable, is easy for customers to walk around, and holds large quantities. Feature-garment displayers can be placed in the center. (Courtesy of Dan Dee Display, Chicago.)

Mixing short and long sleeve or skirt lengths on rounders creates a cluttered and confused look. Use the color theory (rainbow) to develop color arrangements. Mixing unlike textures can be visually disturbing. Hang lightweights together, woolens together, and sheers together. Do not intermix prices, lifestyle groups, or other features that will disturb the customer's concentration. See Figures 8–5A, 8–5B, and 8–5C.

The Supermarket

In supermarkets, fixtures are arranged in grid patterns beginning at the checkout. These grids that extend to the rear of the store allow customers to walk through and around classifications for easy shopping and orderly merchandise location. Merchandise classifications in supermarkets are normally presented in order of sales volume. Store locations with high traffic and visibility are better than those with low traffic and low visibility. The latter are areas for slow sellers. The former are for strong sellers. Not all space can yield high volume because of customer demand.

Close to the supermarket entrance is the high-volume produce department, which requires fixtures that provide light, cooling services, and water, and are deep enough to hold quantities of produce. Impulse items like breads, deli and lunch meats, and some prepared dairy products, are located in the first grocery aisle. Along the back wall meats progress to the adjacent wall where frozen and dairy products such as milk and yogurt are generally presented. End-cap fixtures are used to remove products from the lineup of each aisle for focus and promotion.

Because diets are changing, product location in supermarkets should be reviewed frequently. Hot items that once drew customers to the rear of the store eventually may not do so.

Fixtures must be designed to develop long, uninterrupted rows that reach from the front of the store to the back. In addition, these fixtures should be multishelved to hold product from floor level to the highest customer viewing point.

Customers look from top shelves to bottom shelves for merchandise classifications. Their width of vision is narrow from right to left and top to bottom. If the product is spread out too far left or right, it is beyond the customer's lateral vision. Also, customers find it difficult to bend down in busy aisles to select product. Items that are too low or too high are not picked up as frequently as others. They just are unnoticed. The hot zone is at eye level or the visually active level.

Intermerchandising, or cross merchandising, is becoming part of the supermarket's plan. For example, French breads can be presented next to meat products one day and moved to picnic foods on another day. Intermerchandising encourages multiple selling but, because of staffing limitations, it requires small, flexible, and easily moveable fixtures.

New merchandising plans indicate that food markets are now presenting product based on lifestyle. New fixtures designed to meet these criteria are developed and shown at each Food Market Industries (FMI) trade show. Store and fixture designers are moving away from the ultra clean, serviceable, sterile look of mass presentation of the 1970s and are now focusing on mood and making the mass arrangements of product look more individual. Metallic gold is replacing chrome, black is a new interior color

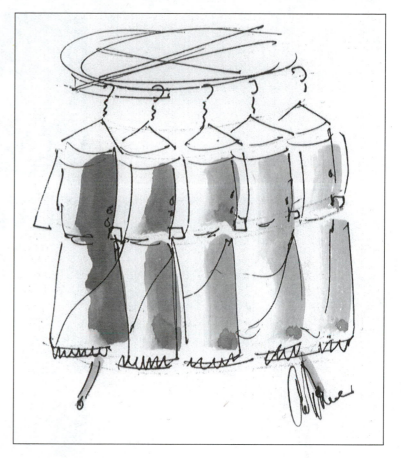

FIGURE 8–5C

Hang the same styles, colors,

silhouettes, and fabrications

together in a color sequence

created using your color plan

as a placement guide. The

impact will be clear and

strong, allowing the customer

to concentrate.

THE QUAD AND THE TRI-WAY

The quad holds eighty-eight garments and the tri-way holds forty garments. Each is available in an assortment of finishes with adjustable arms that are either straight or waterfall in design. These second-tier fixtures are best placed on the floor behind the mannequins and T stands (see the next section) and close to the department's front. When placed between the T stands and the rounders, quads make another pleasant transition in merchandise quantities.

Quads are best used for showing groups of merchandise such as coordinates and separates. If possible, present only one manufacturer's group on a quad because a common design, color, fabrication, and lifestyle was used to develop the **line**. A harmonious grouping creates a greater impact and helps generate sales. See Figures 8–6A, 8–6B, and 8–6C.

FIGURE 8–6A

This is one of the quads. When planning fixtures, explore all possibilities by considering variations of the basic fixture. (Courtesy of Dan Dee Display, Chicago.)

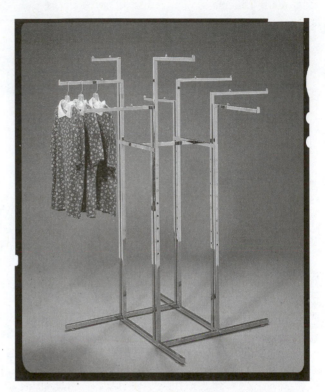

FIGURE 8–6B

The quad, which is smaller than a rounder, is ideal to position behind a mannequin. (Courtesy of Dan Dee Display, Chicago.)

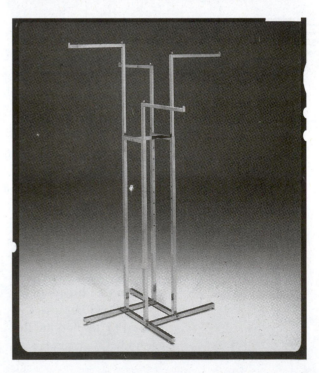

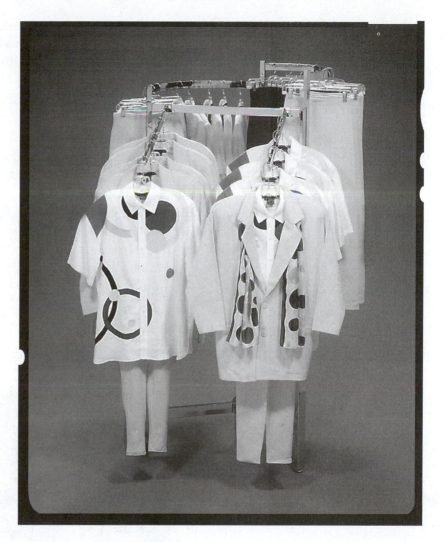

FIGURE 8–6C

Half-rounders, like quads, are small, which makes them suitable for presenting coordinates. (Courtesy of Dan Dee Display, Chicago.)

THE T STAND

The flexible T stand holds sixteen garments at most and is designed to serve as a feature fixture. Its adjustable arms are either straight or waterfall, which makes a pleasing mix of heights. The T stand works best when arranged at the front of the department next to a mannequin group showing the garments on the T stand. A customer is attracted by the mannequins and goes to the T stand to find her size and see what other colors are available. Customers attracted by garments on mannequins generally do not want to hunt to find stock.

T stands, like other fixtures, are produced in a variety of designs, materials, and colors. They are attractive when placed alone or in groups of three or more. They are perfect for presenting feature items. See Figures 8–7A, 8–7B, and 8–7C.

THE SHOWCASE

Enclosed showcases protect exotic merchandise from customer handling. A large assortment of premade or custom-designed showcases is available in many finishes and designs. Premade or standard showcases fit general floor plans and hold many merchandise categories. Whatever showcase is chosen, it must enhance the merchandise and present it clearly. The showcases' design should match the store interior in style and finish.

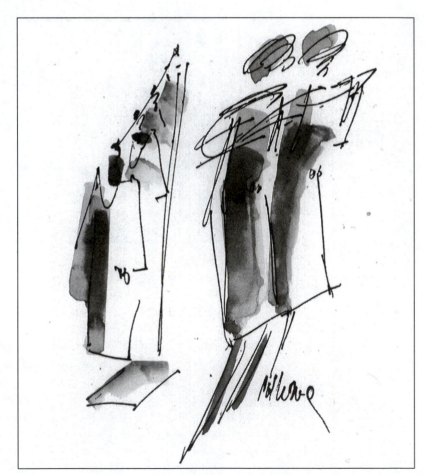

FIGURE 8–7A

Garments in different color

and size ranges are best

presented alongside the

mannequins on T stands.

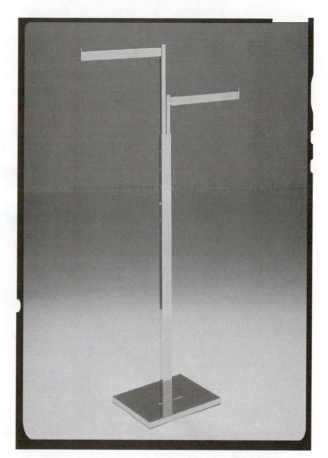

FIGURE 8–7B

T stands are excellent for showing small groups at the front of the department because they do not block sight lines and they encourage the customer to walk into an unobstructed department. (Courtesy of Dan Dee Display, Chicago.)

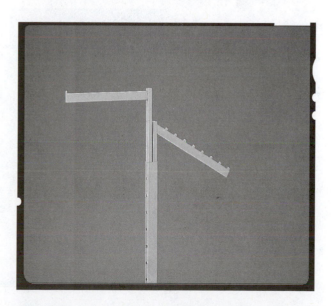

FIGURE 8–7C

T stands are available with straight or waterfall arms, which encourages a variety of arrangement possibilities. (Courtesy of Dan Dee Display, Chicago.)

Upscale stores use showcases frequently to deter shoplifting and to protect expensive merchandise from excessive handling. Enclosed fixtures, often called "service cases," require additional staffing to remove the merchandise to show to customers. Mass merchants, however, prefer self-service fixtures to reduce payroll costs. See Figures 8–8A and 8–8B.

FIGURE 8–8A

Enclosed showcases protect products from excessive handling. Food fixtures need special wiring for lighting, cooling, and moisturizing. (Courtesy of Store Equipment & Design, Chicago. Photographer: Andy Snow.)

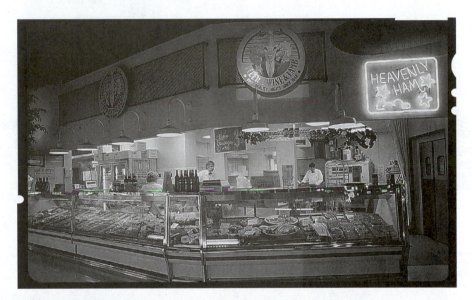

FIGURE 8–8B

Hypermarkets and mass merchandisers prefer open self-service fixtures to enhance convenience and to reduce labor costs. (Courtesy of Store Equipment & Design, Chicago. Photographer: Steve Reynolds.

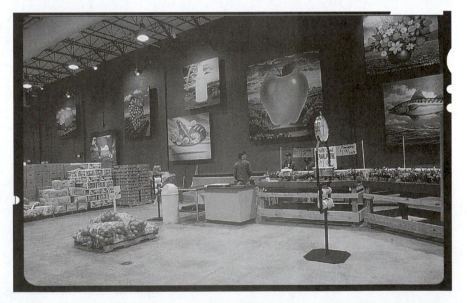

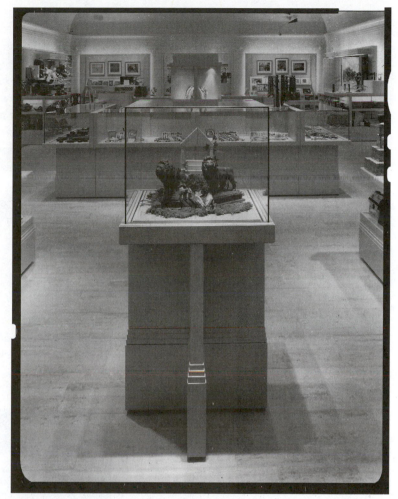

FIGURE 8–9

Showcases in the Art Institute of Chicago Museum Store, Chicago, are lighted by ceiling spotlights focused downward on the cases. This is an excellent idea because showcases are often poorly lighted. (Courtesy of Charles Sparks + Company Westchester, IIIL.)

Showcase lighting is an important consideration when planning. Although most cases use fluorescent lighting to reduce heat, the light may be too intense and poorly color corrected for the merchandise. New showcases are being lighted effectively by ceiling spotlights focused downward. See Figure 8–9.

In-supermarket showcases require permanent locations because an electrical outlet must be on the floor for lighting and refrigeration needs. Unlike general fixtures that can be moved easily for each seasonal merchandising change, moving showcases may require the assistance of an electrician and a tradesperson to reroute wiring. When planning showcase locations, make sure that electrical requirements are included on the floor plans.

SLAT WALL

Departmental back walls and side walls are often clad in slat wall. Three-foot slat wall rods hold thirty-six garments. Countless clever fixtures mounted in endless arrangement possibilities create added impact. Such fixture possibilities include shelving, hang rods, shoe and leg forms, jewelry displayers, waterfalls, straight arms, mirrors, and face outs. Endless colors and finishes make this system work easy to install.

Freestanding and wall-mounted modular tubular and wooden wall fixtures come with hang rods, shelves, and apparel hooks. Create-a-shop systems are suitable for **hard lines** and soft lines. These systems are put together in exciting arrangements. Designers call them "form-a-wall systems," "systems to create with," and "component systems." Some modular units are equipped with lighting systems.

CUBES

Small Plexiglas cubes are just right for presenting jewelry in showcases. Large wooden cubes are used on the selling floor as fixtures for presenting small appliances, china, and food. In fact, cubes are less expensive and more

FIGURE 8–10A

Cubes began as an alternative fixture. Now they are important in the store scheme because they are flexible, transportable, and fit any decor. (Courtesy of Newood Display Fixture Manufacturing Co., Eugene, OR.)

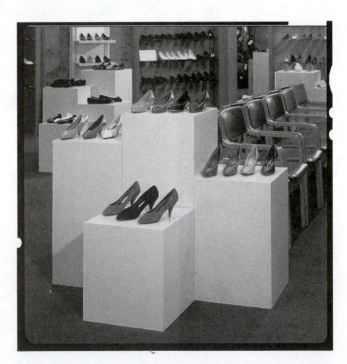

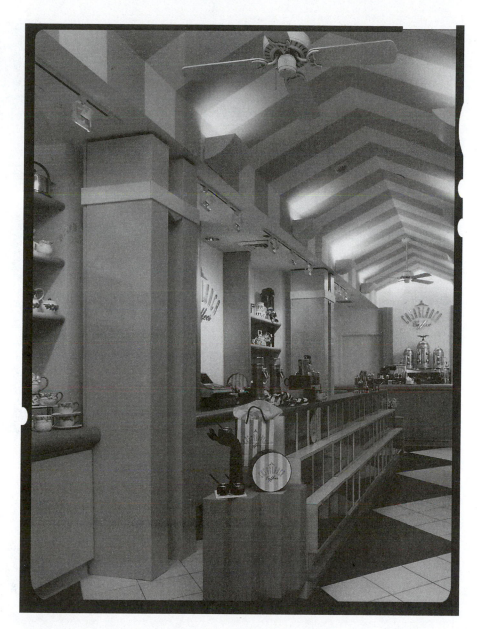

FIGURE 8–10B

Feature cubes make wonderful end caps for feature classifications as at Casablanca Coffees, Chicago. (Courtesy of Schafer Associates, Inc., Oakbrook Terrace, IL.)

flexible than many traditional fixtures. Department heads and selling staff like them for their flexibility. A selling associate can usually present merchandise on a cube without VM supervision. Their portability solves the need for presentation flexibility in contemporary retailing. Fixture vendors provide standard and custom-made cubes. See Figures 8–10A, 8–10B, and 8–10C.

FIGURE 8–10C

The Kubala Washatko's design firm draws shoppers into a small space with illusions of space. Goldies in Chicago is a stage for dramatic cubes. The design team here avoided using traditional fixtures. (Courtesy of Kubula Washatko Architects, Inc., Cedarburg, WI. Photographer: Mark Heffron.)

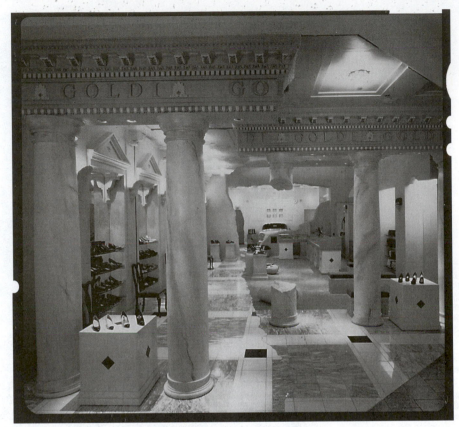

TABLES

Merchandise planners use hundreds of parson-style pine tables and round, skirted tables for assorted merchandise displays. Round, soft, romantic skirted tables are perfect for displaying a cosmetic line. Changing the table covers creates a new look or mood instantly. See Figures 8–11A and 8–11B.

PARALLEL HANG RODS

Five-foot parallel hang rods hold 120 garments. Like rounders, hang rods accommodate large quantities of merchandise. Place them at the department's rear to avoid blocking traffic aisles. They are often traffic blockers and limit customers' views of the sales floor. They look better with a back wall as a perimeter. See Figure 8–12.

FIGURE 8–11A

Tables, like cubes, are flexible. Their possibilities are endless. At Younkers, Omaha, NE., tables are borrowed from the furniture department to present china and gifts. Cross merchandising generates additional sales. (Courtesy of Schafer Associates, Inc., Oakbrook Terrace, IL. Photographer: Brisky Photography.)

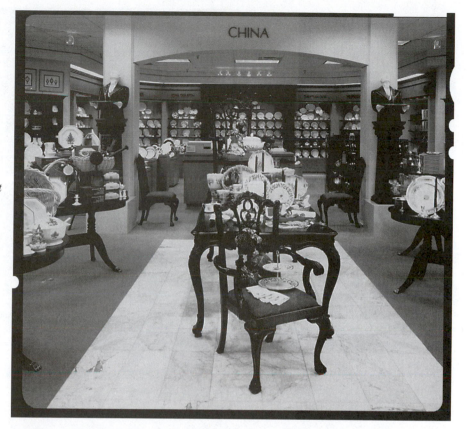

FIGURE 8–11B

Fixture styled tables add height to the merchandise, adding visual variety and enabling the VM to isolate and present groups. (Courtesy of Newood Display Fixture Manufacturing Co., Eugene, OR.)

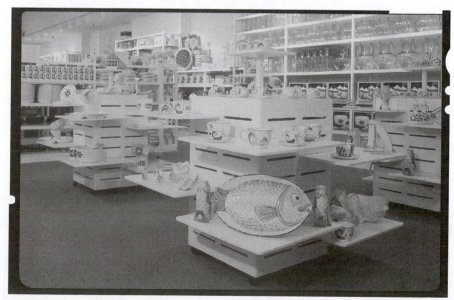

FIGURE 8–12

Hang rods can be wall mounted or used as floor fixtures. Like rounders, hang rods hold many garments. Place them toward the rear of the department to avoid crowding the department's front. Also, avoid hanging small groupings on them because they will become lost and will create a congested, haphazard look.

(Courtesy of Dan Dee Display, Chicago.)

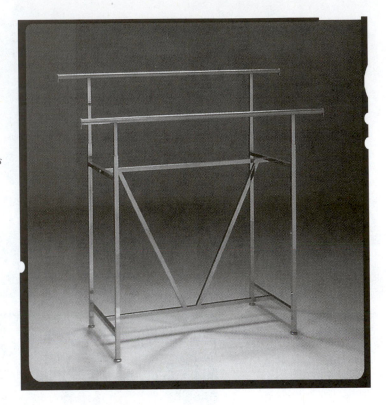

JEWELRY DISPLAYERS

Ring holders, pin and ring trays, earring pads, and bracelet T stands are available in many sizes and are covered in many colors of silk moiré, velvet, and felt. Jewelry displayers like these help organize an endless variety of shapes and materials, including metals, stones, gold, and silver. Colorful, multilevel displayers make monotonous, horizontal showcase interiors exciting. Ring and bracelet displayers hold jewelry in perfect viewing position.

APPAREL ACCESSORIES

Many kinds of countertop garment costumers, such as T stands, hanger-topped drapers, bra displayers, and valets are available. Some of the many fixtures that add height to a countertop include merchandise organizers such as tie displayers, hosiery kiosks, and scarf holders.

The Supermarket

In supermarkets, fixtures are arranged in grid patterns beginning at the checkout. These grids that extend to the rear of the store allow customers to walk through and around classifications for easy shopping and orderly merchandise location. Merchandise classifications in supermarkets are normally presented in order of sales volume. Store locations with high traffic and visibility are better than those with low traffic and low visibility. The latter are areas for slow sellers. The former are for strong sellers. Not all space can yield high volume because of customer demand.

Close to the supermarket entrance is the high-volume produce department, which requires fixtures that provide light, cooling services, and water, and are deep enough to hold quantities of produce. Impulse items like breads, deli and lunch meats, and some prepared dairy products, are located in the first grocery aisle. Along the back wall meats progress to the adjacent wall where frozen and dairy products such as milk and yogurt are generally presented. End-cap fixtures are used to remove products from the lineup of each aisle for focus and promotion.

Because diets are changing, product location in supermarkets should be reviewed frequently. Hot items that once drew customers to the rear of the store eventually may not do so.

Fixtures must be designed to develop long, uninterrupted rows that reach from the front of the store to the back. In addition, these fixtures should be multishelved to hold product from floor level to the highest customer viewing point.

Customers look from top shelves to bottom shelves for merchandise classifications. Their width of vision is narrow from right to left and top to bottom. If the product is spread out too far left or right, it is beyond the customer's lateral vision. Also, customers find it difficult to bend down in busy aisles to select product. Items that are too low or too high are not picked up as frequently as others. They just are unnoticed. The hot zone is at eye level or the visually active level.

Intermerchandising, or cross merchandising, is becoming part of the supermarket's plan. For example, French breads can be presented next to meat products one day and moved to picnic foods on another day. Intermerchandising encourages multiple selling but, because of staffing limitations, it requires small, flexible, and easily moveable fixtures.

New merchandising plans indicate that food markets are now presenting product based on lifestyle. New fixtures designed to meet these criteria are developed and shown at each Food Market Industries (FMI) trade show. Store and fixture designers are moving away from the ultra clean, serviceable, sterile look of mass presentation of the 1970s and are now focusing on mood and making the mass arrangements of product look more individual. Metallic gold is replacing chrome, black is a new interior color for service cases, and slate and faux finishes are prevalent. These new colors and materials reflect residential interiors.

An example of a supermarket with trends grounded on lifestyle is the new Hen House Market in Lenexa, Kansas. The Hen House Market uses design motifs and themes to bring in customers. The store has developed a clean, contemporary, post-modern theme with colors, textures, graphics, and patterns that produce the "Metropolis" look. Clean-lined fixtures with post-modern mood-creating colors replace the congested and unhappy mix of assorted unrelated fixture styles of less current stores. See Figure 8–13.

Bernard Narcy, president of Arizona Western Fixture & Display, had atmosphere in mind when he collaborated on ABCO Foods in Phoenix with Neil True, vice president of store development. Their mood-creating store has a definite "desert market" theme. Large cacti in pots, Indian textiles, and Southwestern colors and textures echo that theme. Wallscapes and produce tables are constructed with Pueblo designs. See Figure 8–14. Note the absence of ceiling light cans, however. The perimeter light over the cornices produces bounce (reflected) light for overall store light. Downlight is balanced by uplight under the produce tables.

FIGURE 8–13

The homogeneous look at McCaffrey's, PA., is developed by a fixture and arrangement theme that is repeated in all of the store's interior elements, creating an uninterrupted flow. (Courtesy of Off The Wall Co., Inc., Telford, PA. Photography: Bob Hahn, Bethlehem, PA.)

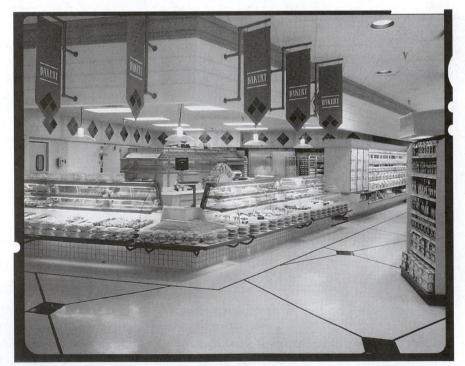

FIGURE 8–14

Thematic store interiors are based on customer desires. This theme, which is based on regional lifestyles, has substantially increased sales. (Courtesy of Arizona Western Fixture & Display, Inc. and ABCO Foods, Phoenix, AZ.)

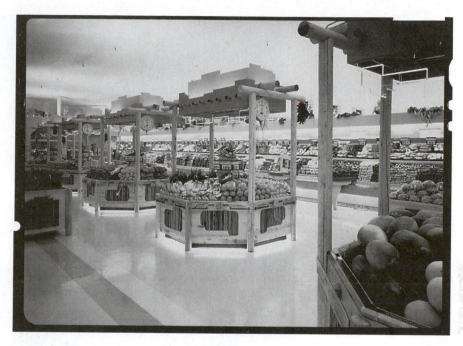

Narcy said, "My client was very supportive and understanding for this project." True said, "Sales have increased in every unit we have designed, the look has won many design and lighting awards."

Food fixturing requires complex installations and equipment for lighting, cooling, and freezing. Both dry and moist product conditioners are needed. Fixtures have to accommodate products as diverse as dinner rolls, milk cartons, carrots, and pop bottles. Colors and cleanable textures are needed to enhance food colors. The VMs in supermarkets refer to a color wheel when planning warm, natural colors to enhance foods. Many small food stores use baskets, innovative crates, and boxes for presentation.

The Exclusive Boutique

Fewer fixtures are seen in upscale boutiques because they carry only one or two samples of each item. The most expensive materials are used in boutique fixtures to produce a luxe look. Overcrowding is avoided. Some merchandise may be brought from stockrooms to show customers. High-end customers do not care to see rows and rows of the same expensive merchandise. See Figures 8–15A and 8–15B.

FIGURE 8–15A

The back wall of this exclusive boutique was inexpensively fixtured with uprights. The light pods on top add an air of elegance. The space was designed to present short runs of merchandise attractively. (Courtesy of Bell Design Consultants, Inc., Toronto, Canada, and Portfolio, Eaton Center, Toronto, Canada.)

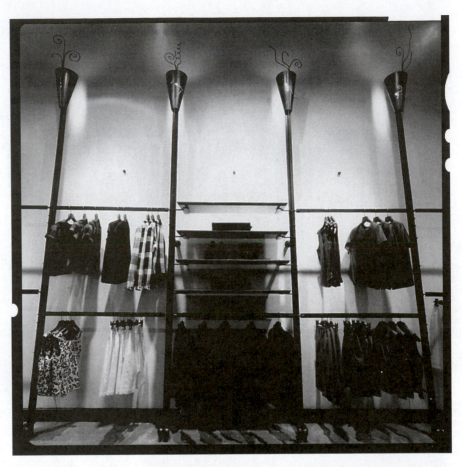

FIGURE 8–15B

The elegant use of light pods and simple hardware add a luxe look to these wall units. (Courtesy of Bell Design Consultants, Inc., Toronto, Canada, and Portfolio, Toronto, Canada.)

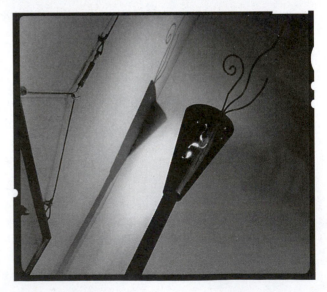

Superstores and Warehouse Clubs

Endless **superstore** and warehouse club assortments require clean fixturing to appropriately present large quantities of merchandise in cartons or groups and to merchandise lots. Care is given to present merchandise groups at eye level. A sample of the boxed product is adjacent to the group for customer inspection.

Some warehouse clubs are adding fresh bakery products and other products to their shelves to provide a personal touch. In huge home stores, pallets show twenty-five kitchen sinks in color order. Items are presented in bulk form to encourage large impulse sales.

Sales Goals and Floor Planning

Normally, about 150 garments can be hung on a rounder. Fewer fit in the fall/winter, however, because of heavyweight fabrics, shoulder pads, and large collars. Knowing the number of garments a fixture holds can assist in floor planning. A scaled floor plan clearly illustrates how many fixtures fit in the selling space. The business plan confirms the quantity of garments needed to meet the sales goals. Multiplying product quantity, units, and price points by fixtures yields the correct product mix. If the space will not accommodate the needed fixtures, adjust the sales goals downward or acquire more square footage for the inventory.

When developing a floor plan for food fixtures, determine the number of classifications and the annual sales goals of each. Divide sales into selling days and units of merchandise needed to reach these goals (sales and units). Then, determine how many items you must sell each day at a given price to meet sales goals. Select fixtures that will adequately hold daily stock. For example, to easily determine how many loaves of bread a fixture will hold, draw a layout, physically stock the fixture, or ask the fixture representative for this information. Determine each fixture need by size, capacity, and quantity, and select the fixtures that meet your criteria.

Overplanned fixture quantities, capacities, and spaces result in crowded, congested stores and create an unappealing, negative environment. If fixtures are underplanned, there will never be enough stock presented to meet sales goals and the floor may look empty and understocked.

ANALYZING SPACE

Begin studying the interior space by using an architectural blueprint. If a blueprint is not available, accurately measure the space. Use a scale ruler to draw the physical dimensions of the space on a 1/4 inch-equals-1-foot scale. A one-eighth scale is used for huge space drawings that can be accommodated on a transportable blueprint or sheet of paper.

Next, use mechanical drafting tools to draw all openings, electrical outlets, walls, windows, doors, fixed features, and elevation changes (step-ups).

Then sketch in traffic patterns. Major arteries and secondary aisles should be planned, according to these patterns. This divides the space into zones. Plan zones that are large enough to accommodate groups of merchandise and fixtures.

Study the merchandise and the use of the space, and plan specific details that will reinforce that use. For example, apparel requires a specific architectural style, decor, and look; foods require another. Then consider the activities and support. Plan equipment and tools for it, such as POS areas, stockrooms, fitting rooms, mirrors, wall fixtures, counters, **gondolas**, wrap areas, and chairs, to name a few.

After making any necessary modifications, calculate the approximate floor space. Determine the size of each fixture and the quantity of merchandise it holds. Determine sales goals and model stock programs to meet those goals.

Now draw all fixtures on the plan. Do not forget any columns. Do a tracing overlay of the plan and indicate where electrical sources should be. Plan lighting and electrical supplies for merchandise fixture displays and POS.

The floor plan confirms the amount of space the client needs, and can help determine the project's cost. The designer can now see the elements required to make the design a reality. Re-drawings are important to get the design just right.

DISCUSSION QUESTIONS

1. What factors determine fixture design?
2. What conditions determine fixture placement?
3. How do sales goals influence fixture quantities?
4. How do sales plans influence fixture stock levels and fixture counts?
5. When can managers easily determine inventory levels by looking at fixtures?
6. What is the function of a T stand?
7. What are some special fixturing needs for supermarkets?
8. How are cubes used as fixtures?
9. Describe the fixturing philosophy for boutiques.
10. Use your imagination and discuss the different varieties of tables that could be used for merchandise presentation.

CHAPTER PROJECT

Project Objective: To plan fixtures.

Project Instructions:

As a team, visit a specialty store in a local mall. Review the merchandise classifications on the mall level. Take notes to guide you in creating your own floor plan. Do not assume that the store has located the classifications correctly. Make your own floor plan noting critical suggestions on the drawing whenever needed. Do not create detailed drawings. Draw only rough zones on your plan.

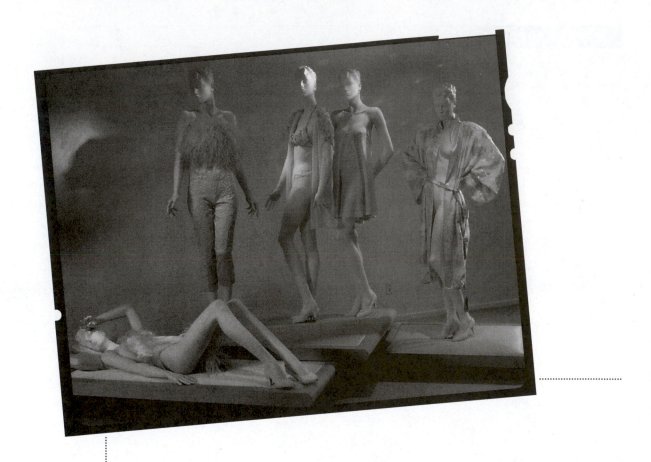

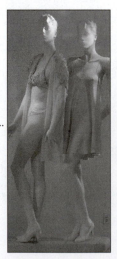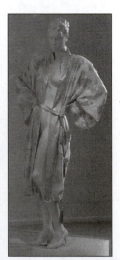

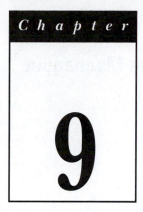
The Mannequin

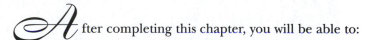

fter completing this chapter, you will be able to:

1. Explain the purpose of a display mannequin.

2. Plan mannequin locations.

3. Dress mannequins and forms.

4. Identify many styles of mannequins.

5. Describe how to buy new mannequins.

The Mannequin

Well-dressed mannequins make an impressive apparel presentation, far more than do any other display props. If you dress mannequins well, accessorize them with style, and locate them correctly, you will create a strong sales generator and fashion image. See Figure 9–1.

Customers are attracted to mannequins because they are fun to look at and their image teaches fashion. See Figure 9–2.

Customers expect that any apparel shown on a mannequin is the latest in fashion and is stocked well in the store. When the stock of an item gets low, change the display. Too often customers inquire about a garment on display and are disappointed to learn that it is out of stock. See Figure 9–3.

Mannequins in display windows and in interior presentations should wear the store's newest fashion merchandise which represents the appropriate selling season and the store's major merchandise classification. Remember, the selling season begins earlier than the actual season.

FIGURE 9–1

Well-dressed mannequins make an impressive apparel presentation. (Courtesy of Rootstein, London, author's personal collection.)

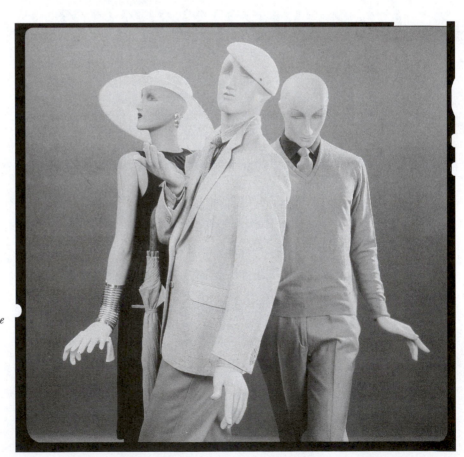

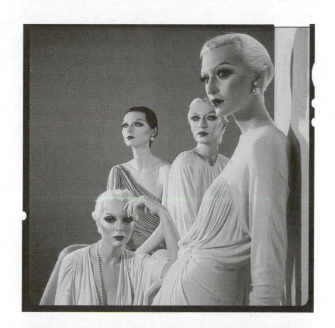

FIGURE 9–2

Customers love to look at mannequins because they are fun and educational. (Courtesy of Rootstein, London, author's personal collection.)

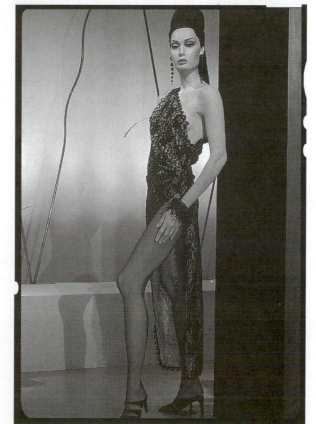

FIGURE 9–3

Mannequins in display windows should wear the store's newest glamour looks. (Courtesy of Patina-V, Industry, CA.)

Abstract Mannequins

Abstract mannequins tend to look animated but they do not represent true human anatomy. For a proper presentation, clothing should be shown on an anatomically correct torso. The finish, face, arms, hands, and hair of the mannequin do not need to be realistic, however. The garments on these forms should be displayed in ways that customers can comprehend. Even paper-doll-type mannequins should show garments in ways that are clear to the customer.

ARM PADS

Arm pads are made of soft, padded fabric in the shape of arms to provide support for a suit or jacket sleeve. Without support, a sleeve turns in or collapses.

Display Forms

An assortment of display forms is needed to present a diverse group of apparel and accessories. Anatomically suitable forms are needed for all apparel classifications: socks, hats, underwear, dress shirts, sport shirts, gloves, suits, and jackets. These forms are generally made of plastic or fiberglass with colors depicting skin. Some are covered in fabric for easy pinning. Women's display forms include hosiery, scarf, wig, millinery, lingerie, 3/4 dress, blouse, and coordinate costumers. New forms are created with each new apparel market to present new clothing. See Figures 9–4A, 9–4B, and 9–4C.

RIGGING

Rigging, which is the art of selecting fashionable merchandise for presentation on forms, includes pinning, fitting, padding, and accessorizing to create a presentation that attracts customers and generates sales. See the Rigging Forms section later in this chapter for more information.

PINNING. Presenting well-fitting merchandise generates sales. Special pinning and padding is required for that perfect fit. The perfect fit represents how the customer will look. A form's active pose may require a garment to be pinned radically to fit and look normal. For example, lifting one arm of a mannequin severely pulls and stretches the garment out of alignment. Pinning is necessary to make the garment appear to be balanced.

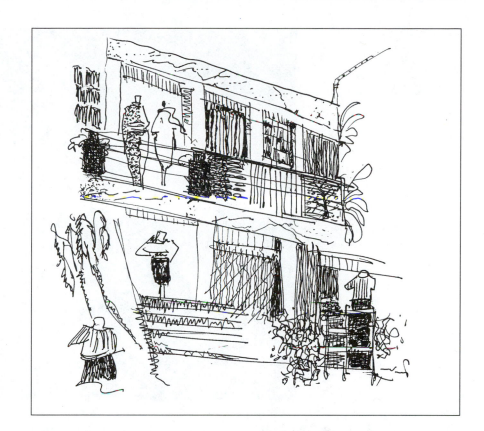

FIGURE 9–4A

An assortment of apparel forms are available for just about any style of apparel and presentation.

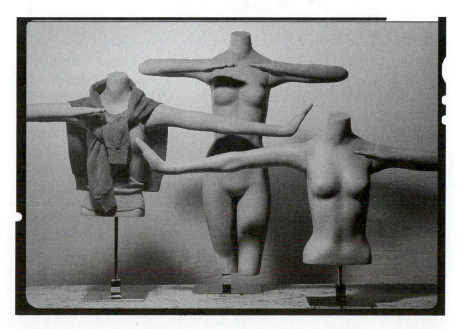

FIGURE 9–4B

New display forms are created with new fashion directions enhancing their looks. (Courtesy of Vogue International, Whittier, CA.)

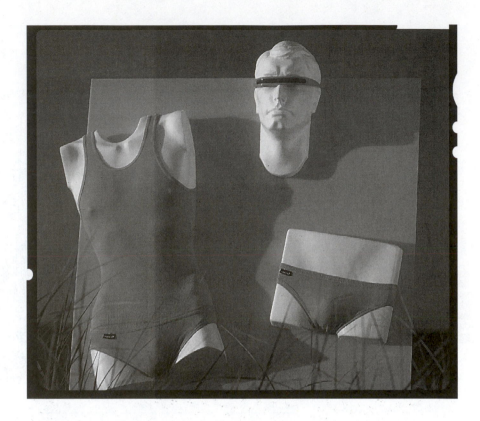

FIGURE 9–4C

Easy-to-dress underwear

forms are stylish.

(Courtesy of Carol

Barnhart, New York, NY.)

Mannequin Chronology

In the fourteenth century, mannequins were three-quarter wooden torso forms with detachable arms. They were made in assorted sizes and were dressed for religious festivals and placed in a cathedral or carried through the streets on a barge. Jewelry worth millions was presented on them. In the early 1800s, retail mannequins depicting the full figure with detachable arms were made of papier mâché and carved wood. Others were headless dress models covered in fabric and metal that were fashioned after a seamstress's sewing model.

As ready-to-wear became more popular in the late 1800s, a larger assortment of mannequins became available. The mannequins were some-what realistic replicas of the human body, but in each period their designs and proportions reflected current fashion trends. For example, in the art deco period, the mannequin's face and makeup became stylized to emphasize the current art deco, sleek look. Until the 1980s, most mannequins were anatomical replicas of the human. Later, in the 1970s, designers inspired by post-modern lifestyles began to develop abstract mannequins and dress forms. See Figure 9–5. Mannequin parts are molded at a plant. These molds are patented and used through a model period. New molds are produced from a sculpted model portraying the new look. See Figure 9–6.

Bob Currie[1], at Henri Bendel's NY 1976, created the famous "overdose window," which featured elegantly dressed mannequins in red and white, grouped in a corner looking curiously at a poisoned mannequin lying face down on the floor. Pills and broken glass were strewn on the floor. In 1977, Candy Pratts[2] placed a single mannequin on a daybed reading Agatha Christie's[3] *Sleeping Murder*. The mannequin's red hair was standing high in the air with fright.

In December 1975, Victor Hugo[4] at Roy Halston[5] featured four evening-gowned, silver-finished mannequins having a champagne party amidst broken glass, smashed televisions, and an array of electrical cords winding across the floor. These trendy windows (display theater) established the minimal look by emphasizing storytelling mannequin groupings. The abstract mannequin was created soon after.

FIGURE 9–5

Celebrities are the real models who pose for the mannequins. This face mold is typical of production. It began as a sculpture. From it a mold was produced. (Courtesy of Greneker/Wolfe & Vine, Los Angeles, CA.)

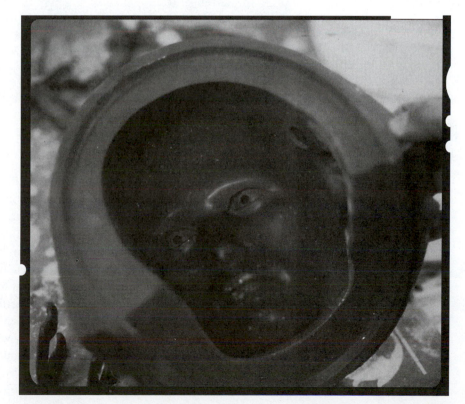

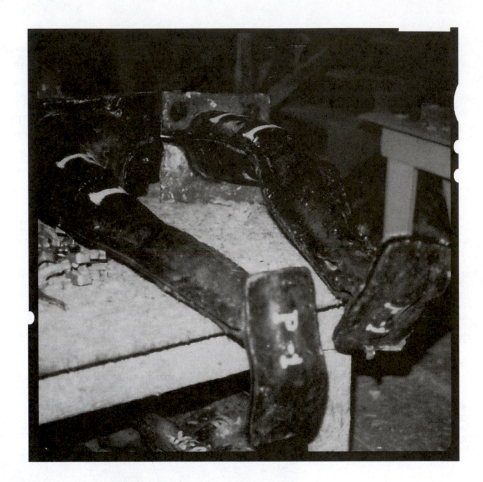

FIGURE 9–6

These leg molds are being prepared for a mannequin. (Courtesy of Greneker/Wolfe & Vine, Los Angeles, CA.)

The Function of Mannequins

Studies reported in *Women's Wear Daily* indicate that customers gain more fashion awareness from apparel shown on mannequins than from fashion shows, magazines, and advertising. Because mannequin presentation is a strong sales tool, VMs should dress mannequins in the freshest fashion apparel in their stores, accessorize them carefully, light them correctly, choose the best locations for them, and maintain them properly.

Customers look to mannequins to learn how to combine separates and coordinates and how to wear new colors, silhouettes, textures, textiles, and accessories. Excellent mannequin presentation zeros in on the newest jewelry, illustrates colors the jewelry can be worn with, suggests compatible garments, and shows the special moods created by the coordinates. Customers can identify their personal lifestyles by seeing a dressy or sporty presentation and imagining how they will look in it. See Figure 9–7.

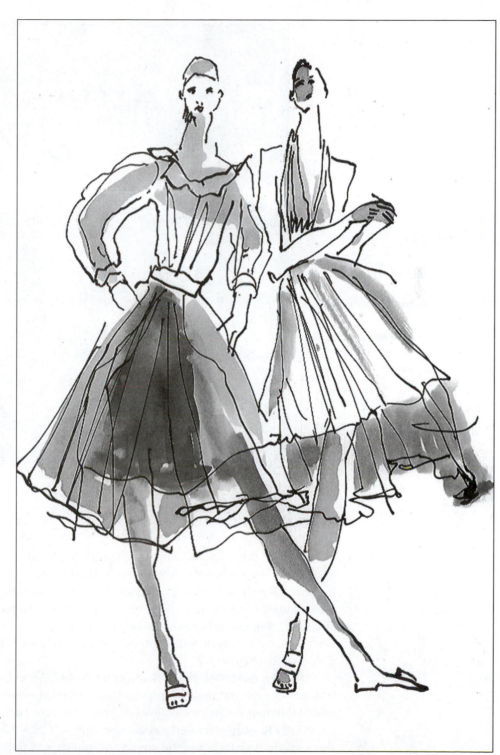

FIGURE 9–7

Customers look to

mannequins to learn

how to combine

separates, coordinates,

and accessories.

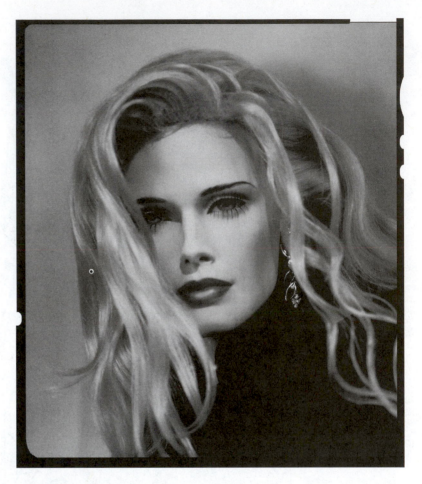

FIGURE 9–8

Glamourous-looking mannequin makeup is very important. It should reflect the makeup shown in the current European designer collections. (Courtesy of E.T. Cranston-Almax USA, New York, NY.)

POSE AND STYLE

Choose the appropriate mannequins to wear your merchandise. Mannequin manufacturers create many mannequin styles: some are high-fashion, elegant, and create a glamour mood, while others are casual and more suited to displaying sportswear. Some mannequins represent a specific age. Sun-tanned mannequins with active poses look great wearing swimwear. Others with sedate poses and pale skin look better in late-day fashions. See Figure 9–8.

Mannequin design changes as quickly as fashion styles. Although most VMs choose natural makeup for their mannequins, some prefer an exotic look. Designers create new mannequin body styles to enhance current fashions. Adel Rootstein created a collection called "Classy Lady Long Legs" to show off miniskirts. When the empire silhouette was popular, mannequins were high-waisted. At another time, mannequins with large shoulders were needed to present the "mega top" look.

In the 1960s, Twiggy was a popular model who created a body type with arms outstretched high to the sides. Runway models and display mannequins replicated Twiggie's look. This look was replaced in the late 1970s with runway models and display mannequins who had their arms close to their body, often with their hands in their pockets. See Figure 9–9.

A mannequin's foot is redesigned whenever shoe designs change. Because a mannequin's foot is unbendable, a new foot is needed for each newly styled shoe. In the 1960s, very high heels were in vogue, which created a need for a high-arched foot. Later, in the 1970s, flat shoes were popular. This required a new mannequin foot. Shoes must fit snugly because the foot is one of the balance points for a standing mannequin. High heels

FIGURE 9–9

The mannequin's pose reflects model types and how they walk on the runways at European designer collections. (Courtesy of Rootsetin, London, author's personal collection.)

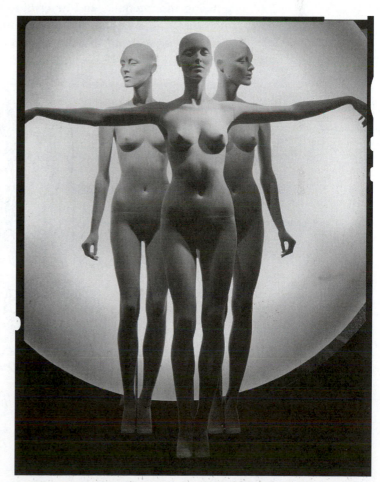

require an arched foot; flat shoes require a flat foot. Flat shoes on a foot with a high arch soon loosen, and destabilize the mannequin, causing it to tilt forward or to one side.

LOCATION

The floor layout or floor plan and the store's traffic patterns determine if a mannequin's location will be at the department front or in a special feature zone. The mannequin's high visibility attracts the customer's attention and the garment sells out in a few days. A group of mannequins at the front of the department can be propped with beach equipment, bicycles, or other merchandise relating to the activity and lifestyle depicted. See Figure 9–10.

To determine and mark mannequins' placement, work with the floor plan overview. Choose locations that will allow even placement without being monotonous, and determine quantity and style. When selecting a group of mannequins for placement, make sure that they have matching skin color, makeup, and attitude (pose).

FIGURE 9–10

Mannequins and

forms can be

propped to

establish a theme.

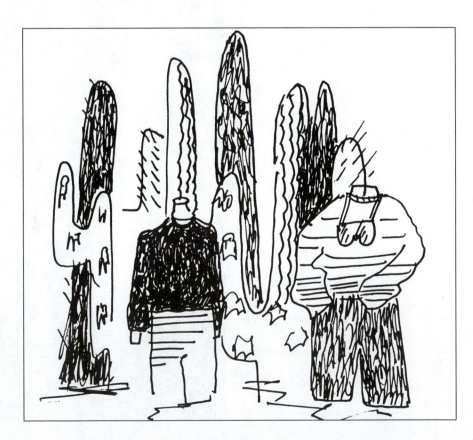

After determining the mannequins' placement, plan the location for all other apparel forms, such as shirt and blouse displayers and boards. The location of such items as mannequins and forms should be upfront in the department, and a straight line of apparel fixtures should follow to the back of the department on the grid pattern. Allow adequate aisle space to flank the configuration from the front of the department to the back so that customers can walk through the department easily. Mannequins placed in the center or to the rear of the department are not highly visible and can be knocked over easily in such crowded space.

Merchandise displayed on mannequins should be close to the mannequins on fixtures such as quads, T stands, rounders, and waterfalls. Well-planned merchandise adjacencies help customers locate colors and sizes at a glance. In contrast, poorly planned merchandise adjacencies upset the customers' sensibilities and require them to spend their valuable time searching through your stock for their selection. See Figure 9–11.

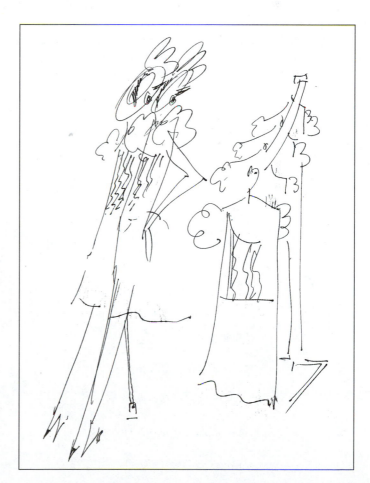

FIGURE 9–11

Merchandise displayed on

mannequins should be adjacent

on a T stand or other fixture to

afford customers easy discovery.

Newly purchased mannequins should be placed in key display windows and key fashion locations. Assign the best fashion presentations to the freshest mannequins. Rotate the older mannequins to secondary locations, rehabilitating their looks to fit other merchandise classifications.

Rigging Forms

Dressing men's forms is called rigging. Men's suitforms are generally headless and armless. They have necks and torsos which extend enough to fit suit jackets and to show collars. These suitforms are mounted on adjustable wooden or metal stands to control height and are covered with fabric for easy pinning. The garment size is stamped on the form's back.

To begin rigging the form, first fit a freshly pressed shirt on the form. See Figure 9–12.

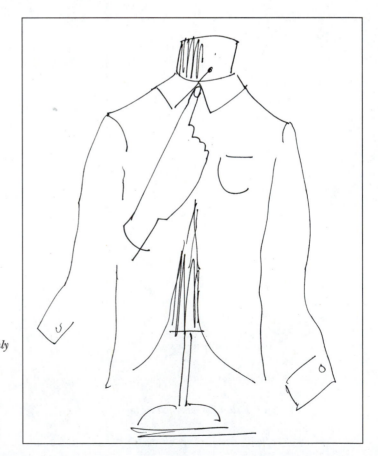

FIGURE 9–12

Dress the form with a freshly pressed shirt. Anchor the shirt by pinning the front collar to the form.

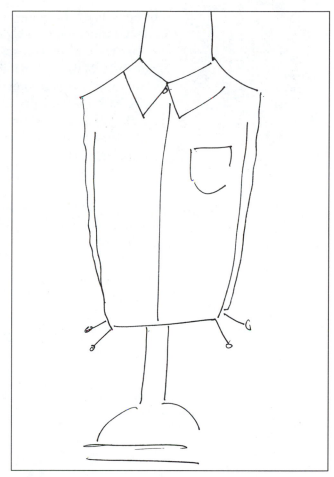

FIGURE 9–13

Pull the shirt down

all around the form to

make it look crisp and

wrinkle-free.

Anchor the shirt by pinning the front collar to the form. Then align the seams and the shoulders of the shirt and temporarily pin them to keep the shirt from riding up. Pull the front shirttail down and under the form and align it while keeping the button placket vertical with the form's center. Next, pin the shirt tail to the pinning strip under the form. Continue pulling the shirt down and pinning it on the back and sides to make it look crisp and wrinkle-free. See Figure 9–13.

The back of the shirt can be pinned under with a box or shirred pleat to eliminate a rumpled look. Make sure the shirt pocket is aligned. Remove any unwanted wrinkles.

Next, pull the sleeves tightly to the back, crisscross them, and pin them. If the cuffs of the shirt are meant to be seen, pull them through the sleeve. Choose the appropriate fashion tie and knot it so that the tie's width matches the collar style. Lift the collar all way around and fit the tie, adjusting it with your other hand. Keep the tie centered, wrinkle-free, and as flat as possible. To tie the knot, bring the big end of the tie face under the small end.

Take the long end up, over, and down, establishing the knot's base. See Figure 9–14. Make sure that the tie edges do not turn under. Place your fingers on top of the base knot and pass the long end over your fingers, wrapping it back under. Bring the long end up behind the knot and down through the opening with your fingers.

Hold the knot firmly with your other hand and slide the knot, adjusting it for the perfect fit. See Figure 9–15.

Now, fit a correctly sized jacket to the form, because too much pinning and padding is required for a jacket that is too large, and a jacket that is too small looks pulled and unnatural. Pull hard on the chosen jacket in a downward direction all the way around the form, making sure that its vent and rear seam are centered vertically. The shoulders, pockets, sleeves, and lapels must also be aligned. The jacket collar and lapel should not stand away from the shirt collar. If they do, shove the jacket collar up in back or pull the lapel

FIGURE 9–14

To tie a knot, bring the tie face under the small end to establish the knot's base.

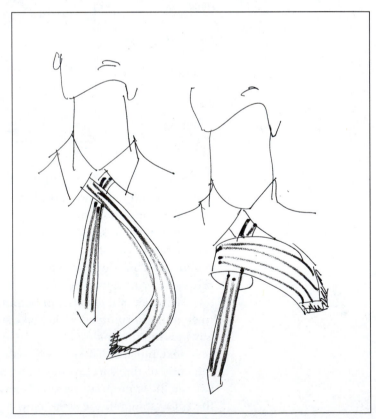

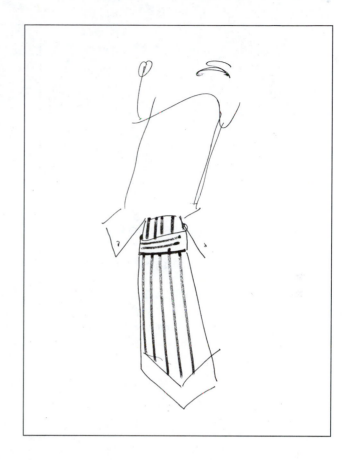

FIGURE 9–15

Slide the knot,

adjusting it for

the perfect fit.

inward and toward the front. This should create enough tension to pull the collar in line. Smooth the jacket by rubbing it in a downward direction. If the lapels pucker as they touch above the first button, blind pin them in place.

Pad the shoulders of the jacket with tissue paper for a snug look. If the sleeves begin to twist or look limp, insert a sleeve or cuff pad. See Figure 9–16.

To make a sleeve pad, trace the sleeve on firm cardboard. One edge should be straight and the other curved to fit the elbow contour. Next, trace the shape on felt, staple it to the cardboard in upholstering manner, and stuff it with tissue paper. Insert the pad in the sleeve, pinning it at the shoulder.

A silk handkerchief in the breast pocket of the jacket might add a fashion touch. Measure the pocket's depth, fold the handkerchief to size, and add one-half inch. Use cardboard if the handkerchief needs stiffening.

Matching slacks can be shown next to the rigged jacket. First, press and cuff the slacks. See Figure 9–17.

To show the crease, grip the sides of the slacks with the fly facing you; shake the pockets down, stretching them tight; fold the slacks in half at the

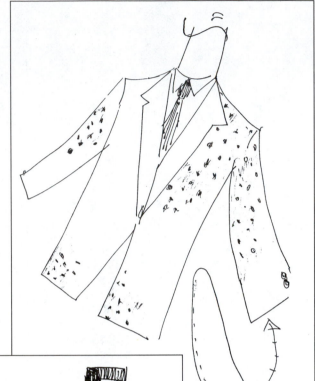

FIGURE 9–16

A sleeve pad makes the jacket sleeve and shoulder look tailored.

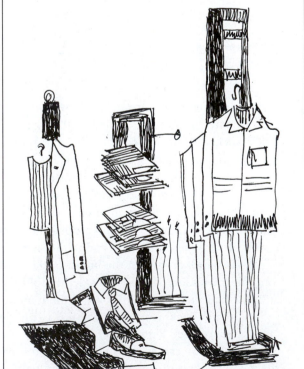

FIGURE 9–17

Matching slacks can be folded neatly and presented next to a rigged jacket.

fly; and bring the hip pockets together. Then, hold the slacks in the folded position and drape them over a T stand or display cube. For added interest, tuck a shoe part way into the pant leg and pin it in position. Also add a belt, cologne, tie, or a prop.

A jacket can be displayed appropriately folded neatly on a parson's table or display cube. Fold the front quarter of a pressed jacket away from you, folded at the seams. Insert a sleeve pad and fold the sleeve on top of the pocket. Grip the sleeve and the quarter side of the jacket and fold it over the other quarter. Lift the sagging shoulder by stuffing it with tissue paper. Vertically align the front edges of the jacket, the hem, the lapels, and the sleeves in a central geometric form.

Shirt and Blouse Forms

Shirt and blouse forms are made of papier mâché or fiberglass and are painted to match skin colors. Their hollow interiors are lined with a pinning strip at the bottom edge. Some have heads and arms, but most have short torsos and necks. Their short torsos, shorter than jacket forms, are based on shirttail length. These easy-to-dress forms are excellent for displaying casual shirts, T-shirts, and muscle shirts. See Figure 9–18.

To dress a shirt or blouse form, press the appropriately sized garment; flip the form over; and pull the shirt down all the way around, pinning it neatly and avoiding harsh puckers. Then set the form upright and align the collar, seams, and shoulders.

For a long-sleeved sport shirt or flight jacket, allow the sleeves to hang neatly at the sides. For dress shirts, choose a flat-fronted (nonmuscular) form for a crisp look. Knot and fit a tie; pull the long sleeves down; and pin them under at the sides, making them look tailored and neat. With a hand steamer, press out any unwanted wrinkles.

These forms look great placed on top of shirt cubes with the same style and color of shirt folded neatly below. The small sizes of shirts should be at the top; the larger shirts should be at the bottom. These forms provide interest and identity when placed on shelves in a back wall and mixed with face outs and hang rods. They draw customers into the department. They also create a focal point at the front of the department when shown in groups of three on a display cube or on display furniture. Some accessories, such as cologne, shoes, sunglasses, scarves, and a simple house plant, add more interest to the group.

A large assortment of lingerie and underwear forms is designed to enable the associate to fit these garments easily. Because it is elastic, lingerie requires little or no pinning. Lingerie forms are available in many new colors and finishes. Some are abstract and others are anatomically correct and finished with realistic skin colors. See Figure 9–19.

FIGURE 9–18

Shirt forms are made of papier mâché for easy pinning. Their torsos are short, enabling pinning all around. (Courtesy of ALU, NJ.)

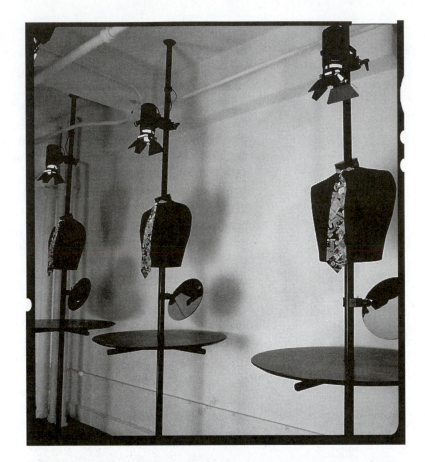

FIGURE 9–19

Softly colored mannequins flatter lingerie. This is a popular color for underwear forms. (Courtesy of E.T. Cranston-Almax USA, New York, NY.)

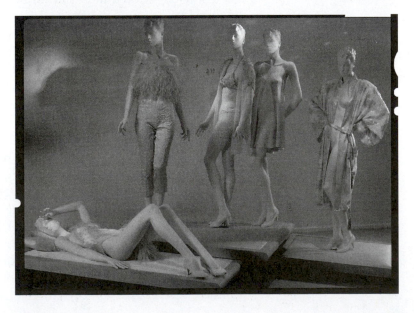

SHIRT AND SWEATER BOARDS

When limited space precludes the use of three-dimensional torsos, shirt and sweater boards provide alternatives. They can be fastened to a back wall, above shelving, on flat columns, or on light cornices in simple geometric arrangements. All shirts or sweaters look better if they have a common collar, weave, fabrication, and style. Refer to the store's color plan when arranging the merchandise. The rainbow sequence, either from dark to light or light to dark, is excellent. Buy the display boards or make them by cutting them out of one-inch-thick Styrofoam. Cut the boards so fabric can be pulled all the way around to the back for pinning.

Dressing Mannequins

Making sure that the store's mannequins are dressed in the most current fashions requires excellent timing, fashion awareness, research, and the help of buyers and fashion staff. These knowledgeable professionals help present the correct merchandise in the best locations at the best times. Poorly dressed mannequins in uncoordinated clothing and accessories jammed between apparel fixtures can be big turn-offs for the customer. See Figure 9–20.

Dressing quality mannequins is a time-consuming art with few shortcuts, but the spectacular results are rewarding. Customers do not like seeing poor mannequin groupings without a good fashion image. They are also disappointed to see the results of too little time spent on coordinated apparel, correct makeup, the correct accessories, proper pinning fitting, striking poses, and figures that are in style with the merchandise.

Management in upscale, fashion-forward stores allocate one-half day for two associates to properly dress, light, and pose three or four mannequins. In contrast, mass merchants and chain department store managers expect one associate to dress twelve or more mannequins per day.

Dressing mannequins for glamour requires the ability to select, **edit**, and coordinate merchandise based on image. The mannequins' look, grouping, pose, and lighting must enhance their garments and flatter the surrounding apparel and store. Dressing the mannequins in a display window or a **studio** is rather easy because of the tools that are available and the luxury of private space. However, mannequins are difficult to move when dressed and groomed because their arms, legs, and torsos detach easily with the slightest movement. Also, their perfectly styled hair can be instantly ruffled. It is awkward to dress and groom mannequins when crowds of customers are shopping in the department, so try doing it early in the day before traffic builds.

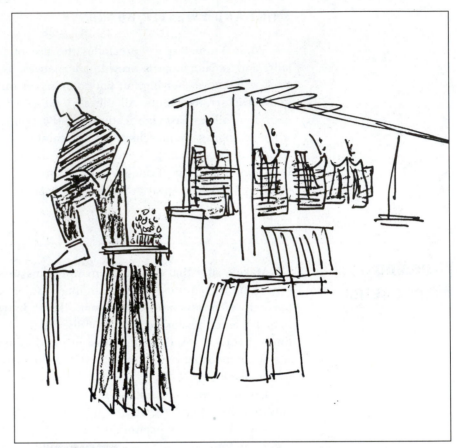

FIGURE 9–20

Buyers and the fashion staff help present current merchandise in the correct locations.

Some seated mannequins are difficult to dress because of their poses. Slacks cannot be pulled up over the waist easily because their waistbands are too narrow. Fabric will not stretch enough to pull the pants over the seat and the tension causes the pant leg to ride up. Jacket sleeves are hard to pull over active arms, especially when the arms are folded tightly over the chest. To visualize this, try on a jacket, lift your arms high, and notice how the jacket awkwardly rides up.

DRESSING A FEMALE MANNEQUIN

Begin dressing the mannequin by inverting its lower torso and fitting color-coordinated hosiery or pantyhose. See Figure 9–21.

If the mannequin's legs are spread, it may be necessary to remove one leg to slide both legs through the pantyhose past the tight waistband. See Figure 9–22.

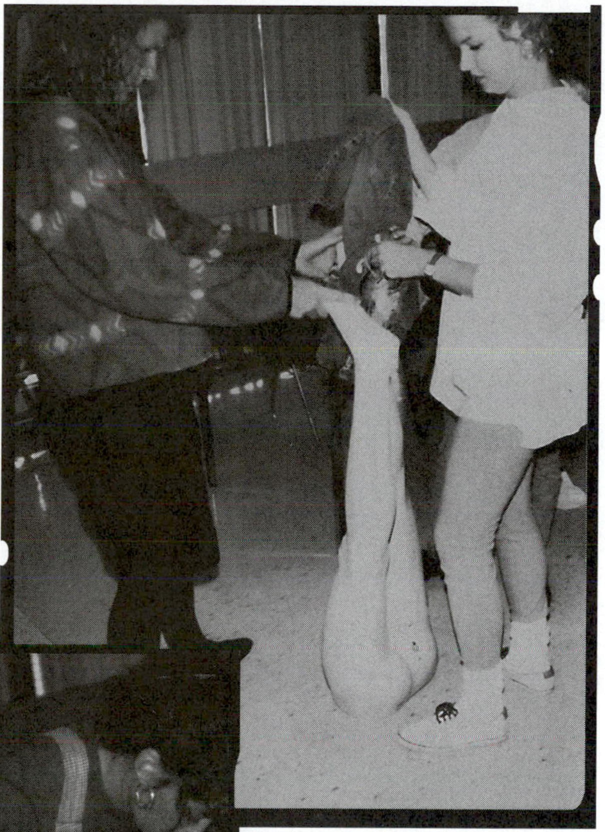

FIGURE 9–21

Begin dressing a

mannequin by inverting

its lower torso and

fitting hosiery.

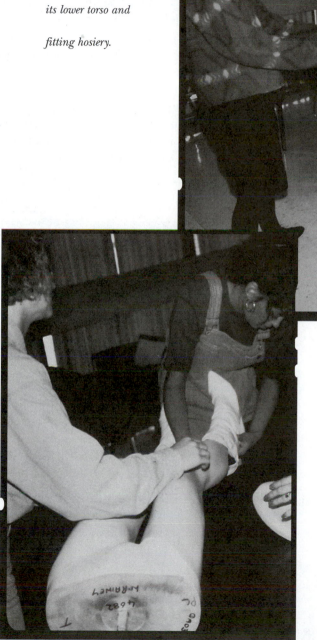

FIGURE 9–22

Remove one leg to fit

garments with tight

waistbands easily.

Then fit the shoes.

This procedure is somewhat awkward and may ruin the stockings. A rugged stocking can withstand rough handling and still look sheer on a mannequin's leg. Ask an associate to assist you in fitting the hosiery carefully while you hold the legs firmly.

After fitting the hosiery, fit the shoes with the help of a shoehorn. Make sure that the shoes' arch conforms to the arch of the mannequin's feet.

Because the mannequin's feet are unbendable, choose a shoe size that is slightly larger than the shoe size impressed on the sole of the mannequin's foot. Stuff tissue paper in the shoes for a snugger fit. Mannequins stand appropriately only when correct-fitting shoes and support rods are used. The heel and sole must make firm contact with the flooring. Mannequins that look out of balance or lean forward or to the side are either poorly mounted on a support rod or are wearing poorly fitting shoes.

After the shoes are fitted properly, stand the lower torso upright, mount it securely to the support rod, and tighten all set screws. See Figure 9–23.

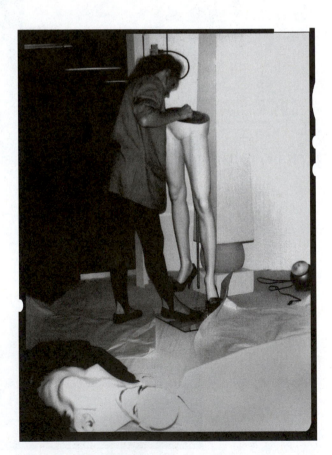

FIGURE 9–23

Stand the lower torso

and secure it to the

support rod. Then

tighten all set screws.

FIGURE 9–24

Slacks must be fitted and seam split to a support rod before a blouse is added.

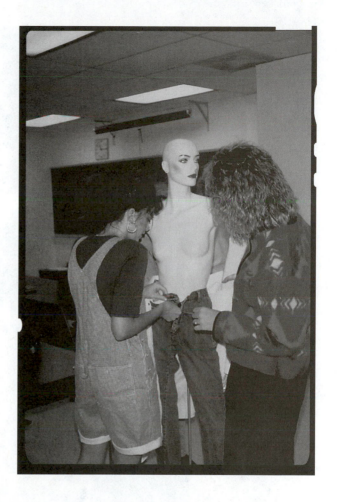

If a support rod and base are not used, strike the pose and secure it with wires fastened to the flooring. This is known as wiring mannequins. When the mannequin wears slacks, the pant seams must be opened carefully before inserting the support rod. See Figure 9–24.

Next, mount the upper torso without wig and arms and fasten it securely to the lower torso. The fastener can be a twist-lock socket or a friction pull-apart fitting. Then, drape an unbuttoned blouse, a blouse and a jacket, or a blouse and a coat over the mannequin's shoulders. Button the blouse loosely first and then pull the outer garment (the jacket or coat) over the blouse. Pull the blouse sleeves through the outer sleeve and align both garments. See Figures 9–25 and 9–26.

Starting from the shoulder, slide the arms, without the hands, down through the sleeves and out through the cuffs. See Figure 9–27.

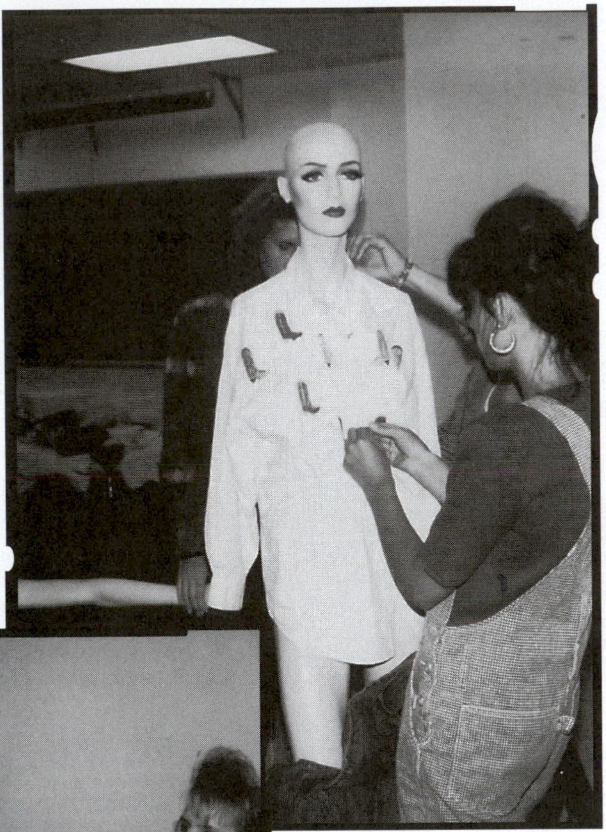

FIGURE 9–25

Drape an unbuttoned blouse over the mannequin's shoulders and button it loosely.

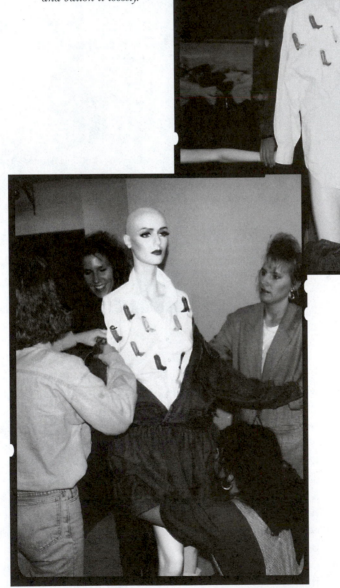

FIGURE 9–26

Pull outer garment over the blouse, pulling the sleeves through and aligning both garments.

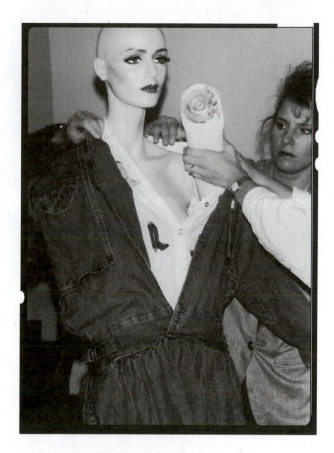

FIGURE 9–27

Slide the arms, with-

out the hands, down

through the sleeves

from the shoulder

and fasten them to

the body.

Then, fasten the arms to the shoulder sockets and fasten the hands to the arms. When fastening the hands and arms, be careful not to chip the mannequin's delicate lacquer body finish and not to chip and ruin the fragile arm sockets. To avoid this damage, the mannequin's arms are designed to fit only one position. Do not try swiveling or forcing them into any other position as you fasten them.

After fitting the garments, fit the wig. Comb, style, and trim it; add hair ornaments; apply new makeup; and add a scarf, jewelry, or other accessories. See Figures 9–28, 9–29, and 9–30.

Fun bracelets, earrings, sunglasses, necklaces, and pins can emphasize a fashion point. Tuck in or remove their price tags, but keep the tags for use later in identifying the merchandise when it is returned to stock.

The heat generated from display spotlights can cause fabrics to wilt and sag, which necessitates additional strategic pinning. A garment can look fresh after fitting, but after a few days heat may cause it to wilt. Always check

FIGURE 9–28

Apply natural makeup that washes off easily. Do not use lacquers or permanent paint because you will need to redo the makeup.

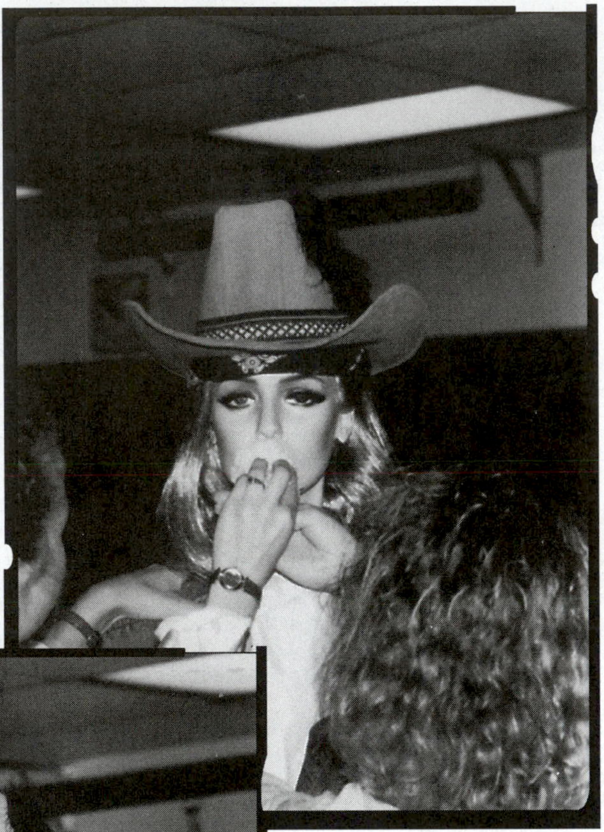

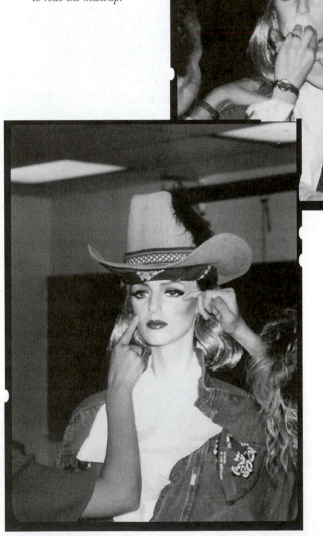

FIGURE 9–29

Blush adds color to the mannequin's face. Blend it in by rubbing your finger in a circular manner.

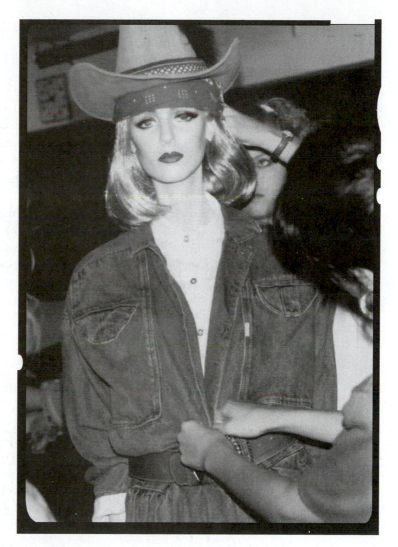

FIGURE 9–30

Add hair ornaments

and scarves and

comb or trim the hair.

the tightness and stability of a fabric's weave to determine how much additional padding and pinning is necessary.

If the garment sags, pin it. For a perfect-looking fit, begin by pinning the back of the skirt on the garment's axis. Then, pin the skirt's waistband tightly without pulling the fabric and align its seams and hem. Be sure that the shoulders of the blouse or jacket are aligned and that the bodice on the model is not twisted. Holding the jacket firmly at the back collar, align its pockets, lapels, and seams.

DRESSING A MALE MANNEQUIN

Before dressing a male mannequin, measure its inseam to ensure that the pant leg is the appropriate length. Tape the cuff or steam or sew it to achieve the length that is correct for shoes or boots and that represents the current fashion.

Dressing a male mannequin is much like dressing a female in that the body parts are sectioned in the same way. To dress a male mannequin, follow the steps in the preceding Dressing a Female Mannequin section. Additional help might be required, however, because male mannequins are much heavier than female mannequins. Their flat feet support them better than do the female's. Also, their different rod support makes them easier to balance and stand. Support rods for male mannequins fit into the ankle socket, which makes them possible to hide beneath pant legs. Wigs for male mannequins require less styling but any rough edges must be trimmed. Makeup can be applied to hide facial and body chips and scratches. Use a makeup foundation cream close in color to the body lacquer.

The male mannequin requires additional pinning for a well-groomed, tailored look. During the day, the temperature range in a window can reach 110 degrees Fahrenheit and 32 degrees at night. As mentioned earlier, fabrics can wilt and sag, which necessitates pinning. Center the shirt collar and the seams and align the shoulders. Open the fly of the trousers and pull the shirt down neatly all the way around. Pin the shirt to the trousers in back at the waist and pin the trousers in the rear, eliminating any fullness. Crease the leg to fit the current look. The tie should be knotted carefully but it can be ruffled in a stylized manner. For the traditional look, fit the tie and back pin it neatly between the jacket lapels. All cuffs, lapels, pockets, and seams should be aligned neatly and the fabrics should fit snugly without looking pulled. For suits, use a hand steamer to smooth out any wrinkles.

UNDRESSING A MANNEQUIN

When dismantling the display, the mannequins should be undressed carefully to prevent damage to the merchandise and mannequins. When removing pullover blouses and shirts, protect the mannequins' wigs and makeup by placing bags over the mannequin's head. To avoid chipping or scratching the finish, do not force the removal of any body parts. Mannequins should be disassembled totally and covered with protective dustcovers before they are moved. After moving the disassembled mannequins, select different mannequins that are suitable for the new apparel presentation.

Account for the apparel on an inventory sheet "Loan Bill" before returning it to stock. The status of the merchandise could change while it is on display. Verify items that are sold or are being held for customers and identify items that should be returned to the manufacturer or shipped to another store. The merchandise must be priced before it is returned to stock. Spot clean, press, repair, and freshen the merchandise for sale.

Budgets and Repairs

Mannequins are expensive and should be charged to a capital expense fund for tax reasons. Because mannequins are not a display expense, adequate money should be budgeted for them in annual purchases. Mannequin body type, makeup, and pose can change every couple of years. You should keep your collection current. Presenting new fashions on outdated mannequins is distressing for the customer.

Although salespeople will call on you to show you photographs of their new mannequin lines, you should see mannequins on display locally, in New York, or at the two annual display shows. See Figure 9–31. Seeing mannequins in showrooms verifies their poses for easy dressing, which is something you cannot do by looking at photographs.

When you purchase new mannequins, repair your old ones. Mannequins get knocked around by associates and customers and need restoration. A repair service will add updated makeup, eyelashes, wigs, and body colors to your mannequins. A rotation plan for buying and repairing mannequins will enable you to keep abreast of new trends.

Use this quick checklist when buying new mannequins:

1. Choose styles that best fit your store's look and merchandise.

2. Check the mannequin's poses carefully to ensure that your merchandise will fit. Some poses, such as folded arms or exaggerated arms and shoulders, are difficult to dress.

3. Hairstyles and makeup should match your merchandise by lifestyle.

4. Be sure that the mannequins fit current silhouettes, skirt lengths, and waistlines.

5. The mannequins' overall look should match your customers' fashion expectations.

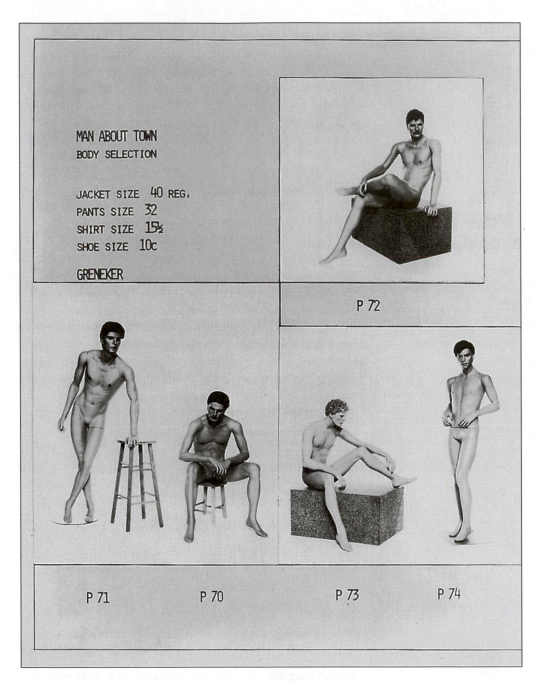

FIGURE 9–31

When mannequin vendors call, they will show you composites of mannequins which include size and a variety of poses for the body selection. (Courtesy of Greneker/Wolfe & Vine, Los Angeles, CA.)

BUSINESS HIGHLIGHT

Mannequin Feature:
Body Perfect

The following is an interview with Nellie Fink, Executive Vice President of Adel Rootstein U.S.A., New York, NY.

Author: Describe how your mannequins fit fashion.

Nellie: Our design teams research and design mannequins to fit the right look eighteen months in advance of the immediate fashions—twelve months to produce the mannequin and about three months for the customers to get them. When the VMs see the mannequins in the showroom, they know that by the time the mannequins arrive, they will fit the fashions the buyers have purchased. Our design teams do a lot of research to get the right look. We have always been on target with the correct mannequin body, makeup, and hairstyle.

Author: You produced the collection "Classy Lady Long Legs." These long-legged mannequins enhanced the current silhouette. Tell me about that.

Nellie: To use as a model, we find the right people with the right body language to fit the right fashion look. In 1970 we produced the collection "Body Gossip": ramrod straight bodies, wide shoulders, and clenched fists. These mannequins fit the style at that time. Later the look became relaxed. Our collections are always fashioned after real people.

Author: Clothes always fit your mannequins so beautifully. Anatomically they are always perfect for a correct fit. How do you do that?

Nellie: We never stylize our bodies. We feel that they must sell clothes. Even though our mannequins are works of art, they are a vehicle to sell. Unless clothes fit, customers will not buy them. We produce beautiful women and hope that customers will think, "If I buy that dress I'll look as good as she does." That's what it's all about.

Author: I have noticed that fashion designers like your mannequins. Why is that?

Nellie: Everyone understands us. We did the La Croix fashion show on mannequins at Bergdorf's, and he was thrilled about how it worked. His clothes fit beautifully.

Author: Are your mannequins accepted by all markets across the country?

Nellie: Yes, we sell worldwide. Germany and Spain are very good markets. They love mannequins.

Author: How do you trend spot?

Nellie: Our design teams travel the world to look at people on the streets, in clubs, and in theaters. They observe social, economic, and life styles, and pull it all together. That's what apparel designers do, and you get the look right.

Author: What advice do you give students who come to your showroom?

Nellie: Look around, develop style and fashion awareness, and buy quality. Learn quality. Understand it. Our mannequins look great and last a long time.

Author: How does one update your mannequins to maintain that "body perfect"?

Nellie: Redo your mannequins every time there is a makeup change, about every two years. [Redo] wigs more often. We have a refurbishing and production facility in New York. Ship the mannequins in.

DISCUSSION QUESTIONS

1. Should you apply new makeup, and restyle and trim a wig each time you dress a mannequin?

2. Why select new shoes and accessories each time you dress a mannequin?

3. Why present mannequins in groups?

4. How do you plan the location for mannequins?

5. Is it necessary to inspect a mannequin before buying it?

6. How long do mannequins stay in vogue?

7. Describe the steps for fitting a man's jacket to a form.

8. Can mannequins be repaired and updated? If so, explain how.

CHAPTER PROJECT

Project Objective: To gain experience in dressing a suit form.

Project Instructions:

1. Select a suit, shirt, and tie.

2. Dress, rig, pad, and pin the suit on the form for a perfect fit.

3. Accessorize the suit and fold the slacks neatly, presenting them to the side. Add a display prop for interest.

ENDNOTES

1. Bob Currie, master of window display for Henri Bendel, New York, NY, in the mid-1970s, created street-theatre style windows.

2. Candy Pratts was the *enfant terrible* display director first at Charles Jourdan Shoes, New York, and then at Bloomingdale's, New York, in the mid-1970s. She was noted for creating brash, daring windows.

3. Agatha Christie, the well-known mystery novelist, was born in England in 1891.

4. Victor Hugo was the VM for Halston, New York, in the mid-1970s. He called the windows he created "my weekly paintings."

5. Halston was considered the greatest New York fashion designer in the mid-1970s. He designed for Jacqueline Kennedy. Originally from Evansville, Indiana, he studied at the Art Institute of Chicago.

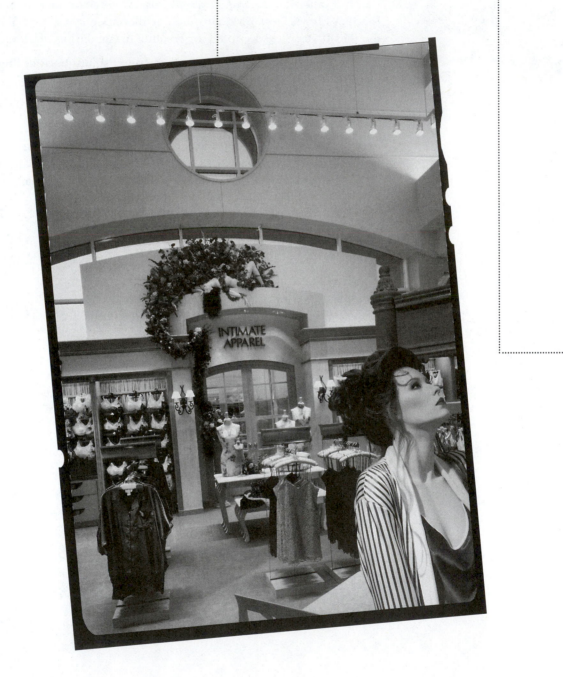

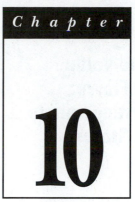

Flowers

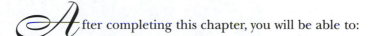

*A*fter completing this chapter, you will be able to:

1. Explain the importance of flowers and plants in stores.

2. Tell why you should use a florist's services to help design and select floral arrangements.

3. Discuss why a theme is important when choosing flowers, containers, and arrangements.

4. Explain how professional rental services and florists can help plan effective presentations with floral displays.

The Value of Flower Arrangements in Stores

Flowers have been important parts of displays for years. Because flowers are used increasingly in displays, it is important to learn about them and about florists.

It is a wonderful feeling to walk into a store and be greeted with an arrangement of cut flowers and a smile from a sales associate. Flowers help create a civilized air of well-being that prepares the shopper emotionally to begin shopping. A smart retailer would therefore establish a liberal budget for flowers to create a desirable selling environment. However, only deluxe stores budget for and plan flower displays. Neiman-Marcus, Dayton's, Marshall Field's, Bloomingdale's, Tiffany, and Saks Fifth Avenue keep local florists busy supplying flowers for the fashion shows, special events, cosmetics department, and dress salon consoles. See Figure 10–1.

Sonia Rykiel's favorite florist, Christian Tortu, adds magic to Rykiel's St. Germain boutique in Paris by festooning exterior architectural details with flowers. See Figure 10 –2. Inside, wonderful arrangements add glamour to round display tables. In Dallas, Mrs. Stanley Marcus[1] made a tradition of supplying the store with quantities of tropical flowers from her residential greenhouse. The VM staff carefully planned strategic locations for these grand arrangements.

FIGURE 10–1

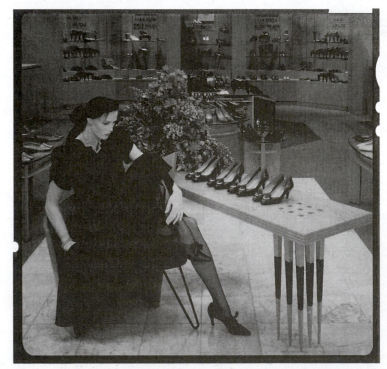

It is a joy to walk into a store and be greeted with an arrangement of flowers. (Courtesy of Schaffer Associates, Inc., Oakbrook Terrace, IL, Younkers, Inc., Omaha, NE. Photographer: Bob Briskey, Chicago.)

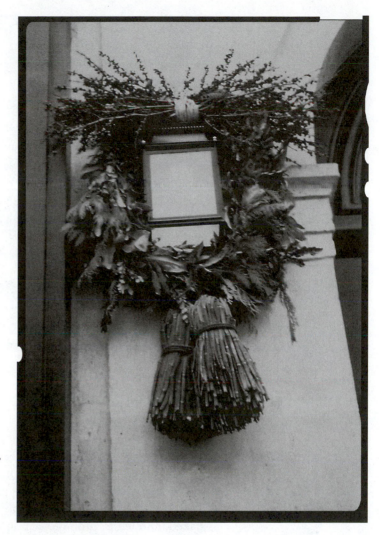

FIGURE 10–2

Sonia Rykiel's favorite florist,

Christian Tortu, created this

wonderful arrangement of berries,

greens, and snake grass for her

St. Germain boutique.

The Florist

Many fashionable and sociable New York and Chicago floral designers have made their reputations by creating unusually spectacular flower arrangements for deluxe stores. The VM directors of deluxe stores search out floral designers who can create flower arrangements to enhance the VMs' presentations. The VMs rely on florists who are knowledgeable about wholesale suppliers of flowers as varied as symbidian orchids, French tulips, and calla lilies. Not all flowers are available in every season and many wholesalers specialize rather than sell complete assortments. Your florist will supply you with the available plants and flowers. See Figure 10–3.

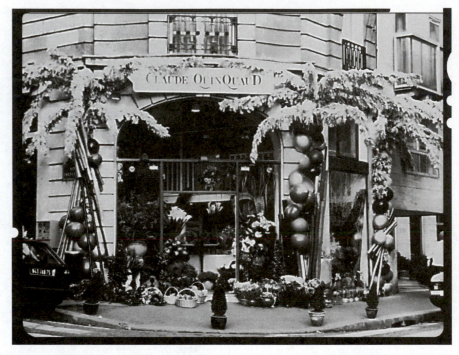

FIGURE 10–3

Creativity is recognized instantly in this florist's shop. This is Christmas in Paris.

KEEPING FLOWERS FRESH

Floral designers provide basic botanical information and characteristics of plants, including their needs and longevity. These professionals inform the VM of the best conditions and locations for plants and floral arrangements—hot, dry, moist, or in the sun—and explain how to care for flowers so that they survive beyond one day. Flowers must be trimmed, soaked, and fed to promote lasting freshness. A florist has the appropriate conditioning workrooms and makeup tables to do these things.

ARRANGEMENT TECHNIQUES

Professional arrangement techniques can prolong floral freshness. The ways in which flowers are wired and taped into position affect how long they last. Some basic stock flowers last longer than other types of flowers. Orchids have become popular because they last a long time.

EDITING FLOWERS IN ARRANGEMENTS. Glamorous flower arrangements should be edited by removing unwanted blossoms or pruning

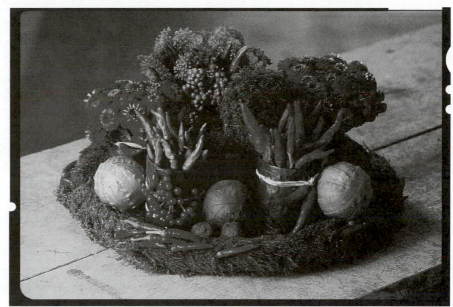

FIGURE 10–4

Flower arrangements should be edited to emphasize beauty. (Courtesy of Christian Tortu, Paris.)

branches and leaves. One flower, the Casablanca lily, blends beautifully with other flowers if many blossoms are eliminated. Florists know which flowers create specific moods and which flowers blend with others in an arrangement. Leave all of these decisions to the true artist, the florist. See Figure 10–4.

FINDING A COMPATIBLE FLORIST

When searching for a florist who can create arrangements that fit and enhance your display style, visit the smartest stores in town and review florists' work. Interview florists to determine if they can meet your deadlines and provide you with the correct style, price, quality, and quantities. Then choose the best florist for you.

Flower Motifs

Floral design motifs have always appeared on decorative materials, home furnishings, garments, textiles, and architecture. Over time, floral motifs have appeared as sophisticated, primitive, or abstract designs. In many cultures and periods, flowers have decorated useful household objects. Their dominant presence in literature and culture has affected nearly everyone.

FLORAL THEMES

Because store looks are based on themes, a VM can easily select specific floral groups that will enhance those themes. Some flowers project a country look, while others have a romantic look. Others suggest a tropical morning; some fit a Victorian theme. Still others portray a Georgian theme.

Many **flower themes** are based on seasons. Flower growers and wholesalers provide lists of available stock by season. January flower offerings include begonias, cyclamen, primula chinensis, oboconica, malacoides, and azaleas. Bulbs that are available in January include tulips, hyacinths, daffodils, and freesia. Early Easter stock includes rambler roses, heather, marguerites, lilies of the valley, Easter lilies, hydrangeas, bougainvilleas, chorizemas, azaleas, tea roses, geraniums, heliotrope, ageratum, bellis daisies, and pansies. During the first week in March, flower stocks increase to include carnations, roses, snapdragons, sweet peas, anemones, myosotis, pussy willows, and pansies. Daffodils and tulips also abound in growers' greenhouses during this season. Each month, endless new blooms appear on fresh flowers and bulbs.

CONTAINERS

Some florists arrange flowers in containers by formula. They repeat dome arrangements of carnations and chrysanthemums without realizing how innovative simple twigs, freesia, Queen Ann's lace, and rambler roses can be. Although the flowers reflect a theme, specific themes are also attributed to the floral containers. Because there are endless examples of china, stone, metal, and glass containers, a flower and display theme can easily be made to match a container. One should strive for complete harmony in flower arrangement, container, and location. Hiring a professional to design arrangements that fit your valuable containers is well worth the expense. Be sure that the store's containers are sent to the florist on time.

Small boutiques sometimes pleasantly surprise their customers by arranging flowers at the counter that are picked fresh from the associates' gardens.

Each display prop room should be stocked with an array of containers. Some container possibilities are watering cans, fine glass jars, baskets, urns, crocks, antiques, and cooking pots. The store's china or art department might have a selection of interesting containers. See Figure 10–5.

MOOD

Skilled florists can create any imaginable mood with flowers. Instruct your florist carefully about your theme, color plan, and display location. They will suggest specific sizes and flowers that will work for you.

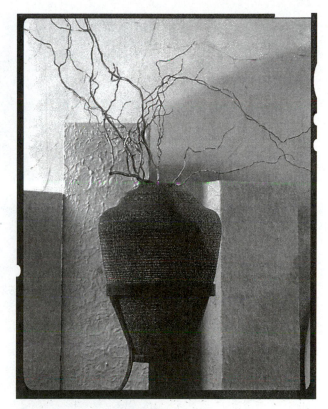

FIGURE 10–5

Collect an assortment of flower

containers. Anything that can

hold an arrangement can

make a perfect container.

(Courtesy of Flute, Chicago.)

PLANTS

Many companies rent and maintain plants. Their consulting services instruct customers on where best to locate plants. For example, a specific store location might need a visual lift. A begonia tucked in an antique cabinet is one possible solution. Large plants can enhance or hide weak architectural details. Rental systems that maintain plants can save associates many hours. One VM spent the first half of each day watering and caring for the many plants in his store.

SILK AND DRIED FLOWERS

Silk flowers are sensational on many occasions and are necessary in some instances. See Figure 10–6. For example, overscaled main aisle floral trims that remain in one place throughout a season should be artificial to minimize maintenance and eliminate watering and pruning. Huge sprays of

FIGURE 10–6

Silk flowers can, on occasion,

make sensational statements.

Cut flowers do not stay fresh

for long in the heat of a

tough window environment.

(Courtesy of R & K

International, Inc., NY.)

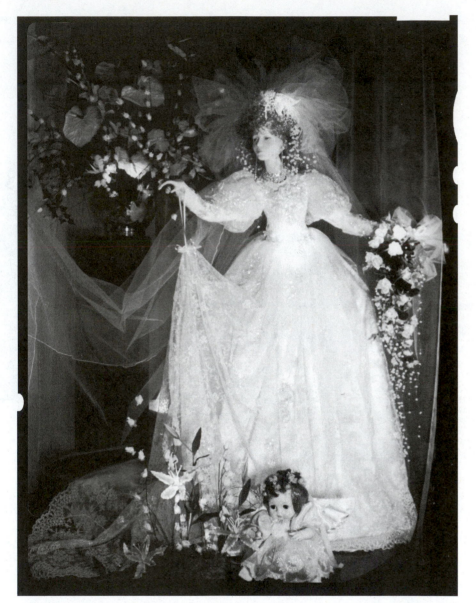

artificial pine boughs, wreaths, poinsettias, and pine trees are seasonal florals that are in one location through the Christmas season (November 1 through January 4). R & K International Inc., Spaeth, and Colonial Display, New York, are custom display houses that make wonderful seasonal arrangements. Some are superscale and are perfect for huge store interiors. Many are eight to twenty feet tall, including containers. See Figure 10–7.

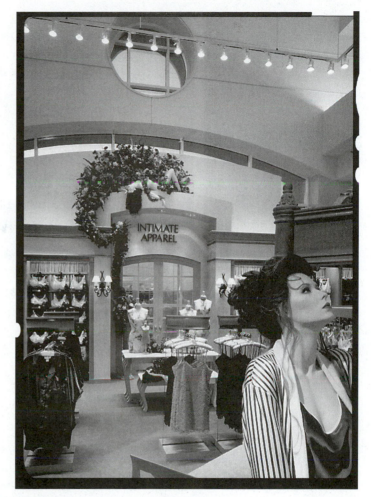

FIGURE 10–7

Special fresh overscaled floral

arrangements may not be easy to

maintain because of their sizes and

locations. Dried or silk flowers are

excellent for such applications.

(Courtesy of Schaffer Associates, Inc.,

Oakbrook Terrace, IL. Photographer:

Bob Brisky, Chicago.)

Dried flowers are always perfect in the fall and require little maintenance. Their subdued colors enhance fall apparel collections, textural antiques, woolens, and country cabinets.

Flowers are the hallmark of beauty. To use them is to confirm style.

Giant Floral Supply Wholesalers

In major cities, wholesalers who sell endless varieties of floral supplies—tools, containers, wired picks, stemming sticks, electric equipment, easels, foliage, frames, ribbons, fresh-cut and dried flowers, and plants—"to the trade" are located in giant warehouses. They present design seminars and design shows each season. Nationally known guest artists and commentators who represent floral associations show how to create designs that inspire the florist and the designer. These guest speakers present the newest arrangement techniques and clever design solutions in a cocktail-party atmosphere, which gives designers the chance to network.

DISCUSSION QUESTIONS

1. Why should a flower arrangement fit a display theme?
2. What is the value of renting plants?
3. When is it advantageous to use silk or dried flowers?
4. Why use a florist's services?
5. What special charm do fresh-cut flowers add to a store's interior?

CHAPTER PROJECT

Project Objective: To learn the importance of flowers in a display by creating flower arrangements.

Project Instructions:
Gather weeds, dried flowers, and branches. Edit, prune, and wire the material. If necessary, spray the weeds and branches a color that will enhance the display. Select containers that fit your display theme, and create two arrangements that are at least four to five feet tall.

ENDNOTE

1. Mrs. Stanley Marcus is the wife of the owner of Neiman-Marcus specialty stores of Dallas, Texas.

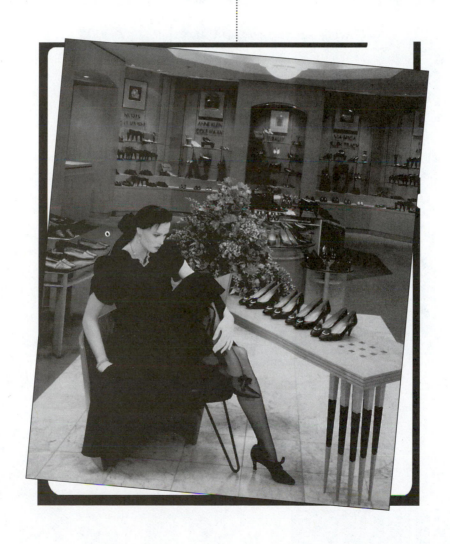

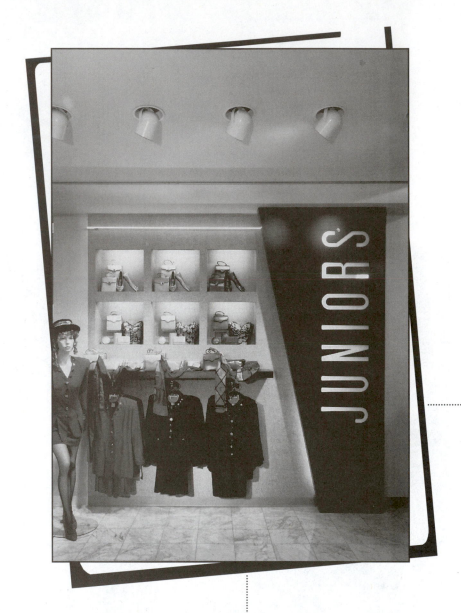

JUNIORS

Signs

After completing this chapter, you will be able to:

1. Determine the kinds of merchandising signs that a store needs.

2. Identify general store and information signs.

3. Outline production processes.

4. Describe the buyer's role in assessing sign needs.

5. Specify the special sign needs of different retailers.

6. Differentiate between the styles of store signs and choose one to fit a retailer's image.

Self-Service Creates Need for Signs

As retailers stress self-service, signs become more important as selling tools. Signs are still excellent communicators and replace sales associates to some degree. Signs provide basic information about a product and its location. A sign with ambivalent copy such as "New Arrivals" is ineffective. Customers assume that all of a store's stock is new. They want to know a product's price and its significant benefits. See Figure 11–l.

First Customer Contact

Signs are often a customer's first contact with a store. Effective signs identify the store and each department, describe the store's merchandise, advertise sales, and inform customers of special events. Signs can also describe the theme of a window or interior display, direct customers to selling and nonselling departments such as the credit department and rest rooms, and warn customers about wet floors or inoperative elevators. See Figures 11–2A and 11–2B.

FIGURE 11–1

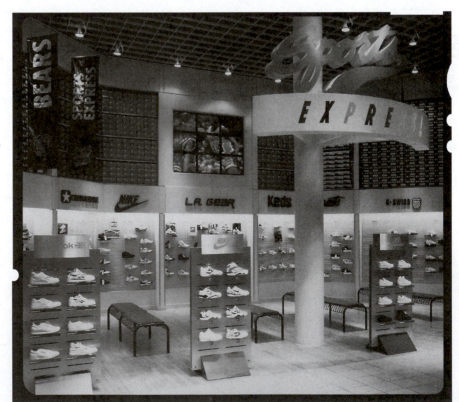

At Chernin's Shoes in Chicago, the athletic shoe classification is clearly identified. Along the perimeter, each vendor is identified, which makes merchandise visible to the customer. (Courtesy of Charles Sparks + Company, Westchester, IL.)

FIGURE 11–2A

In Canada, the entrance to The Candy Lab is designed with a dominant logo which harmonizes with the store's interior and merchandise. This design order creates store identity and an inviting shopping environment. (Courtesy of Bell Designs Consultants, Toronto, Canada.)

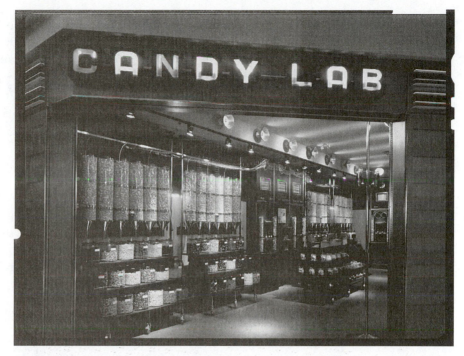

FIGURE 11–2B

A sign should incorporate a typeface that enhances the store design and sends a message about the store's merchandise. Elements such as color, texture, size, location, style, and balance are some of the design principles to consider. (Courtesy of Kubala Washatko Architects, Inc., Client Bare Bones, Bloomington, MN. Photographer: Shin Koyama, Bloomington, MN.)

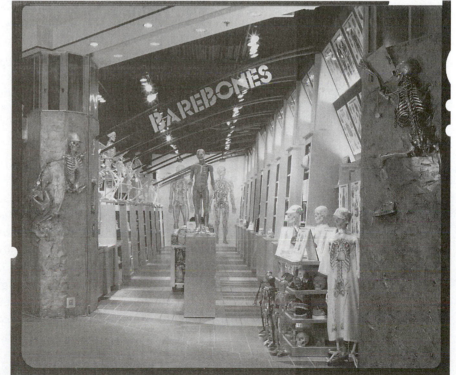

Merchandise Signs

Merchandise signs inform the customer of specific merchandise characteristics: price, use, size, fabric content, lifestyle, construction, or other benefits. Legible and clear signs are critical because busy customers have no time to stop and ponder a sign's meaning.

PRICE

In some exclusive fashion-forward stores, price is not included on merchandise signs because a designer's name may be more important to the customer than price. In contrast, mass merchants shout their prices in large typefaces because price is important to their bargain-minded shoppers. In Wal-Mart, for example, a sign on inexpensive, fast-moving merchandise such as assorted kitchen gadgets might simply state "$1.00 each." Retailers who do not put price tags on their merchandise rely on signs to communicate with their customers.

LOCATION

The VM carefully considers where to place merchandise signs. Most signs are mounted on fixtures or close to products. Placing prices too far from products confuses the customer. Sometimes, however, retailers place large merchandise sign holders called bulletins (22 inches x 28 inches; a **half sheet** is 14 inches x 22 inches) at the store entrance some distance from the merchandise to announce specific departmental sales, events, or promotions. Bulletin copy is less specific than that on merchandise signs and might simply announce "All Woolen Sweaters 10% Off" or "Donna Karan[1] shows her new collection in Better Sportswear today at l P.M." See Figure 11–3.

END CAPS

Many mass merchants and supermarkets effectively display samplings of their merchandise that are advertised in daily newspapers at the front of their department or on end caps[2] with highly visible tie-in bulletins or half sheets. Most of the stock is on its home shelf in the department. The signage combined with its location creates a strong focus on the display of advertised merchandise. Customers shop for the product on the end cap or in the department. For additional attention, the corresponding newspaper advertisement is often dry mounted to the sign card.

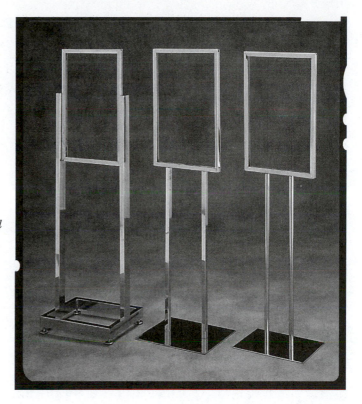

FIGURE 11–3

Merchandise signs are

available in such favorite

materials as metals, wood, and

plastic. Bulletins are used to

announce events and provide

information and directions.

(Courtesy of Dan Dee Display

Fixtures, Chicago, IL.)

Alternative Typeface Materials

STICK-ON LETTERING

As an alternative to printed lettering, some boutiques use stick-on lettering[3] to describe their merchandise. Stick-on letters are available in a variety of typefaces, colors, and sizes and are made of plastic, wood, metal, foam, **acrylic**, and other material. They can be dimensional or flat.

MOUNTING SIGNS

Signs can be mounted on walls, glass showcases, or plateglass display windows. Use graph paper to assist in placing the letters and in writing the copy. Or, tape a leveled ruler to the surface.

For dramatic graphic signs, make letters of branches, straw, or other inventive materials. Basic design principles and design skills help the VM work through sign design problems. Joining creativity with interpretation and adding good copy suggests many solutions.

FIGURE 11–4

As alternate signage, information can be printed on shopping bags and boxes to reinforce image. (Courtesy of Schafer Associates, Inc., Oakbrook Terrace, IL. Client: Casablanca Coffees.)

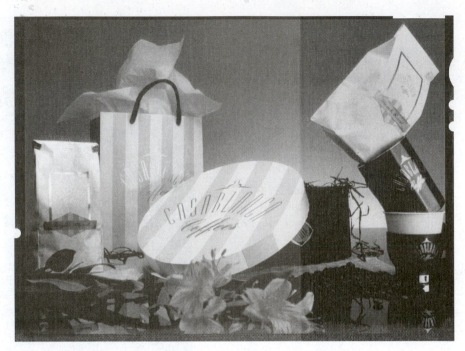

DECORATIVE GRAPHICS

Fashionable retailers combine highly decorative graphics with signs. Instead of using traditional signs to highlight a sale, these creative retailers print information on shopping bags, colorful kraft paper, stylish banners, and ten-foot-high backlighted graphics with identical patterns and colors. Others project messages on walls or employ motion light boxes, fiber optics, or video technology. See Figure 11–4.

Departmental Signs

Departmental signs in mass-merchandise stores usually hang from the ceilings and are printed in easy-to-read typefaces and colors. They hang over the center of the merchandise classification (department) and must be conspicuous from some distance to be seen by hurried customers. Departmental signs are visible from some distance when they hang high and are separated from stacks of merchandise. These signs must also be unambiguous, highly readable, and visible from other parts of the store.

Upscale fashion and department stores mount departmental signs on back walls or on light cornices, which create decorative backdrops for their merchandise. See Figure 11–5.

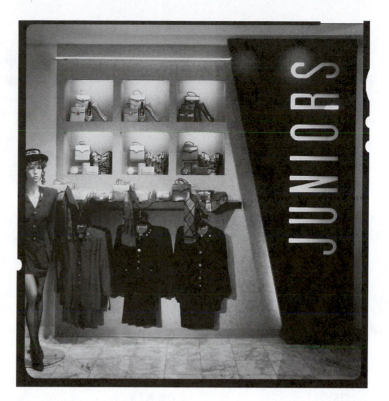

FIGURE 11–5

Very visible, well-designed departmental signs help busy customers locate merchandise classifications quickly. (Courtesy of Schafer Associates, Inc., Oakbrook Terrace, IL. Client: Younkers.)

Creativity and style are the criteria for sign creation. These stores coordinate typeface, colors, and style to enhance their interior decors. Visibility and large scale create an impact—the signs must be readable from the store or department's front. The shape, color, texture, and style of the sign are limited only by the store's decor. Custom typefaces, materials, and designs are available from custom manufacturers. The design of signs often coordinates with the store's architecture and often repeats a current fashion apparel color.

NEON, PROJECTIONS, AND BACKLIGHTING

When customers enter a department or a mall store, they may be delightfully entertained by huge, backlighted graphics on which store logo and departmental information is stylishly overlaid. Fiber-optic designs and neon that spell out fashion messages and product lifestyles add light and color to the graphics and draw the customer into the department. A dozen synchronized video projectors may provide product information and show how merchandise is used with product information. Color, movement, and sound work together to grab the customer's attention.

SIGNS AND PROPS

Fashion stores often place thematic mannequins and display props alongside departmental signs. Huge banners are designed as parts of the store architecture. In a minimalist, high-tech interior, the design of departmental signs is integrated into the store as part of the original architecture and lighting plan.

Sign Production in Supermarkets

Some supermarkets still print signs by hand with Magic Markers. Handmade signs look unprofessional and send a negative signal to the customer. Their haphazard look gives the impression that the products they advertise are damaged, defective, or soiled. Other supermarkets use computers and printers in tandem with **silk-screen** printing. In giant warehouse stores, signs are printed by computer with software tied to computerized inventory and price information. As merchandise arrives, signs are printed immediately from information on the purchase order.

Sign Production in Fashion Stores

In fashion stores, either corporate or in-store staff print signs by calligraphers or with sign machines, computers, or silk screens. To reduce labor costs, many chain stores farm out sign printing to silk-screen printers and graphic services that can handle large-volume accounts. Graphic services generally produce professional-looking signs. They are equipped with correct sign production tools and are staffed by professionals.

By working with a print-service shop to plan sign layout, style, color, and size, a VM can organize a printing system to meet store signage needs for one year with a few days. Sign copy, revisions, and additions can be faxed or sent through a computer modem by the VM staff. A computer operator in a central location can, with the correct software, design, write copy, and edit any sign and have it printed in each store within minutes. Removing sign production tasks from the display responsibility enables VMs to concentrate on merchandise presentation.

Sign Sizes

Traditional department stores base sign sizes on divisions of standard 22 inch x 28 inch card stock. The home store often uses 22 inch x 28 inch vertical cards in floor stands because products are large and when special events are announced. Apparel areas use 11 inch x 14 inch (half-card size) vertical cards in floor stands to convey information about design and sales events. Specific merchandise information such as price, size, fabric data, and designer credit is conveyed on 7 inch x 11 inch and 5 1/2 inch x 7 inch landscape (horizontal cards) on fixtures and countertops. Smaller 2 1/2 inch x 3 1/2 inch cards are used for showcase interiors. Fixture companies stock these smaller card holders as standard size. (See the following Card Holder section.) See Figures 11–6 and 11–7.

FIGURE 11–6

The retailer's favorite merchandise sign size is a 7 inch x 11 inch landscape card. These cards can be mounted on walls and fixtures and placed on countertops. (Courtesy of Dan Dee Displays, Apparel Mart, Chicago, IL.)

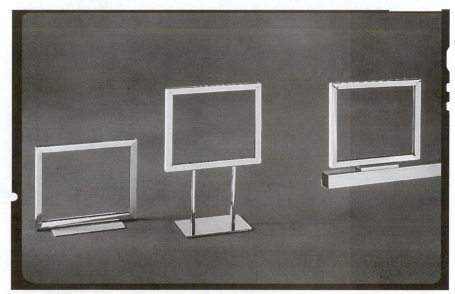

FIGURE 11–7

Frequently used sign holders are 5 x 7 1/2, 7 x 11, and 11 x 14. These plinth-based holders are made of plexi for a clean look. (Courtesy of Dan Dee Display, Apparel Mart, Chicago, IL.)

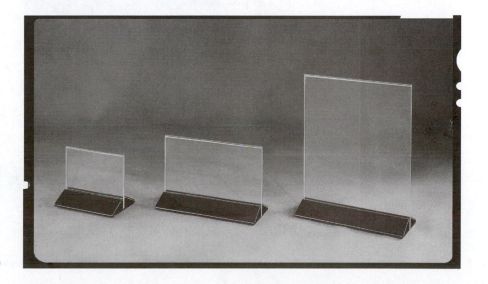

BANNERS

Banners printed by silk screen on felt or fashion textiles can deliver attractive, highly visible events messages when hung from the ceiling or on floor banner hangers. They can replicate any fashion color or copy and can be printed in dramatic typefaces. Their custom size and shape can fit any interior. At ceiling level, banners are imposing architectural elements, especially in gigantic interiors. See Figure 11–8.

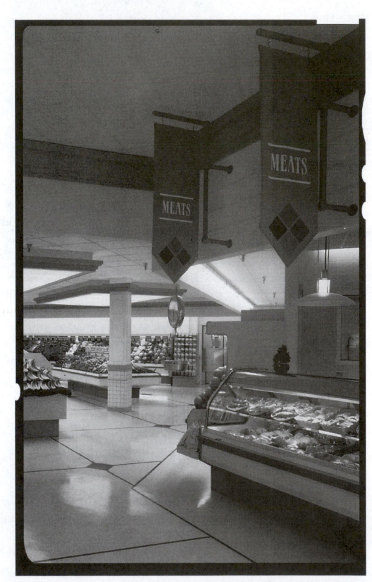

FIGURE 11–8

Banners hung from the ceiling are decorative and provide readable merchandising information. They look best when matching the store's interiors and architecture.

(Courtesy of Off The Wall Co., Inc., Telford, PA.)

CARD HOLDERS

Card holders come in several lengths for mounting on tops of dress fixtures, hang bars, or showcases. They either have screw-in stems at both ends or clips at one end. Holders with clips are for wallboard and hang-rod mounting and serve as bases for countertops.

SIGN HOLDER MATERIALS

Sign holders are made from an assortment of materials. Choose a material and color finish that will enhance and repeat the design motif of the fixture and store decor. Mixing materials and finish colors within a department creates a visual disaster.

Merchandising Staff

Buyers are responsible for ordering signs after they have placed merchandise orders, which is long before the merchandise arrives in the store. Buyers know the arrival date, price, and quantity of merchandise. They also know on which fixtures the merchandise will be placed and can determine sign size and sign holder style. If a sign does not fit a fixture because the wrong fixture size was ordered, production time is wasted by costly remakes and delays. Lacking signs for new arrivals or advertised merchandise is unacceptable to store management.

In addition to anticipating merchandise arrivals and quantities, buyers have information about the merchandise that can be included in sign copy. They often know in advance about co-op advertising (advertising that is partly paid for by vendors) that needs tie-in signs, for example. Unfortunately, buyers often write copy that is too wordy and want too many signs in a department. A clutter of signs of different sizes and styles confuses the customer and gives the merchandise a bad image. The VM staff should assist buyers with copy and help determine the appropriate number of signs. Some large signs should be arranged to create a focal point. Smaller supportive signs should be used to provide less emphasis. Some merchants want the largest sign to be on every fixture. The buyer can provide the merchant with a system to create order.

Customers in a hurry do not have time to read a paragraph. They only have time for one or two lines. When writing or editing signs, be specific and to the point. A rule of thumb is that about all a customer can absorb on a 7 inch x 11 inch card is three lines: a headline, a line of copy, and the price.

When possible, the VM should be sure that the copy conforms to the retailer's specific identifiable style which appeals to the target customer.

Building Signs

The name of a store must appear on its exterior. See Figure 11–9.

Building signs can be wall mounted or freestanding and can be made from a variety of materials. Letters can be lighted internally, backlighted, or lighted with exterior spotlights. The style of the sign and the letters should reflect the store's image and quality and enhance the building's architecture. The retailer's logo can be incorporated into the sign to reinforce store identity. See Figure 11–10.

Signs that are too garish can affect the customer negatively. Some malls and towns have sign ordinances that mandate sign material, location, and size. A sign should add to the total architectural look of the building and create an aesthetically pleasing look. Neon signs are not accepted by many shopping malls and some villages.

FIGURE 11–9

This "Portfolio" sign adds to the store's total look and immediately identifies an upscale fashion boutique. (Courtesy of Bell Design Consultants, Inc., Toronto, Ontario.)

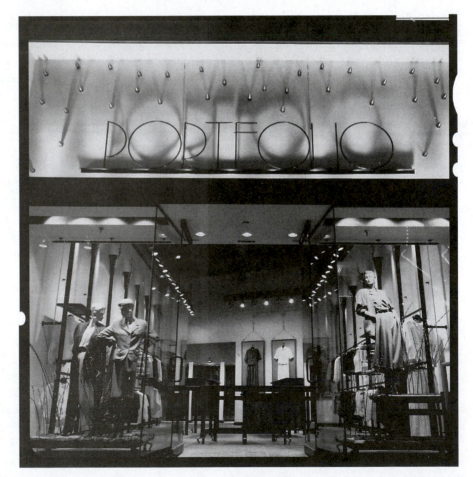

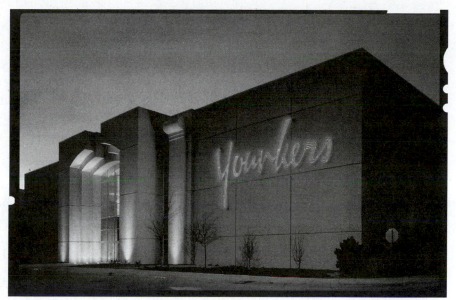

FIGURE 11–10

Exterior signs must identify the retailer and establish mood and image. Younker's sign enhances its building. (Courtesy of Schafer Associates, Inc., Oakbrook Terrace, IL. Client: Younkers.)

Sign Maintenance

The VM staff should direct sign maintenance. Signs can become soiled and tattered within a week. Because signs are visible, any blemish and soil attracts attention. Clean signs regularly and promptly remove floor signs announcing sale ends to avoid confusing customers.

VENDOR SIGNS

Vendors usually love to provide fixtures for presenting their products. Some fixtures are acceptable according to your store's fixture manual but many are not. Most come with attached vendor signs that are printed with corporate logos, colors, and materials. Often the sign's colors, typefaces, and card sizes do not fit the store's sign style. Sometimes the signs may aesthetically detract from other fixtures. Be firm with contributing vendors when communicating the store's needs. Perhaps the vendors will supply materials that fit the store's design scheme. Vendors are usually cooperative.

Savvy retailers believe signs should communicate the store's message, not the vendor's. For instance, a vendor's jewelry fixture might be topped with the name "Monet." Some stores display a dozen different vendor names in assorted typefaces, styles, and materials on one jewelry counter. This cluttered look annoys many customers. Also, the forest of sign cards hide stock presented in showcase backdrops.

TYPEFACES

The typeface and ink colors in a store should be consistent. Black, dark green, and dark blue are the most readable ink colors on white card stock. White card stock is widely used, but other colors are acceptable if they are aesthetically pleasing and easily read. Signal colors such as orange, yellow, and red on white stock produce excellent headlines for clearance sales.

A typeface that repeats the distinction of the store's logo is effective. If copy, typeface, and card color are consistent, customers will be able to read the resulting signs easily.

Some typefaces are traditional, some are modern, some are novelty, and some are display typefaces. Bodoni is the name of a traditional typeface family that comes in several variations, including italic, bold, light, and truface. A typeface retains its basic characteristics through all family variations. These variations are self-explanatory: "light" means that the type is its lightest style, "italic" means that the type is slanted. Evaluate and assess a typeface in terms of its aesthetic design and use.

FONTS

A **font** is a complete assortment of type of one style and size in both **uppercases** and **lowercases** (see the following Uppercase and Lowercase section). Some fonts contain eight *A*s and two *Z*s, at least eight of each of the other vowels, and only four *R*s.

Good design is always practical. It is balanced to fit the right size. The designer's task is to marry typeface to the store's architecture, decorative elements, and interior decor. However, typeface on a sign isolated in a display showcase or a display window can match the display theme and the style of the merchandise but need not entirely match the store's basic typeface.

POINTS

The size of letters is defined in terms of points, with 72 points equaling 1 inch. Type size varies according to placement and function on the sign. Forty-point type is somewhat large and is suitable for headlines on a 7 inch x 11 inch card. Eighteen-point type might be used to describe the merchandise on the card. Headlines look best in the largest size types. Subheads require intermediate sizes, and regular text in the smallest. Some type looks distorted when enlarged too much because its basic design does not lend itself to increased size.

PICA AND CHARACTERS

Pica is a linear unit of measurement expressing the width of a line. The number of all characters, spaces, and punctuation marks combined in the creation of copy creates a measurable line. If the number of characters in the copy is 1,750, and the type size is 8 points, use a type chart to help determine how many characters fit on one line of 8-point type. If the number of characters is 45, divide 45 into 1,750 to yield about 39 lines of 8-point type.

UPPERCASE AND LOWERCASE

Uppercase is the term used for capital letters. Lowercase is the term used for noncapital letters. See Figures 11–11, 11–12, and 11–13.

FIGURE 11–11

Uppercase is the term used for capital letters.

36 Point
ABCDEFGHIKJKL

FIGURE 11–12

Lowercase is the term used for noncapital letters.

bcdefghijklmno

FIGURE 11–13

The number of characters, spaces, and punctuation marks combined in the creation of copy creates a measurable line.

Character Count

1 2 3 4 5 6 7 8 9 10 11 12 13 14 15 16 17 18 19 20 21 22 23 24 25 26 27 28 29 30
HOW IS ONE TO ASSESS AND EVALU

BUSINESS HIGHLIGHT

Robert Schafer
Talks About Signs

Robert Schafer, CEO of Schafer Associates, had this to say about his company's design for Sears in Bloomingdale, IL: "We discovered that it was more important to have a high-speed and accessible store than a high-style store. Good signage enhances the store's accessibility. The sign band that extends along the perimeter of the store replaces hanging signs and banners that shoppers associate with Sears. The sign band gives customers information that they need when they need it."

Barry Vinyard, Schafer's VP and corporate design director, talked about Krochs & Brentano's Chicago bookstore. "The most difficult aspect of designing a bookstore is arranging departments and signage so that customers can quickly and easily find what they're searching for," he said. "The large perimeter category signs are visible from all parts of the store, and even from the mall through the glass storefront."

At Casablanca Coffees, Chicago, Schafer Associates developed signs based on the need to communicate visually. "In a competitive retail arena where similar customer services are offered by a variety of outlets, the Casablanca Coffees image required a unique appeal in order to create a differential. This was achieved by cleverly combining a sense of humor and tongue-in-cheek attitude with the style and savvy of the 'Casablanca' design concept. This attitude is illustrated in every aspect of the business, from the signature gray-and-white awning-stripe motif, to the names of the blends, to the detail above the logo borrowed from a piece of deco metalwork."

DISCUSSION QUESTIONS

1. What is a sign's purpose?
2. Who is responsible for ordering signs and writing sign copy?
3. Why is it wise to standardize signs?
4. Why maintain signs?
5. How do you determine the design of an outdoor sign? What restrictions are placed on outdoor signs?
6. When should you use the services of sign shops?
7. How do you correct the vendor sign problem?

8. Name each sign size and its general purpose.

9. Why should buyers assist in writing copy for signs?

10. Why limit sign copy?

CHAPTER PROJECT

Project Objective: To practice choosing graphics and typefaces that represent a store and its fashion merchandise.

Project Instructions: (Choose one)

1. Design a shopping bag based on a product (such as cosmetics, jewelry, or other) or on a store image (such as a high-fashion retailer). Design the bag with logo and graphics that instantly identify the product or store. Match type style with product and store image.

2. Buy a small shopping bag at Hallmark's in a fashion color that enhances your subject. (If your subject is fashion jewelry, you could choose a bag with a metallic finish, for example.) From a current fashion magazine, cut photos of jewelry and photos of a vendor or store logo. Combine the photos in a composition and paste them on the bag's face using a collage technique. Use your layout design skills when creating the bag. Remember that the art of composition is putting things together that belong together. Choose items that have such commonalities as color, texture, and balance.

3. Create a window, showcase, or tabletop display using a store logo and create a display that reflects its image.

ENDNOTES

1. Donna Karan, the New York fashion designer who produces upper-end, trendy sportswear, also owns DKNY, New York, a cheaper sportswear line. Karan designed for Ann Klein before becoming **entrepreneurial**.

2. End caps are semicircular shelf display fixtures placed at the ends of aisles of back-to-back shelving. They are used in supermarkets, mass retail stores, and superhardware stores to present featured merchandise.

3. Stick-on lettering is available in fonts of varied typeface, color, and size. The letters have an adhesive backing that can be pealed off to apply the letter to any surface. A grid is available for setting the letters. Before appyling the letters, level and tape a ruler to the surface.

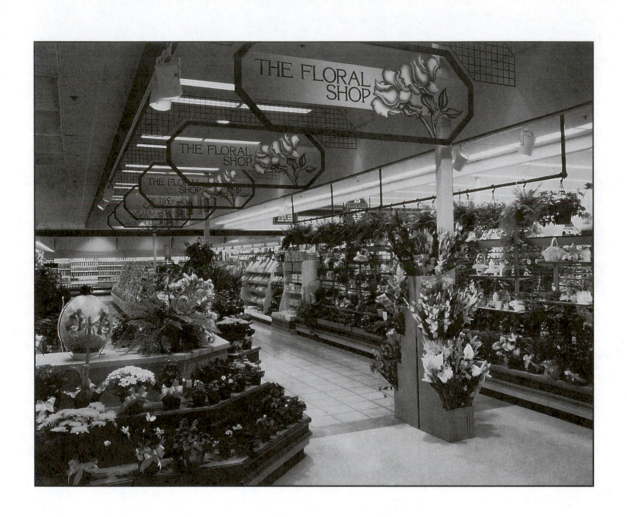

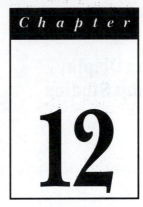

Supplies— Setting Up Shop

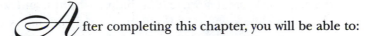

After completing this chapter, you will be able to:

1. Determine what supplies are needed for various retailers.

2. Identify the storage needs for supplies.

3. List the art supplies that will help you do a job.

4. Tell what materials and equipment are needed for a carpentry shop.

5. Know what materials and equipment are needed for a paint shop.

6. List the tools needed to install a typical display.

The Display-Shop Studios

Well-equipped display-shop studios fulfill the needs for building props and installing displays. They also handle ongoing remodeling, maintenance, fixture building, and repair tasks. A staff of carpenters and painters is needed to operate these shops. The carpentry shop, paint shop, and display workroom are often in a warehouse where props are stored, like at Bigsby & Kruthers, or they are on an upper nonretail floor in the flagship store such as at Marshall Field's.

CARPENTRY SHOPS

The display-shop studio in a large store or department-store chain has a complete carpentry shop. The shop contains industrial saws, planers, sanders, drills, lathes, and other modern power tools used by the building trade. It also contains large workbenches; tables; sawhorses; metal utility bins; and storage shelves for lumber, fiber board, wall board, and foamcore. Cabinets and bins under workbenches hold every size screw, bolt, and nail in every finish. The carpenter should have every available power tool to expedite production.

PAINT SHOPS

A complete paint shop should be located adjacent to the carpentry shop, with well-vented industrial spray booths, air compressors, spray guns, dusting hoses, paint storage bins, industrial sinks, and solvents. The paint shop should be stocked with industrial-sized containers of basic latex and oil paint in every color and tint needed to create any color. Skilled painters are experts at mixing color from basic color tints. Large quantities of paint are cheaper. Seldom are premixed colors bought unless large amounts of the same color are needed.

VM DIRECTOR'S OFFICE

The display studio next to the carpentry and paint shops should have space for the VM director's office, which is equipped like any other business office. Individual drafting tables and art supply cabinets filled with hand tools and art supplies should be close by for the VM associates to use. The display studio should include drawing supplies such as drawing pencils; inks; water colors; **tempera**; acrylics; brushes; drafting tools; architectural scale rulers; pads of drawing paper; tracing papers; colored markers; and graph papers to make basic presentation boards, sketches, and drafting floor plans. A small reference library containing shelter magazines (interior design), fashion periodicals, design books, and **trade publications** should also be provided. Computer and printer hardware with Auto**CAD** applications installed, placed in quiet, uncluttered areas on functional computer furniture, are terrific tools for store planning tasks.

WORKROOMS

The workroom area should provide space for dressing mannequins and forms and should house large worktables for making and cutting decorative panels, cutting large sheets of foamcore, cutting large bolts of fabric, and working on seamless and Kraft papers. The worktables must be large and sturdy for assembling props before installing them in display areas. Adequate space and tables are needed for special, handcrafted signs. Drafting tables are often used to make these signs. Props should be made in the workroom, and mannequins should be dressed before they are installed in windows. Equipment, props, merchandise, and mannequins are often damaged when constructed or assembled in cramped window displays.

STORAGE UNITS AND SPACE

As has been discussed in previous chapters, many assorted items are used in creating displays. Some are quite small and others are huge and difficult to handle. Display materials must be stored in an orderly fashion and classified by color, design, texture, or size so that they can be easily handled. Organization is essential because many VMs work with all or some of the materials at the same time. Storage units either made in the carpentry shop or bought from a utility storage company must aid in organization.

In addition to needing storage space for display items, storage space is needed for large decorative panels. These panels are often sleeved into utility units that are eight feet high. Mannequin closets help keep fragile mannequins grouped in order and protect them from dust and chipping. Because textiles are used in quantity, large roller or textile shelves are helpful. Cabinets are needed for storing the huge assortments of ribbons, braids, cordings, and trimmings that are used daily. Drafting cabinets keep posters, drawings, prints, and matte boards organized. Seamless papers, because of their size, become awkward to handle if they are not stored in cabinets.

Floor coverings such as cork, grass, sand, gravel, shredded raffia, plastic chips, and bark chips take up space and need to be stored in adequate cartons by type and color. Three-dimensional props such as antiques, artificial flowers, signs, sign holders, auxiliary sign-making equipment, lighting equipment, flowers, flower containers, and other needed materials also need adequate containers and space.

Well-equipped shops and studios are necessary because most materials cannot be purchased locally, and the supplies should be on hand to keep the work going. Management often requests displays at the last moment, and you will not have time to run out to buy materials.

BOUTIQUES, CHAIN STORES, AND SMALL RETAILERS

Because boutiques, chain specialty stores, and smaller retailers farm out much of their carpentry and refinishing work, they do not need paint and carpentry shops. However, their VMs will want a workspace for one or two associates, an area for sign equipment, a place to facilitate minor additions and touch-ups on premade props, and a small storage area. The workspace should include an area for painting and fabricating simple props and storage space for ribbons, trims, papers, signs, three-dimensional props and large decorative panels, textiles, floor coverings, small props, hand tools, art supplies, hardware, wire, nails, screws, fasteners, lighting equipment, antiques, flowers and containers, and sign holders.

Most small stores have little VM workspace. Props are prepared by corporate representatives or by freelancers and are installed by regional display teams, the store VM, or another freelancer. All hand and power tools, art supplies, and props must be supplied by these installers. When a display is dismantled, the props are discarded, returned to the display workroom, or shipped to another store or warehouse because storage space is limited.

A CENTRALIZED STUDIO EXAMPLE. The Florsheim Shoe Co. in Chicago where VM-VP Gunter Albers has a showroom, assembly area, and design studio is an excellent example of a centralized chain-store studio. At Florsheim, fixtures and displays are first designed, then the designs are farmed out to display manufacturers, fabricators, suppliers, and design companies for costing, production, and sampling estimates. Albers said, "I prefer that one company supplies all the decorative materials in the display such as flowers, textiles, and graphics. This creates a uniformity of style. Coordinating any subcontracting would be time-consuming, labor intensive, and costly."

Albers's design staff submits a display design under his direction and a vendor makes a sample (prototype). The sample display is then shown to management (department heads). If it is approved, the display goes into production. The displays or fixtures are either drop-shipped to the stores from the contractor or they are shipped to the central warehouse with photographs and installation instructions for corporate shipping to all

Florsheim stores. "At one time all the displays were made in their work-rooms," Albers said. "It was too costly and [the displays] were always limited by their production capabilities. If plastic injection or backlit graphics were needed and it was beyond the staff's capabilities, it wasn't done. This problem limited creativity and limited the end result."

The Toolbox

To execute displays on location, the VM should carry a well-equipped toolbox containing dressmaker pins, "T pins," staple guns, "T tackers," pliers, screwdrivers, side cutters, picture-hanging wire, filament (invisible nylon fish line), a tape measure, claw hammers, utility knife, Exacto knife, assorted glues, fine sandpaper, erasers, and scissors. The toolbox should also include masking tape, duct tape, double-faced tape, and cellophane tape. **Hot-glue** guns are a must for fast, heavy, and secure gluing. Because every display task is different, list the tools and supplies needed beforehand. When dressing mannequins and forms you will need a portable steamer, clothes brushes, masking tape, a small, portable vacuum cleaner, cleaning solvents, and extension cords for portable power equipment in addition to the toolbox.

Shop Materials

TEXTILES

The VM uses large amounts of textiles to cover display boards, jewelry pads, table pads, pinning boards, tablecloths for tabletop displays, showcase linings, and backdrops in all displays. The fabric stock should contain a variety of textiles for these endless display needs. Fabric is a great instant cover-up for walls when the VM is redoing a boutique within a store.

Fashion textiles are excellent for draping display backdrops or creating textile sculptures as parts of a display. As props, fashion fabrics can enhance apparel. Wide fabrics such as upholstery fabric, which is 54 inches wide, and felt, which is 72 inches wide, can be used for tablecloths because their seams are almost undetectable. Narrow dressmaker fabric, which is 36 inches wide, is appropriate for draping. Felt is stretchable, is available in many clear colors, and is perfect for upholstering furniture pads and decorative furniture.

Choose the correct fabric for the job: one that is attractive and that meets the physical requirements of the job. Consider a woven, print, or solid when choosing textiles. Some fabrics such as velvet, satin, silk, and rayon, are elegant and drape and fold easily while others are somewhat stiff and are better suited for covering decorative boards. Burlap comes in many colors, adds texture, and is excellent for covering huge background pads. In addition, consider whether to use metallics, synthetics, or natural fibers. Moiré is a VM favorite because it adds glamour and comes in many colors. Many VMs prefer novelty fabrics. They are often synthetic, wide, and are known for their bold thematic prints.

Some local fire codes might require the fabric to be fireproofed. How the fabric is used can be a factor in fireproofing because some textiles ignite readily. As a result, hot lighting fixtures must be placed some distance from the fabric. Intense light beams are very hot and care should be taken when focusing them on textiles.

WALLPAPERS

Wallpapers are used frequently and are available in a color range from solid to patterns. They also come in textures to fit any historical period or mood. They are decorative and are quick cover-ups for display backdrops, pad covers, showcase linings, and box covers. Some wallpapers are plastic coated or vinyl and may be scrubbed. Silk and hand screened wallpapers, however, are fragile. Trompe l'oeil (fool the eye) papers are display design-er favorites. Wallpaper that looks like marble or pebbles add whimsy and exotic surfaces to mundane items.

Because retail decisions happen quickly, a VM might be given short notice to convert a selling space to another merchandise classification. Wallpapers provide a quick and convenient cover-up. The savvy VM keeps a selection of wallpapers and textiles on hand.

FOAMCORE

Large amounts of foamcore are consumed daily for props, stiffening boards, decorative panels, sculptured effects, and tasks that are as varied as your imagination. It is portable, inexpensive, cuts easily with a utility knife, paints well, and pins easily.

FIBER/HOMASOTE BOARD

Other than foamcore, **homasote** board is a mainstay for the VM. It is made of compressed paper, 4 feet x 8 feet, and varies in thickness from 5/8 to 3/4 inch. Homasote's stiffness makes it desirable for making pads. It also lends itself to upholstering techniques such as back stapling, maintaining rigid box pleats, and stretching fabric. It is lighter, cheaper, and more disposable than drywall, plywood, or other building materials. It is strong, paints well, nails easily, cuts handily, and looks permanent. These are important considerations because displays are short-lived. VMs usually love to make display and merchandising cubes with homasote because of its low cost, strength, finish, and construction ease. Homasote is better than foamcore for making rigid displays and is lighter than plywood.

PLYWOOD

Plywood is indispensable and should be on hand for stiff, durable, and permanent wall and partition construction. It is best used for props, dividers, and quick interior construction. It is also appropriate for shelves, fixture repairs, and fixture construction.

GLASS

Glass shelves, showcases, glass cube fixtures, doors, and glass unibuilt fixtures often break. Replacement glass should be available for quick fixes.

EXOTIC WOODS

Exotic woods such as walnut, birch, oak, and mahogany should be kept on hand to repair and construct fixture and furniture trim.

SEAMLESS PAPER

For window display backgrounds, seamless paper is a must. It comes in seemingly endless colors. It is exciting because it is wide (8 to 14 feet). It can cover a whole back wall, providing instant color. Add-on surface treatments are popular. Seamless paper can be sprayed over and drawn on. Designers love to glue decorative items to it to create collage effects.

WRAPPING PAPERS

Wrapped gift boxes are used as props throughout the store for any gift-giving occasion. Huge amounts of boxes and wrapping papers are needed, especially at Christmastime when they are included storewide in all trims, garlands, wreaths, and trees.

PAINT

As mentioned earlier, large amounts of basic paint colors and good tints are necessary. Any expert painter mixes most colors to specifications with latex or oil-based paint. Tempera, casein, acrylic, and watercolor paints are necessary for detail and art work.

ART PAPERS

Buy art papers, such as illustration boards, watercolor papers, bristol boards, and graph papers, to draw on. Keep exotic Japanese and Italian papers for interesting accents.

DISCUSSION QUESTIONS

1. Explain why large retailers need fully equipped carpentry shops.
2. What tools would you find in a VM toolbox?
3. Name some props and equipment that need storage space in a VM studio.
4. Why should you prepare and create props before installing them in small stores? What tools are needed for prop installation? Who installs the display?

CHAPTER PROJECT

Project Objective: To practice cutting foamcore by cutting shapes.

Project Instructions:

Using a utility knife, experiment by cutting the following lines and shapes from small scraps of foamcore: straight lines, curves, and complex geometric shapes. Use bevel cutting for strong precise corners. Do not use an Exacto knife because the blade is too weak and produces a wavering line. Draw the line and cut into it many times until the cut penetrates the foamcore. If you try cutting through the foamcore with the first cut, your hand will waver and you will not cut a straight line. If the blade is not sharp, the edge will shred. If the line is not exact, use sandpaper to clean it up and smooth it.

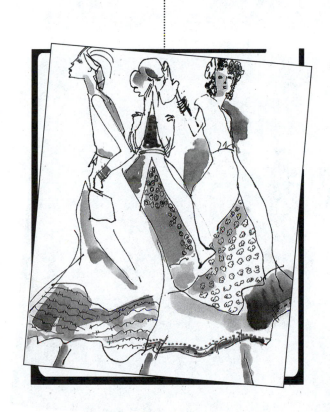

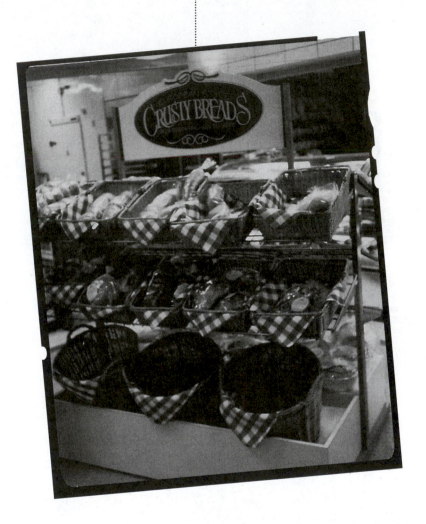

Chapter 13

Vendors
and Markets

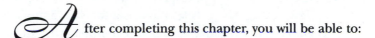

*A*fter completing this chapter, you will be able to:

1. Tell when and where display markets are held.

2. Understand the importance of good resources.

3. Identify where to look for props.

4. Comprehend the value of searching home furnishings and apparel markets for presentation ideas.

5. Recognize flea markets as a valuable resource.

6. Appreciate the value of developing good relationships with vendors.

Finding Display Materials

Display is a decorative art. To create the many displays needed in a year, the VM requires numerous props and decorative materials such as mannequins, fixtures, signs, graphics, florals, and art pieces. Anyone who can provide a useful material can be a supplier. Finding these useful materials, however, is time-consuming.

Creative people usually want to use materials that are different, original, or unique. The search for new and different things may take you to the local hardware store, to trade shows, and to foreign countries. Using materials creatively might mean using a common, everyday material in a way no one has thought of before. You might find an unusual object at an antiques flea market like the ones in Kane County, St. Charles, IL, or Marche Pouce, Paris, France. Both flea markets are huge collectors' affairs filled with exotic, extraordinary objects.

The National Association of Display Industries

The **National Association of Display Industries (NADI)**, a national display association, organizes two trade shows a year in New York. One is in May and one is in December. *VM & SD* magazine has cosponsored the shows since 1994. These shows provide a selling stage on which VMs can personally inspect display materials that are exhibited by worldwide display suppliers. Suppliers from Europe, Asia, the Orient, South America, Canada, the United Kingdom, and Mexico provide an exciting mix of stylish items. New York is a logical location for the shows because it is the site of the largest number of display vendors, workrooms, and showrooms.

The spring show is a showcase for fall and Christmas trim; the December show features spring and summer trim. In the past, the shows have been located in the Javits Center, the NADI headquarters building, on the Pier (1990 and 1992 New York Harbor). Many New York vendors participate by exhibiting at the show, while others convert their studios and showrooms into exciting showcases.

The vendors who exhibit in their permanent New York showrooms provide hospitality bars, luncheons, and snacks. Attendees are invited to pause, see a striking line, mingle with other buyers, and recharge for three or four rigorous, fourteen-hour days of buying. Seminars are conducted to share and upgrade current skills and knowledge.

PRODUCTION PLANS

Productive VMs are out early and work at the show until five. After five, over late dinners, VMs and vendors work together discussing custom work and production plans. Many busy display manufacturing executives attend the VM shows and are available to help the VMs with planning custom projects.

PLAN AHEAD

If you want to work with a vendor on special projects, make an appointment far in advance. Do not arrive in New York and expect last-minute appointments. Make the appropriate vendor appointments long before a market trip and take a list of items needed for the season. If you do not plan ahead and make priority lists, you might overlook items in the show's confusion. With so many items to look at, you might easily become frantic. To maintain focus, know what merchandise has been purchased and what advertisements and special events are programmed. An events calendar will help identify specifics. If you buy yellow props when merchandise buyers purchase red and advertising has projected red for spring campaigns, your career is in serious trouble.

PLANS BECOME A REALITY

For the Christmas show in May, many VMs bring detailed illustrations of their intended Christmas trims. They plan production meetings with sales-people and New York production people who will make their plans reality by determining material and production costs and providing manufacturing and shipping suggestions. Some parts of the trim are manufactured in New York. Other parts are made in Asia and returned to New York for assembly. Because parts of the trim are huge, such parts as twenty-feet-tall Christmas trees need special coordinating, crating, shipping, and receiving. Some of the display components may be shipped early while others that are too large to be received at the store are not shipped until installation time.

A VM may have a terrific trim idea only to find that the manufacturer must use an alternate material for production. Some materials are available only in certain colors. It is best to work all of these details out while in New York. Your regional vendor-salesperson will always be on hand later back at the store to assist with any changes, measurements, and other details. Insist on production progress reports. You probably do not want to hear days before the expected delivery time that the manufacturer could not fabricate your trim. By November, which is generally Christmas installation time, you would probably hate to find that your store will have no Christmas trim.

Although decorative items and trim represent half of the items at a trade show, additional vendors showcase mannequins, alternate mannequins, apparel forms, and fixtures. Sign specialists exhibit sign-making equipment. Fixture vendors exhibit sign holders. Christmas animations are a big business. In May, they are well represented in glamorous exhibits. Just about any trendy display item can be found at trade shows.

REGIONAL SALES REPS

Because many VMs, cannot visit the New York VM show for a variety of reasons, traveling sales representatives of major companies make calls on them. When not on the road, these representatives are in home-based showrooms. Representatives make calls on major accounts at least twice a year and at other times by appointment. They show major seasonal collections and help plan custom work. Secondary collections, such as cruise and other minor seasonal materials, are shown with spring/summer and fall/winter/ Christmas lines.

Other Shows and Sources

CHICAGO'S VM SHOW

On April 23, 1994, the Retail Equipment Expo & Visual Merchandising Show was held at McCormick Place, Chicago, with more than 500 exhibitors and about 5,000 VM store planners and designers. About 10,000 pre-registered attendees, including show organizers, absorbed the industry atmosphere. The VMs and others were able to witness teleshopping and other new retailing venues. A banner group of store-planning companies designed and executed a central showcase of model stores called Concept 2000 *the future.* Owing to the impact of the Chicago stores, it will likely continue. In 1995, many more kinds of retailers, such as food/supermarket, auto, and hardware, attended the show. The National Association of Store Fixture Manufacturers (NASFM) sponsors the store-fixturing show and *Display & Design Ideas* magazine produces it.

EURO SHOP

Euro Shop '93 was attended by 92,000 visitors from seventy countries, which made this mid-June market the world's largest trade show for VMs. The show, which was held in Dusseldorf, Germany, was housed in seven exhibit halls. Several of the halls were the size of Chicago's McCormick Place, which is the equivalent of fifteen airplane hangars. Unfortunately, this show is held only every three years.

Exhibitors at Euro Shop '93 showed the world's trendiest mannequins, apparel fixtures, supplies, and store designs. Manufacturers showed exciting fixtures ranging from trendy boutique, department store, and mass merchant to supermarkets. A large group of the supermarket fixtures, which focused on new materials, lighting, and colors, were shown. Vendors set up complete stores to present new display ideas and arrangement concepts.

Some critics believe that Euro Shop '93 display vendors did not understand the VM and that the VMs' taste and needs have moved faster than the vendors'. This seems to be a natural progression because ideas change with each new merchandise classification and lifestyle. The art of VM has moved on from early Chicago and New York and now is totally different. When you attend these giant shows, you must be aware that new updated items are exhibited as well as items that are trending out of "vogue." What might seem old hat to some are fresh and exciting to others, waiting to be presented in new ways.

THE '94 JAPAN SHOP

Japan presented a program of shop interior-exterior designs, VM tools, fixtures, and lighting at its '94 Japan Shop at the Tokyo International Trade Center. Four hundred and five companies exhibited in 1,771 booths.

VM WEST

VM West now replaces the old Western Show organized by the Western Association of Visual Merchandising (WAVM). In 1994, VM West was at the hangar in Santa Monica, CA. It provided another venue for store design and VM professionals to see 120 exhibitors.

ADVERTISEMENTS

Visual trade publications such as *Display & Design Ideas*, Atlanta, GA; *Retail Store Image*, Atlanta, GA; *Store Equipment & Design*, Chicago, IL; and *VM & SD Visual Merchandising and Store Design*, Cincinnati, OH, publish advertisements for suppliers and lists of services and resources. They also review and critique new materials. *VM & SD* Visual Merchandising and Store Design publishes a thorough annual buyers' guide and announces trade show dates, locations, activities, and vendors.

APPAREL MARKETS AND GIFT TRADE SHOWS

Creative inspiration can often be found at apparel markets and gift trade shows. Trade-show designers create exciting exhibits for their clients by presenting their products in the freshest ways. The designers' clients are manufacturers with deep pockets and broad marketing skills who demand that their products are shown to their best advantages. As a result, the most competent design teams in the industry show the products on the newest fixtures with the hottest decorative elements and colors. Supermarket shows are especially worthwhile because many fixture companies that do not attend the NADI shows attend them. Food companies traditionally show their products in fresh innovative ways. See Figures 13–1A and 13–1B.

NEW YORK GIFT AND APPAREL CENTERS AND SHOWROOMS

While in New York at the NADI market, you should check out the apparel, gift, and home furnishings marts and manufacturers' showrooms. Preview merchandise lines that will be delivered to your store. This allows you to correlate decor and make your market visit more meaningful. You will also come away with many new presentation ideas. Some savvy retailers set up appointments for their VMs to visit apparel manufacturers to preview these lines. This provides more insight into how the apparel manufacturer presents a line. Vendors have personal philosophies about their products and how they should be marketed and displayed. Your store's key vendors will happily accommodate you. Make appointments with your buying offices beforehand.

GIFT SHOWS

VMs are always searching for new props—china, glass, metals, wood, art. Many props can be found at the mammoth regional and national gift shows. Although these shows are geared to the buying segment of retail, you can benefit from them by seeing the newest decorative accessories. Floral and basket vendors provide many items that make perfect props. China companies sell huge overscaled containers that are ideal for floral arrangements, fruits, and topiary trees which complement large store interiors. Many decorative items that are marketed for residential interiors are excellent for store decor. The 225 Fifth Ave. Building in New York City is a good source for decorative arts, china, glass, and pottery ideas.

FURNITURE MARTS AND MARKETS

Most VMs use huge amounts of textiles and wallpaper in creating displays. Specialty, decorator-style wallpapers; textiles; and furniture can only be shown and sold through **wholesale** (to the trade) showrooms. Most large cities have a furniture mart, decorator center, or decorator district where major home-furnishing manufacturers have showrooms exhibiting and selling to the trade. These secondary markets are wonderful sources for ideas as well as wonderful places to buy furniture, accessories, and decorative hardware. The furniture industry does an outstanding job of presenting new product lines. They engage

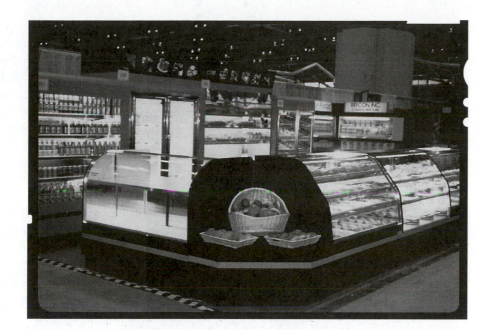

FIGURE 13–1A

At the FMI trade show,

fixture manufacturers

show their newest lines.

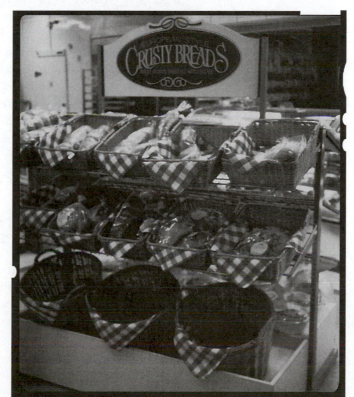

FIGURE 13–1B

Food manufacturers at the

FMI show present products

in fresh new ways.

superstar interior designers to decorate their showrooms with the freshest ideas and newest materials. Many VMs would not miss a major furniture show. Seeing new home furnishing trends is important because the designs of residential interiors, store planning, and displays are closely related.

Fashion trends influence residential textile designs and colors and vice versa. The work of decorative designers, design products, and professionals overlap the display industry.

Antique Shops, Flea Markets, and Auctions

Many VMs regard antiques as their favorite props. The antique classification is huge because it represents things produced in all periods. As a result, it fits countless decorative classifications and uses. Furniture, accessories, china, glass, metal, utensils, rugs, paintings, sculpture, textiles, and architectural fragments are but a few of the useful antique items that could be used as props.

Antique shops, country auctions, and antique flea markets are a terrific source. Some of the largest world markets that offer seldom-seen decorative items that are perfect for a store include London's Portobello Road near Notting Hill, Petticoat Lane on Middlesex Street, and New Caladonian Market at Bermondsey Square; France's Marche aux Puces (five distinct markets), Northern Paris near Porte de Clignancourt, and Village Suisse, near the Eiffel Tower; and Rome's Porta Portese Arcade, near the Tiber River. The United States has Grenekers', Flea Market near Hershey, PA, Kane County Flea Market, near St. Charles, IL and Sandwich Antique Market, near Sandwich, IL. See Figures 13–2A and 13–2B.

If you see something that you cannot carry home on a plane, do not be discouraged from buying it. Call a local freight and forwarding company. Most dealers recommend reliable local shippers who will pick up, crate, and ship the item to your store. Many large markets and auction houses provide permanent space for forwarders, packers, and freight companies.

CRAFT STORES, ART STORES, AND WHOLESALE FLORAL SUPPLY HOUSES

Shop for art materials and supplies in craft and art supply stores. They are the only source for special paints in unusual colors or finishes, unique art papers, ribbons, decorative trims, sable brushes, silk-screen equipment, and hardware. Whether you are painting scenics in oils or acrylics or building three-dimensional props with faux finishes, these retailers are excellent supply resources.

Large metropolitan wholesale floral supply houses are as big as football fields and provide huge assortments of dried and artificial flowers, decorative fabrics, papers, ribbons, flower containers, paint, wire, tape, and hard-to-find specialty tools and hardware.

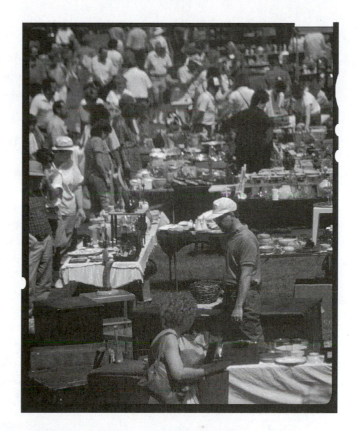

FIGURES 13–2A & B

Many of the best VMs and interior designers from around the country shop at Sandwich Antique Market (Sandwich, IL). Below, an antique vendor shows decorative items that would look great in any store.

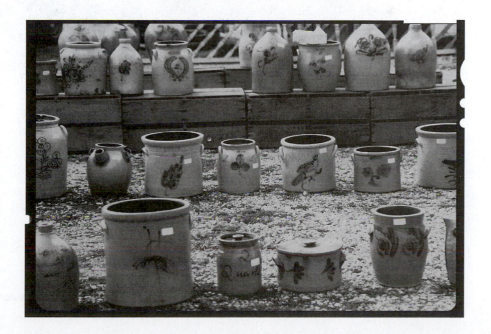

HARDWARE STORES

A huge assortment of tools, nails, screws, hangers, and fasteners are at local mega-hardware and home building supply stores. A good part of your budget will be spent on lumber, tools, foamcore, and hardware.

VENDOR REPRESENTATIVES

Early in your career, you will develop a design style. To make that style a reality, you must rely on representatives and resources that can collaborate by supplying items and custom work that will support that style. Smart VMs develop excellent working relationships with vendor representatives who function as prop locators and suggest other sources for hard-to-find props. A friendly vendor representative can help execute rush orders and locate lost shipments.

Vendor representatives will become aware of your tastes and will communicate your needs for custom work. For example, they assist production designers in interpreting what you want. They also know their company production capabilities and can help you decide what additional resources and fabricators are needed to complete a task. As a customer, you will receive the same personalized service from a vendor representative that you provide to your customers.

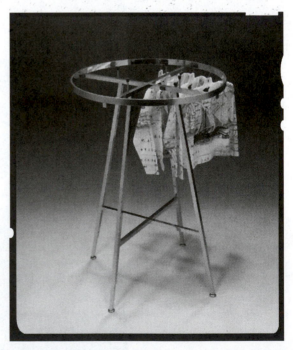

FIGURE 13–3

This rounder is used by a traveling sales representative. If possible, it is better to inspect fixtures personally before ordering. (Courtesy of Dan Dee Display Fixtures, Chicago, IL.)

Vendor representatives will call on you to show you catalogs of fixtures. Inspecting these catalogs personally is important because the photographs become distorted. Photographs may be manipulated to highlight the most distinctive and best features of a product and subdue the poor quality of cheaply made trim. Visiting the showrooms to inspect the product is wisest procedure. See Figure 13–3.

Look closely at fixtures to check the quality of the finish, detail, and construction. Also check to determine if the brackets or shelves are adjusted easily, inspect the weld joints for strength, and, finally, check to determine if the fixtures are strong enough to hold the quantities of merchandise you intend to present on them.

When working with the vendor representative, ask about the shipping point and freight costs. If these costs have not been budgeted, you may be surprised with add-on bills. Try to work out volume discounts and check invoice payment terms. Saving 1 percent of a ten-day payment can save the store needed cash. Some vendors arrange delayed billing to help you address a budget problem.

DISCUSSION QUESTIONS

1. Why is it important to visit a showroom to inspect items before ordering?
2. Why are flea markets good resources of display materials?
3. Are furniture markets beneficial? Why or why not?
4. Why should you create a good working relationship with a vendor?
5. What associations and trade publications can help you locate products and vendors?

CHAPTER PROJECT

Project Objective: To find display materials and resources.

Project Instructions: (Choose One)

1. Make a list of local display vendors, hobby shops, furniture marts, art stores, hardware stores, flea markets, or any other business that might be a good resource of display materials.
2. Visit some of these businesses to find suitable display materials.
3. Write a brief report that lists some interesting items you have seen and explain how you could use those items in displays.

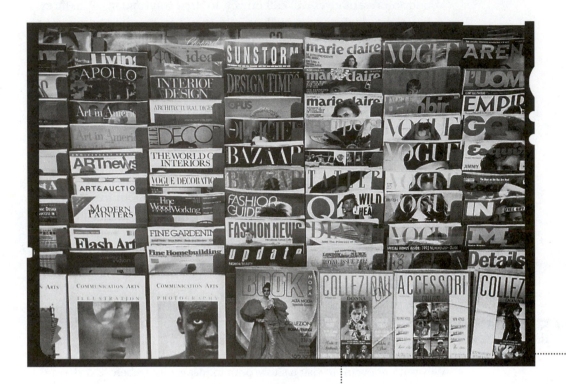

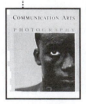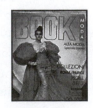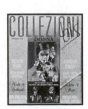

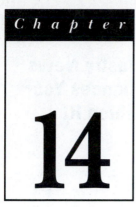
Fashion News
and Communication

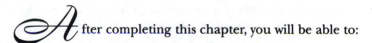

$\mathcal{A}$fter completing this chapter, you will be able to:

1. Discuss the many kinds of fashion news sources.

2. Name various helpful trade associations and describe their services.

3. Identify trade publications and describe the kinds of fashion news each publishes.

4. Describe the reports a VM is responsible for producing.

5. Name consumer publications and their editorial contents.

6. Describe the fashion information published by newspapers.

7. Explain why the merchandising staff should report fashion purchases to the VM.

Industry News Enhances Your Fashion IQ

The design, color, texture, and silhouette of apparel and accessories change frequently. Because new collections are global and markets are expanding, one person cannot possibly see all items. Therefore, you must read accounts of the changing fashion scene. Not every part of a trend changes annually, but some parts do. Color may change more frequently than silhouettes, for example, while textiles may not. Regional looks, Seventh Avenue styles, European and Scandinavian designs, Asian knockoffs, the "street look," and manufacturer's trends all change to some degree.

These changes can also be regional. A new hemline might appear in Paris but not in Milan. Red might be hot on Seventh Avenue but fail on Main Street America. Blue jeans may be trendy for mass merchandising but not for specialty retailing. Savvy fashion editors and writers provide reporting services, and publications furnish information and predictions to help you with your store's presentation strategies.

Information about complex fashions, home furnishings, food trends, and their suppliers and customers requires considerable reporting. Reading these accounts is important so you can interpret trends and keep abreast of their movements. A professional who does not read fashion and industry news is disadvantaged. Successful retailers stay "in the know."

Magazines

Magazines fall into two types. Trade publications are targeted to the industry or **trade**. Consumer magazines, which are available to the general public, target the retail customer or **consumer** for extensive fashion reporting. You must read both types of magazines for your career and work. Trade publications report trends as they are conceived and manufactured. Consumer magazines report fashion news months later, close to the apparel's arrival at retail. Some publications are daily; others are weekly, monthly, or quarterly. Many are international, but some are national or regional. For example, *California Apparel News*, a regional trade publication, focuses on readers west of the Rockies.

TRADE PUBLICATIONS

Almost every business involved in the producing and distributing of goods and services has a trade publication that reports news about deals, manufacturing, prices, human resources, management, and markets. Some examples of trade publications are *American Druggist*, *Supermarket News*, *Chain Store Age*, *Home Furnishings*, and *Hardware Retailer*. Seven current trade publications target VMs. Thirty target druggists and sixty target grocers.

Trade publications target professionals and report on almost everything from the raw product to the finished product. Topics include trade shows, design, manufacturing, marketing, finance, management, and distribution. Many trade publications are linked to manufacturers' associations such as the Men's Fashion Association (MFA).

Retail management must know about product availability, manufacturing, and distribution one year in advance to determine appropriate buying strategies and to organize promotional activities.

The trade magazine *VM + SD Visual Merchandising and Store Design* targets the VM and the store design professional. It broadly covers the VM industry with reports on trade shows and market weeks, prop manufacturing, new display ideas, store interiors, fixtures, signs, resources, new products, careers, and trends. It also illustrates fresh new ways of presenting merchandise. Skilled VM designers share ideas about display creation as well as general information about their profession.

Another VM trade magazine is *Display and Design Ideas*, which is a barometer of the VM industry. This newsy magazine is ideal for news scoops. Its resources and coverage are broad and regularly updated. *Store Equipment and Design* targets the food retailer. It covers new fixtures, food presentation, store design, trade shows, market weeks, fixture manufacturing, and marketing ideas. It also provides excellent coverage of cutting-edge store designs.

Retail Age, a general retail management publication, also targets the VM. By reporting on all aspects of retailing, *Retail Age* editors often scoop new display trends and ideas. Other trade publications such as *Women's Wear Daily (WWD)* and *Textile Age* provide reports to help apparel buyers evaluate clothes during market weeks and during production. Savvy VMs assess these trends so that they can buy props to enhance the selections of the apparel buyers. Research generates fresh ideas and spontaneity.

TRADE FASHION PUBLICATIONS

Daily News Record (Men's)
Women's Wear Daily (WWD), New York, NY
Apparel Executive, Great Neck, NY
Apparel Manufacturer, Riverside, CT
Bobbin
Fashion Accessories & Footwear News
Modern Bride, New York, NY
Retail Week, New York, NY
Stores, New York, NY
Western Apparel Industry, Los Angeles, CA

MASS MARKET FOOD TRADE MAGAZINE

Store Equipment & Design, Chicago, IL

TRADE VM MAGAZINE

VM + SD Visual Merchandising and Store Design, Cincinnati, OH

Display & Design Ideas, Atlanta, GA

CONSUMER MAGAZINES

In addition to reading trade publications, savvy VMs read consumer magazines to keep up on trends that will be marketed to their customers. As mentioned earlier, these magazines cover fashions only slightly before the merchandise arrives in stores. They love to excite the consumer market with fashion predictions. Many fashion retailers, such as Marshall Field's, Hudson's Henri Bendel, or others in your region, run full-page advertisements focusing on looks they will carry that season.

Fashion consumer magazines such as *Vogue, Bazaar, Elle, Glamour,* and *Seventeen* are departmentalized and report on apparel, designers, theater, books, accessories, home furnishings, food, art, architecture, health, and just about anything else that appeals to their upscale readers.

Magazines that report balanced fashion news are preferred to biased magazines that hype their favorite designers and ignore others. VMs should read about Karl Lagerfeld as well as about all other Paris designers, including those showing collections for the first time.

Shelter magazines such as *Architectural Digest, Country Living,* and *Southern Accents* report on trendy interiors and provide readers with information about new color trends, interior furnishings, textiles, and furniture. A VM can identify an upcoming decorative trend after viewing how interior designers dress and accessorize rooms.

Reporting also helps influence trends. For example, if painted faux finishes are reported well, they will be trendy for displays and will appear in store interiors. If blue transfer china pieces are shown in country cupboards in numerous magazines, they can become trendy accessories for home store displays. If Persian birdcages are hot, they can be perfect as display props. Most customers are pleased to see retailers using some of the home furnishing ideas they have read about in magazines because it is like sharing a discovery.

Customers who read *Vogue, Harper's Bazaar, Southern Accents,* and *Architectural Digest* are uninspired when stylish displays are presented with outdated apparel or props. It is disastrous when customers are more fashion aware than the VM staff. Fashion and interior design editors look closely at every fashion retail and wholesale market in Europe and across the world. They look for a new product, who designed it, where, and who is producing it. Like VM professionals, customers also read the editors' reports. No retail staff could provide you with information of the same focus and depth.

In *Vogue* and other fashion magazines, major fashion retailers run full-page institutional spreads advertising the newest international designer's looks that are available in their stores. Therefore, fashion-magazine **target marketers** are interested in readers who are also retail customers. Their close relationships with stores encourages them to research and produce consumer data that can provide some helpful marketing data. See Figure 14–1.

CONSUMER FASHION MAGAZINES

Brigitte, Hamburg, Germany
Depeche Mode, Paris, FR
Elle, Neuilly FR
Elle (USA), New York, NY
Glamour, New York, NY
Harper's Bazaar, New York, NY
Mademoiselle, New York, NY
Seventeen, New York, NY
Taxi, New York, NY
Vogue (USA), New York, NY
L'Officiel (American version), New York, NY

CONSUMER MENSWEAR MAGAZINES

Esquire, Chicago, IL
Gentlemen's Quarterly (GQ)
L'Officiel Hommes, Paris, FR
Playboy, Chicago, IL
Vogue Homme, Paris, FR
L'Uomo Vogue, Milan, IT
Linea Italiana Uomo, Milan, IT

FIGURE 14–1

A wide selection of international fashion magazines are available on newsstands. Many fashion schools and retailers subscribe to these magazines and continue to keep up-to-date on their valuable reporting. (Courtesy of Women's Wear Daily, *NY.)*

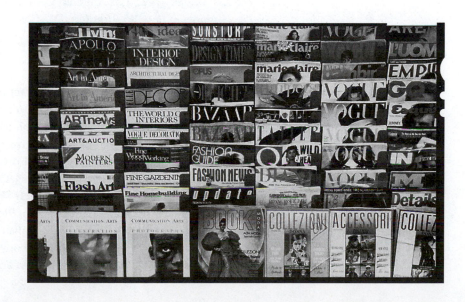

Newspapers

Major and local daily newspapers report some fashion apparel and home furnishing news. The Sunday supplement is a hybrid of the newspaper industry that competes with magazines. *The Chicago Tribune* and *The New York Times* send editors to review fashion shows in Europe and all over the world wherever fashion is happening. Both papers produce strong, upscale Sunday fashion supplements and also report general fashion news during the week.

The Chicago Tribune covers fashions on Thursdays and Sundays. It sells substantial advertising space to local fashion retailers on these days. Newspapers develop strong relationships with local fashion retailers, and often give the stores valuable additional publicity and favorable store reporting. Many papers publish special fashion editions and work with retailers to create comprehensive yet newsy narratives on retailers, designers, lifestyles, looks, manufacturers, and fashion predictions. Local papers that seldom report on fashion sell few fashion advertisements and have not developed relationships with national or local upscale fashion stores. As a result, fashion retailers hesitate to run apparel advertisements in these newspapers. Retailers, like other advertisers, spend advertising resources on those publications read by their customers.

CONSUMER FASHION NEWSPAPERS. The following newspapers send fashion editors all over the world to cover fashion openings and showings:

> *"W,"* New York, NY
> *The Chicago Tribune,* Chicago, IL (fashion sections)
> *The New York Times,* New York, NY (fashion sections)
> *The Los Angeles Times,* Los Angeles, CA (fashion sections)
> *The Washington Post,* Washington, DC (fashion sections)

Government Publications

Freelance VMs and display-prop manufacturers find that government publications supply specific data that can help in business decision making, such as how to start their business or complete tax forms. New entrepreneurs use these publications to start their businesses.

The U.S. government publishes material on almost every topic. It publishes census data (sales data) in the *Statistical Abstract of the United States,* an almanac-like listing of summary tables which show all businesses in each state, county, and city. This sales data can help identify business markets and competitors. The government publishes the abstract for each state following each census. For example, you can obtain a copy of the abstract for Illinois, called the *Census of Retail Trade, Geographic Area Series Illinois,* by writing to the

U.S. Department of Commerce, Bureau of Census, U.S. Government Printing Office, Washington, DC 20402. The abstract lists tables of statistics for counties and metropolitan statistical areas. It lists all towns in Illinois; the number of business establishments and their sales, payrolls, paid employees, and number of partnerships and individual proprietorships. In addition, the industrial classification lists kinds of businesses reporting this information as well as statistics comparing the current year with the last. Census information is also available on a local library's data disk.

Fashion Reporting Services

Trade associations, such as MFA, among others, supply fashion information to the press and the fashion industry about mens' fashions. The FMI focuses on supermarkets, and food manufacturers, mass-food retailers who supply fixtures. It also produces trade shows and provides lectures, reports, and seminars on marketing, education, human resources, management, presentation, fixtures, and store design.

Fashion reports provide paid subscribers with fashion information about color forecasts, designer collections, pret-a-porter (ready-to-wear), and **couturier** trends. The following are a few: *Im, Nigel French, The Color Projections, Tobe, The Fashion Service, Here and There, Sir International, Stylists, Information Services, The Color Box,* and *Video Fashions, Inc.*

Design reporting services supply clients with photographs and printed reports within about eight days after the European collections are shown. Design and VM associations provide the VM with design information, journals, interviews, and educational programs. (See *American VM.*) Design-related associations include:

Center for Design, Chicago, IL
American Institute of Graphic Arts, New York, NY
American Society of Interior Designers, Washington, DC
Association of Registered Interior Designers of Ontario, Toronto, ONT
Association of Visual Merchandising Representatives, Plano, TX
Color Marketing Group, Arlington, VA
Design Management Institute, Boston, MA
Display Distributors Association, Salt Lake City, UT
Institute of Store Planners, Tarrytown, NY
International Council of Shopping Centers, New York, NY
International Exhibitors' Association, Springfield, VA
International Furnishings & Design Association, Dallas, TX
International Mass Retail Association, Washington, DC
International Society of Interior Designers, Los Angeles, CA
National Association of Display Industries, New York, NY

National Association of Store Fixture Manufacturers, Plantation, FL
National Retail Federation, New York, NY
Shop & Display Equipment Association, Caterham, Surry, England
Western Association of Visual Merchandising, San Francisco, CA

Store Communication

GETTING INFORMATION TO THE ASSOCIATES

An important task for fashion merchandisers who see and buy world-wide collections is to inform the many levels of management and store groups about fashion trends. This information should go to every department participating in fashion presentation and selling.

To coordinate activities, the advertising and special events departments need to be informed of which specific fashions have been bought and their delivery dates. This information helps the departments focus on only those looks that the store purchases. Because a retailer cannot buy every fashion, the merchandising group edits, selects, and buys only those looks with sales potential. *Vogue* may report fashion on a broad scale, but a store report must be narrow and tailored to cover its purchases. See Figure 14–2.

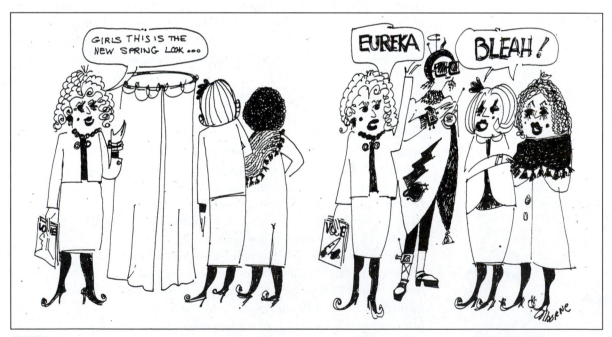

FIGURE 14–2

VM REPORTS

As mentioned in previous chapters, plannograms direct sales and stock associates in placing merchandise on fixtures. Floor plans and elevations should also be provided. These drawings should be accompanied by special written instructions that outline fixture installation and completion dates, as well as any special instructions.

When remodeling and expanding, make ideas about merchandise location, fixtures, electrical sources, and decorative elements known by presenting plans. Weekly, monthly, and quarterly display schedules which identify display merchandise, theme, location, time, price, and duration should be presented to management.

DISCUSSION QUESTIONS

1. Why read fashion publications?
2. How can reporting services help a VM?
3. Can associations help a VM? How?
4. Why does the merchandising staff prepare its own fashion reports?
5. Where would you look for information on color forecasting?
6. If you have design problems, which association could provide a solution?
7. Why read trade publications?
8. How do consumer magazines report fashions?
9. Why do some newspapers and some fashion retailers share special interests?
10. Name five trade publications and five consumer publications.

CHAPTER PROJECT

Project Objective: To broaden your fashion knowledge by reading fashion publications.

Project Instructions: (Choose One)
1. Use the current *Harper's Bazaar* magazine to write a brief report covering fashion trend. Focus on silhouette, color, textiles, and lifestyle. Choose one piece of merchandise and describe how you might display it.
2. Using *Women's Wear Daily,* write a brief report on fashions that will be shipped in the future. Describe what kind of props you will need to display the fashions.

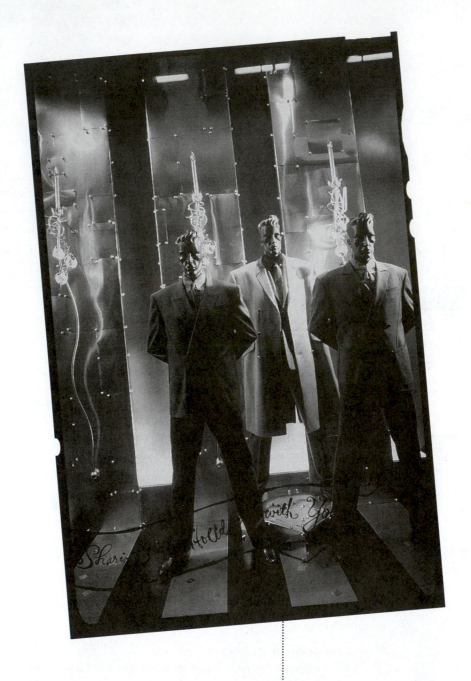

Chapter 15

Careers—
Who Is Doing the
Presentation?

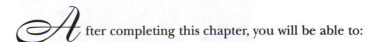

*A*fter completing this chapter, you will be able to:

1. Outline how to develop a career.

2. Recognize college-level fashion-merchandising curriculums.

3. Identify the many career paths open to a VM.

VM Careers

All VMs fit into one of two categories. In one category, VMs design and install super-fashion windows that have international audiences. These savvy designers have enormous strengths in art and design, coupled with merchandising wisdom. They were educated as **apprentices** or earned degrees or certificates in fine arts, interior design, or commercial art. They mastered their trade by taking additional business and marketing courses and by studying core courses in retailing, fashion merchandising, and fashion business.

These VMs center their careers in super-stylish department stores and fashion-leading specialty stores that have large budgets to support their activities and salaries. They create fabulous, theatrical-styled windows and exotic moods for customers. Their goal might be VM-VP of a store group such as Marshall Field's or of its corporate parent, Dayton Hudson. These VMs manage people, budgets, design, purchasing, production, and presentation. See Figure 15–1.

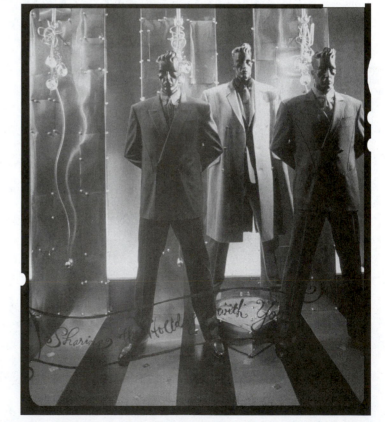

FIGURE 15–1

Savvy VMs install exotic windows and displays for leading, stylish department and specialty stores. (Courtesy of Marshall Field's, Chicago.)

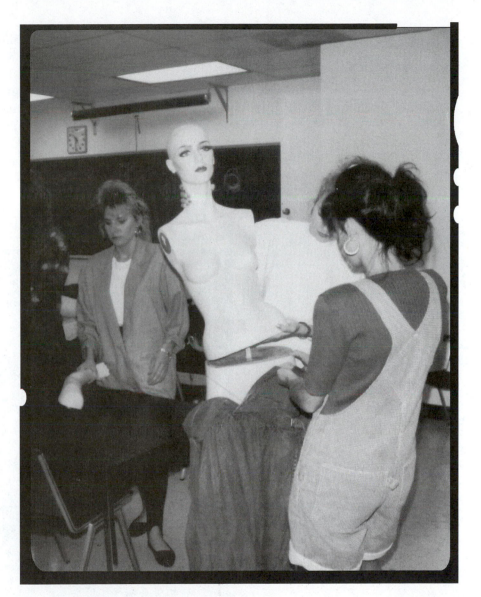

FIGURE 15–2

In a community college class, a VM student dresses a mannequin. VM is a fashion retail core course in accredited colleges.

The VMs in the other category work for national or regional chains. These VMs spend less time creating fabulous displays and focus more on merchandising, store design, and fixturing. They have art backgrounds and were educated as apprentices or earned degrees in fashion merchandising, business, or marketing, depending on the school's core courses. See Figure 15–2.

These VMs, like those in department stores, may aspire to be regional or corporate VM-VPs. They are extremely well compensated for their work, creating shopping environments for their target customers.

VM Careers and Education

The food, apparel, and home furnishings businesses combined are the largest generator of capital in the United States. In fact, two-thirds of our economy is retail. However, fewer jobs are available for VM superstars who produce stellar windows because some central flagship stores have declined or suffered demise. Suburban store branches either do not maintain a VM staff or lack windows for complex decorative displays. Since the 1970s, display budgets have shrunk, leaving meager funds for presentation. Although the market for VMs has also shrunk, some spectacular careers still exist with lots of room at the top. See Figure 15–3.

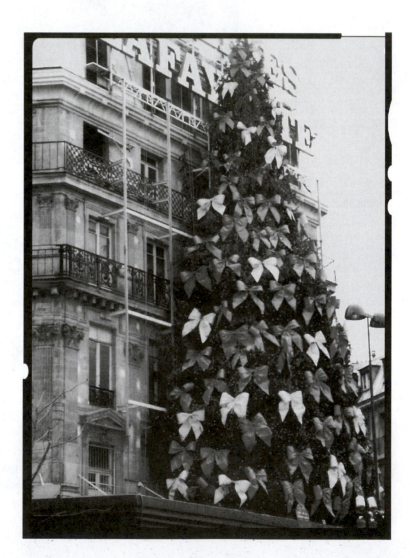

FIGURE 15–3

A sophisticated VM team and a supportive budget created this crowd-stopper at Lafayette Department Store, Paris.

SHOPPING ENVIRONMENT

Many VMs are gainfully employed at department stores and specialty chains that have lower budgets and smaller staffs. These stores focus on creating interior shopping environments. The VMs in stores that are parts of a conglomerate empire receive their display direction from regional corporate staff who manage global design, budgets, schedules, and buying.

The New Communicator

Today's VMs should be communicators, people who can coordinate complex new systems. The display staff can never be large enough to completely handle the presentation of all merchandise in all departments in any store. In response, the VM should instruct store associates clearly and assist the communication with plannograms, drawings, and manuals. In addition to being an excellent communicator, a team player, and an art director, the VM must know basic marketing and merchandising principles and have an excellent art background. Using teamwork, a professional VM working with sales associates can produce a large quantity of displays.

As mentioned previously, the majority of VMs work for smaller retail groups presenting simple window and interior displays and rigging mannequins and forms. Regional VMs work with corporate buyers and merchandising groups to coordinate presentation with merchandising plans at the store level.

Corporate VMs work with and project the retailer's total business plans and goals. Whether the VMs' presentation concepts are national or international, they are developed far in advance. The corporate VMs work with manufacturers as they plan, design, and begin production. These VMs are aware of the product design and marketing strategies developed by the manufacturers.

Alternative VM Careers

A VM career is usually associated with retail. Skilled professionals, however, may also want to teach, write, freelance, or consult. Some may be interested in wholesale, advertising, trade shows, exhibits, design and production, museum exhibits and presentation, art gallery presentations, photo styling, or prop manufacturing.

ACCREDITATION

In high schools, fashion merchandising and retail classes are part of the home economics departments. Some schools have workrooms where garments are designed and made, VM labs, studios, and boutiques where design students present and sell their collections.

Colleges and universities divide their fashion courses into two independent design and merchandising departments, but each may be a part of

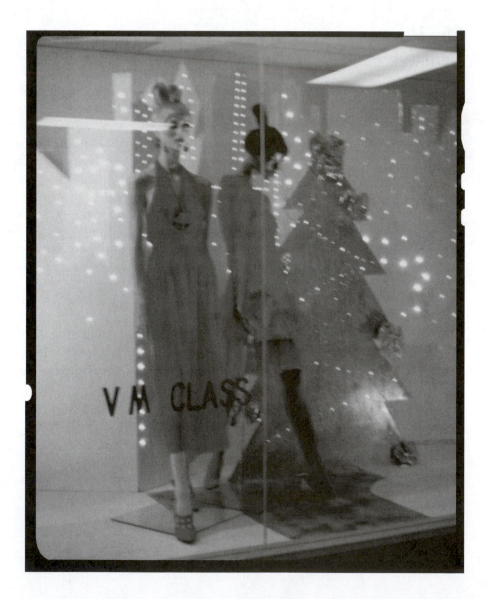

FIGURE 15–4

This student display window was created by the VM class at a suburban Chicago community college.

the marketing, business, or art departments. A master's degree in an appropriate area is needed to teach in a secondary institution. Teaching salaries in high schools and colleges are adequate. See Figure 15–4.

WRITING

The VMs who love to write may publish business articles on fashion merchandising and visual merchandising in many periodicals. Also, advertising agencies often need VMs to write specific fashion advertising copy.

WHOLESALING

To make the merchandise in showrooms look spectacular at market time and to create a buying atmosphere for customers requires the assistance of a VM. Showrooms that remain open in all seasons employ permanent VMs to keep the rooms fresh-looking. These VMs also present newly arrived merchandise.

FREELANCING

Many stores that cannot budget funds for permanent display staff hire freelancers to do weekly or monthly display work. Freelancing allows the designer to be entrepreneurial. Running a business provides the designer with an array of clients with a variety of needs.

CONSULTING

After many years in the profession, a VM may want to consult. Many corporations set up large budgets for consultants who supply needed outside opinions and who solve presentation problems.

Consulting provides corporations with a variety of clients who add occupational diversity. Because consulting contracts are short term, one does not remain with a company through all the trials and tribulations of ongoing projects. Consultants are most often associated with a client at the best of times, and their advice is carried out by the client's internal staff.

MUSEUMS AND GALLERIES

Most museums design, build, install, and maintain complicated internal displays and traveling exhibits of their collections. Their staffs consist of model makers, designers, artists, and visual presentation professionals. Many professionals who love the fine arts especially enjoy the culture of museum work.

EXHIBITS

Many corporations that show their products at trade shows require the expertise of professional trade-show designers who design, build, and install their exhibits. Exhibits can be small for regional trade shows or huge for national shows. At national shows, exhibits can command space equal to one square city block. The VM who designs company exhibits uses many retail techniques. See Figure 15–5.

FIGURE 15 –5

Designing exhibits for trade

shows is an excellent career

that many VMs pursue.

(Courtesy of FMI Show,

Chicago, IL.)

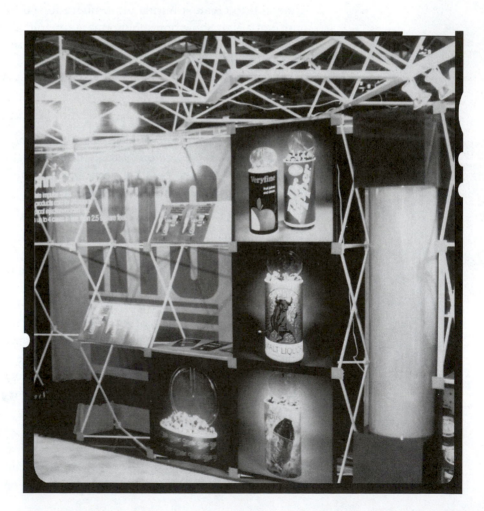

ADVERTISING

Large agencies employ **stylists** with VM experience to find suitable locations for photo shoots. These VMs also assemble props, models, and accessories. Photo studios and advertising agencies provide glamorous, well-paid positions. People who love the fast track and travel do well in these positions.

EDUCATION

Locating a school's fashion program may be confusing because curriculum development can be regional or statewide, depending on the school's state or federal accreditation. Privately owned schools are approved by the Association of Independent Colleges and Schools (AICS). Others are approved by the Counsel of Postsecondary Accreditation (COPA). State and community colleges may be approved by other associations, such as North Central Association of Colleges and Secondary Schools in the Midwest. Each accreditation has its own program. Programs vary, and many classes are not transferable from one school system to another.

A student should first determine which schools will accept credits for higher education. This is called articulation. Students intending to work for a master's degree should carefully check their schools' accreditation and credit transfer requirements.

Fashion Merchandising

Fashion merchandising can be a part of several departments, including art, business sciences, fashion merchandising and design, or apparel and family studies.

Core fashion classes vary. For instance, in a state college, university, or preparatory school, the curriculum might include classes in advertising, introduction to fashion business, marketing, fashion promotion, history of costume I and II, textiles, color and line design, fashion buying, merchandising, fashion illustrating, fashion coordination and show production, retailing, management, and visual merchandising.

Depending on the curriculum, an associate's or bachelor's degree may be awarded. Because choosing a college is an important career decision, one must look at the quality of teachers, facilities, equipment, and students. Check scholarship availability and compare and evaluate tuition costs.

Schools of fine arts, such as the Art Institute of Chicago, prepare students in visual design, volume design, or interior design. Many excellent professionals who design great production windows graduated from an art school. Although fashion merchandising may not be part of an art school's curriculum, art schools offer fine arts and design classes such as volume design, interior design, art history, drawing, painting, graphics, and many other art courses which provide students with qualifying backgrounds for store design and presentation.

FHA-HERO

Many schools include fashion programs in home economics. Gone are the days when students focused on cooking and sewing. Today, home economic students may study food services, interior design, and fashion. The VM curriculum is also part of their fashion retail program.

New high school students are aggressive career builders. The hands-on learning methods in their schools sharpens their skills in career basics. Many are members of Future Homemakers of America (FHA) and Home Economics and Related Occupations (HERO). This group is known as FHA-HERO.

FHA-HERO was founded in 1945. Today it has 281,000 members, 53 state groups, and 11,000 local groups. Young men and women in public and private schools up to grade 12 study home economics and related occupational courses that focus on leadership and career preparation. The second chapter, Home Economics and Related Occupations (HERO), stresses job and career preparation and places special emphasis on homemaker and community leader roles.

Building skills for life is the group's often repeated goal. FHA-HERO encourages personal growth, leadership development, family and community involvement, and preparation for the adult roll of wage earner. This in-school organization is a focus for interior design, fashion, and food service students. Many go on to secondary schools to major in these programs. See Figure 15–6.

Annual state and regional achievement (STAR) competitions are organized FHA-sponsored events that enable members to demonstrate proficiency and achievements in chapter projects, leadership skills, and occupational preparation. Accomplishments in fashion display are included among the many categories of competition. Statewide, as many as twenty-five or thirty high school students are selected to attend. They attend the state conference with their teachers and their counselors. In one project, students create fashion displays based on specific criteria, such as setup time, size, creativity level, clarity, message, and subject. The winners in two classifications receive statewide recognition. In addition, alumni awards and honorary memberships are presented. The group's publication is *Students Taking Action of Recognition*. See Figure 15–7.

FIGURE 15–6

Virginia high school students attend a state FHA-HERO fashion-retail workshop where they focus on presentation. (Courtesy of National FHA-HERO.)

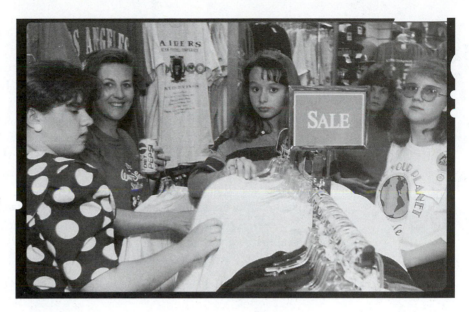

FIGURE 15–7

Jackie Winkel, a student at West Leyden High School, Northlake, IL, created this tabletop display for the state STAR competition.

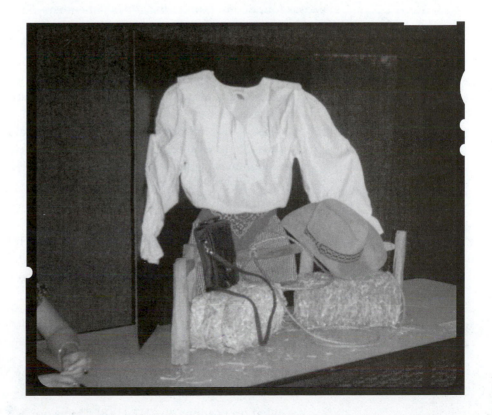

DECA

Distributive Education Clubs of America (DECA) was founded in 1946 for focused high school juniors and seniors interested in the vocations of marketing and retail and wholesale distribution. It currently has 55 chartered associations and 6,000 local groups. Students share class and work time, receive credits from the school, and earn salaries in the workplace. The students also receive leadership evaluation and grades and are supervised by the educator and the employer. In many regions, students work in retail for VM departments. Students focus on learning a trade, developing professionalism, and forming an attitude of teamwork. Students, educators, and employers are honored annually at an awards banquet.

DECA publishes a newsletter reporting on teaching aids, surveys, scholarships, and special events.

VICA

Vocational Industrial Clubs of America (Industrial Education) (VICA) was founded in 1965. It has 272,000 members, 53 state groups, and 14,000 local chapters of young students in trade, technical, and health occupation programs in high schools and junior and community colleges in the United States, Virgin Islands, Puerto Rico, and Canada. Members maintain high standards of workmanship, scholarship, and trade ethics. The VICA leadership encourages cooperation in the community of teachers and labor and business leaders.

VICA sponsors Skills Olympics Seminars, teacher training, and lecture programs. It also publishes the *VICA Journal*, which is a quarterly that provides students with information on education and job development skills.

HEEA

The Home Economics Education Association (HEEA) was founded in 1927 by teachers and supervisors of home economics education. Its current 3,700 members and staff promote effective programs of home economics education.

DISCUSSION QUESTIONS

1. What opportunities exist in advertising for the VM?
2. What is FHA? HERO?
3. What occupations do FHA-HERO focus on?

STUDENT PROJECT 15–1

Open discussion focusing on the development of each student's career.

Project Objective: To help students choose a career and to make them aware of academic courses that will help them develop it.

Project Instructions:

1. Each student should inform the class about their career choices. The students should enter into an open discussion about school curriculum and careers. The instructor should moderate the discussion about those careers and curriculums that will reinforce the students education.

2. Students should bring college and university catalogues borrowed from the school library to reference available career-building curriculum. During the discussion, students should refer to the catalogues and point out which classes and schools can be beneficial.

3. During the student discussion, there should be as many questions as answers provided.

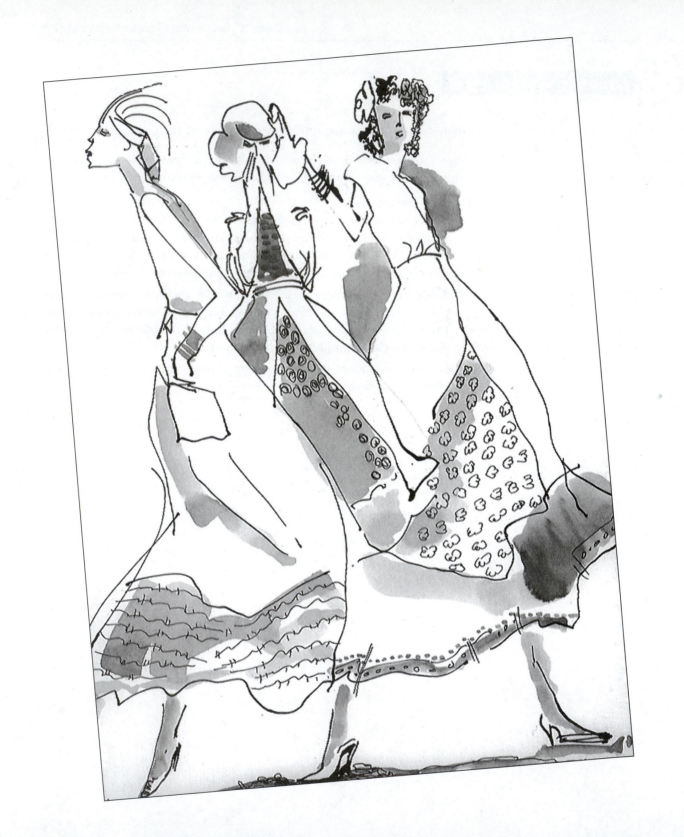

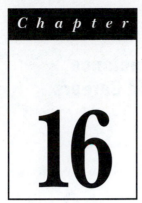
The Freelance Display Designer

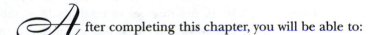

After completing this chapter, you will be able to:

1. Describe the freelance profession.

2. List the materials needed to perform a job.

3. Discuss the importance of excellent communication between the freelancer and the client.

4. Identify the kinds of display projects required by the small retailer.

Freelance VM Careers

Freelance display professionals work for retailers who cannot afford permanent display staff. The ranks of freelancers have increased recently because cost-cutting retailers have reduced staff drastically—and foolishly. Inventory and staff are two major retail costs. Retailers have always chosen to sacrifice staff rather than reduce inventory. Now, many stores must rely on the economies of freelancers to create and install displays. As a result, consultants and freelancers are the norm. From finance and marketing to buying and display, freelancers fill the human resources void.

In the 1970s, retailers were in trouble caused by buyers mistakenly overloading inventories, which resulted in costly mark downs. Poor managers reduced display staff instead of flushing out the ones making buying mistakes. Display staff employees were often released because they were not directly selling units.

In addition, stores that were not designed for self-service were rearranged by redoing old floor plans and fixtures. Store display windows and display feature areas were converted to selling space. Presentation programs were eliminated. These steps reduced the sales staff and ignored the development of an exciting shopping environment. Specific kinds of retailers suffered some negative results.

These events, however, boosted the careers of freelancers. Many outstanding display designers became entrepreneurs and started display-consulting businesses. They created profitable knock-dead presentations for small, upscale boutiques.

Thousands of retailers are potential clients of display professionals. In just one state, Illinois, the number of retail trade establishments in 1993 totaled 63,945, which indicated fertile ground for the entrepreneur. According to the *Census of Retail: The 1993 Census of Retail Trade, Geographic Areas Illinois* (August 1989), RC87–a–14 U.S. Department of Commerce, Bureau of the Census, Washington, DC., of these 63,945 trade establishments, 6,877 were food stores. General merchandising stores numbered 1,290. Of these, 440 were department stores. Of the 6,830 apparel and accessory stores, 826 were men's and boy's clothing, 2,745 were women's specialty, 2,367 were women's clothing, 378 were women's accessories, 690 were family clothing, 1,933 were shoes, 283 were children's and infant's wear, 4,638 were furniture, 1,118 were florists, 1,141 were jewelry stores, and 1,219 were gift stores.

Savvy retail management understands the professional VM's taste level and knows that an image that is created by substituting the store's sales associates for the professional VM may not meet the VM's level. Further, they know they may be disappointed with the results. Nonprofessionals may present the incorrect image or the wrong fashions to customers, which create image problems for the retailer.

The Freelancing Profession

Freelancers schedule their work time to fit the needs of small owner-operators. Because they are not employed by stores, freelancers provide their services once a week or once every two weeks, when a display window change is needed or when new arrivals must be presented on the floor. Some retailers occasionally call on freelancers to help with expansion plans or remodeling.

Many retailers do not know the benefits of working with a freelance display professional and do not know how to go about finding one. Freelancers should aggressively make cold calls on retailers to sell their services. An aggressive freelancer who calls on all stores in a mall might easily end up serving most of them. Consolidating all freelance work in a tight region is an excellent strategy.

Banks, restaurants, and hotels also search out freelancers to design, buy, and install Christmas trim. Mall developers hire freelance designers to design and install props for special events such as Christmas and Easter. Many businesses have one-time-only needs, which could be annual events.

Sometimes a freelance VM will contract to consult with a retailer about its display problems. The designer will present the client with solutions and plans and the retailer will execute them. Trade shows generate freelance work designing and installing exhibits. For example, a manufacturer in Kansas City may ship his exhibit to a Chicago trade show and hire local freelancers to install it.

Fashion clubs, social groups, and fund raisers contract freelance display designers to produce fashion shows and special events. These fashion shows which are held in country clubs and private clubs, need special professional attention. Backgrounds, runway setup, lighting, and music are complex and look second-rate when provided by the relatively unexperienced social group or club.

Large department stores hire freelancers to assist their VM staff in installing storewide promotions and Christmas trim. Display studios such as Niedermaier in Chicago have store-planning divisions and resources for complex promotional installations. The freelancer can help at specified times of the year when the VM staff is overloaded with seasonal promotions.

THE FREELANCER'S OFFICE

As the operator of a small business, a freelancer should record business activities for tax as well as planning, production, marketing, human resources, bill payment, receivables, and purchasing purposes. By law, bookkeeping is necessary for tax reasons. Therefore, regardless of your company's size, establish good accounting procedures. If you are going to freelance, set space aside for an office in the house, garage, storage area, workroom, or commercial space. Do not worry about glamour—you will rarely meet clients there.

The Small Business Administration (SBA) provides information, pamphlets, books, and referrals to help freelancers get organized. In addition, community colleges offer a large variety of inexpensive credit and noncredit business classes for start-up companies. Some of these courses might be part of a VM curriculum. The community service arm of business departments in community colleges provides information and lectures. Low-cost classes in accounting, business, business math, management, human resources, marketing, and business law are all worthwhile in doing business better.

THE WORKROOM

A workroom is needed to create art panels, make display props, and preassemble displays. Low-rent space is usually available in industrial parks, garages, or city lofts. Easy access, no stairs, and large doors and rooms are necessary for erecting large-scale items. Drafting materials for making floor plans and presentation boards should be included in this space.

As mentioned in a previous chapter, small stores have little extra space for staging props or rigging mannequins. Display preparation must take place in a back hall or a back storage room. Affordable premade and assembled props can be brought or drop shipped to the store. Heavy, overscaled props shipped from display suppliers should be shipped to the studio and delivered by truck at installation time. Small boutiques have inadequate storage space and receiving facilities.

The lack of staff and space makes it impossible to create elaborate displays. Everything must be portable. Many clients want simple yet effective merchandise arrangements and window displays. Besides rigging mannequins and forms, other typical projects that must be completed include covering display pads with fresh material, adding fresh floral arrangements, and adding new merchandise signs. See Figure 16–1.

Owning a van or another commonsense utility vehicle is a must for a freelance VM. The vehicle should be equipped with a large assortment of tools, hardware, and craft supplies, plus vacuum cleaners and an assortment of cleaning supplies to clean the display area before installation. A client never supplies cleaning staff. Arrive at the job with all of the installation tools, props, and equipment because a hardware or paint store may not be handy or open when you need one.

THE CLIENT

On the first call, discuss the client's display needs, budget, and expectations. The first conference should be long enough to determine what

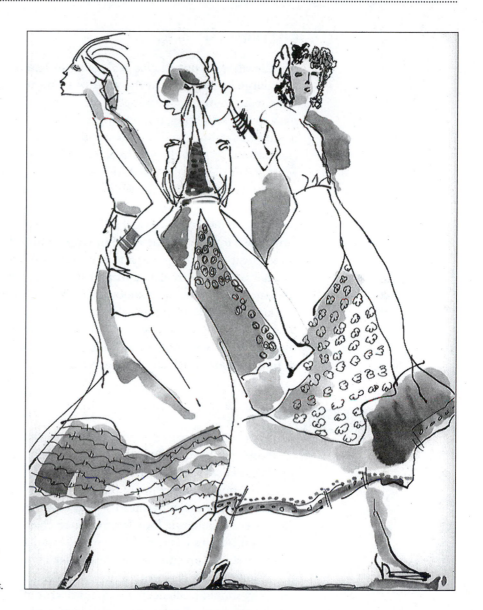

FIGURE 16–1

Many clients want simple yet effective apparel presentations.

image, fashion, and shopping environment the client wishes to project. Determine who will select and condition the display merchandise.

Consider and prepare for any detail that might become a problem. If the detail is internal, discuss it, because clients do not like surprises—large or small—and the VM should be prepared for it. It might be necessary to call the client if he or she wants to see sketches, floor plans, and presentation boards. Simple sketches should always be presented to ensure that the clients understands your solutions.

BILLING

Clearly spell out all charges. Some designers charge by the hour; others charge by the job or by the window. Contracts should state the plan and costs exactly. Also, determine up front if subcontracting is necessary for such things as lighting, remodeling, or custom installations. This eliminates misunderstandings and arguments that could terminate a good working association. To keep the job, freelance VMs need clients to spread the good word about them. Additional freelance jobs are based on networking.

Determine whether the windows and display areas need minor remodeling. Additional lighting may be necessary. Display studios can create part or all of the display and install it. When large jobs such as Christmas installations are totally subcontracted in larger stores, banks, and malls, the VM is responsible for designing and supervising the work.

Because small freelance display designers usually lack a fashion staff, they must read enormous amounts of fashion news to keep current. The freelancer also should attend display markets and FMI shows to see what is new in fixtures, colors, and trend, and to network to find new clients through display vendors or at trade shows. The manufacturers and representatives know which stores need freelance help.

DISCUSSION QUESTIONS

1. How should you prepare props for a small boutique?
2. What about the job should you discuss with the client?
3. Why should you set up an office and establish accounting systems?
4. Why would a client want to see presentation boards?
5. Where should one look for freelance clients?
6. What businesses need the help of freelance display designers?
7. Why should an entrepreneur establish good accounting practices? Why should freelancers write work contracts for clients?
8. Why should freelancers set up a workroom?
9. When should freelancers use outside contractors?

CHAPTER PROJECT

Project Objective: To interview a freelance display professional.

Project Instructions:

Interview a display freelancer, take notes, and be prepared to discuss the profession. Focus on fees, clients, schedules, office, staff, and the workroom.

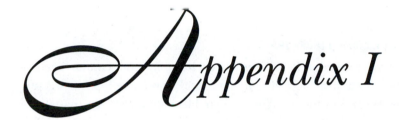

Appendix I

History at a Glance

Each period has produced many exciting fashion designers, authors, celebrities, musicians, and artists whose artistic influence have made fashion stores look great. These people were about international style, possessed a certain presence, and had a unique way of viewing the world.

Fine Artists

Brancusi, Constantin (1876–1957)
A Romanian sculptor who worked in Paris creating sleek, polished steel figures. His Bird in Flight is polished, slick, and simple like a sleek Concorde jet.

Chagall, Marc (1897–1986)
Russian. In 1922, Chagall began printmaking in Paris. His colors were clear and intense, which created mystical works.

Dufy, Raoul (1877–1953)
Painter, textile designs (1926). Worked in Paris. Dufy's quick calligraphic style in oil and watercolors was stylish and intensely colorful.

Erté, Romain de Tiroff (1892–1990)

Russian. Drew *Vogue* covers in 1915 and the 1920s. Erté's designs were fantasies in a fashion illustration style. Designed glamorous, fantasy costumes for Folies Bergère (a supreme Paris nightclub). He became a fashion cult figure in the 1980s.

Johns, Jasper (1930–)

American POP artist working in New York City. His American Flag theme raised questions about the difference between image and reality. His style is urbane graphic.

Laurencin, Marie (1885–1957)

Parisian, worked in Paris, friend of art haute monde. Laurencin created stylish decorative portraits of women in cover story poses wearing designer apparel of the day. Her fashion, illustration style, was pastel and mystical.

Le Corbusier, Charles (1887–1968)

Painter and architect, worked in Europe. Le Corbusier's outstanding building in France is the Swiss Pavilion (1932), Cité University, Paris.

Rauschenberg, Robert (1925–)

Pioneered a certain assemblage look of the 1970s. His collages are pasted, with newsy items and clippings from comic books, magazines, and photographs. Current politics, the war, and space exploration are Rauschenberg's favorite themes.

Warhol, Andy (1928–1987)

POP artist; print and master media maker. Warhol worked in his New York City factory where ideas and new lifestyles flourished. He was a friend of the rich, the socially elite, genius personalities, and artistic celebrities.

Apparel Designers

Cruz, Miguel (1944–)

Cuban; apprenticed under Balenciaga in Paris. In 1963, Cruz began to create exciting knitwear, which made a major impact in Italy. He designs menswear in suede and leather.

Fredericks, John (N/A)

Mr. John owned a millinery business with Fred Fredericks. Mr. John designed hats for the socially elite and for celebrities. From 1926 to the late 1950s, he worked in his salon in New York, and he was famous for his trunk shows and men's ties. Customers loved him, he enjoyed traveling to major cities to meet them. John Frederick was the label for Fredericks ready-to-wear line.

Gaultier, Jean Paul (1952–)

Parisian influenced by London street wear. Gaultier designed skirts for men in the early 1980s. They still appear in his radical collections.

Kenzo, Takado (1940–)

Vanguard Japanese designer. Kenzo's elegant western, stylish looks, especially the layers, have a hint of traditional Japan, and are popular in Europe and the United States.

Mainboucher (1890–1976)

First American designer in the Paris fashion conduit. Mainboucher illustrated fashions for French *Harper's Bazaar* and Paris *Vogue*. He closed his couture house and returned to New York in 1940.

McCardell, Claire (1905–1958)

Created great American ready-to-wear. McCardell's colors and fabrics were specialties that fit perfectly into the prevailing lifestyles. In 1944, she won the Coty award. She also created flat ballet pumps that have never been out of style.

Patou, Jean (1887–1936)

Parisian who dressed Hollywood celebrities, created an innovative sportswear line, and was the first to create simple tennis outfits. Patou's daytime dressing was simple and uncluttered. He produced the epitome of the American country socialite at play. Textile dyes, embroideries, and fabrics were produced by a very large staff in his couture house. His perfume, "Joy," remains one of the world's costliest.

Poiret, Paul (1879–1944)

King of Fashion, Paris. Extravagant, arrogant, grand couture. Poiret was a rich, famous art collector and designer. In 1908, he created a wonderful hobble skirt that everyone wanted. Elegant, simple, lush gowns were his hallmark. He died a pauper.

Rykiel, Sonia (1930–)

France. Worked in Paris in her husband's "Laura" shops, then opened her own boutique in Galleries Lafayette, Paris. Rykiel opened her shop on the Left Bank and the second premier shop on Boulevard St. Germain. A former vice-president of the Chamber Syndicale, Rykiel is considered to be one of the best Parisian designers. Her 1980s' looks were elegant groups of wool jersey with smashing motifs and details.

Simpson, Adele (1903–)

Premier American designer. Simpson was the best Seventh Avenue designer in the late 1920s to the early 1930s. She designed coats and suits, founded the Fashion Group of America, won the Coty, Neiman-Marcus, and Winnie awards.

Trigere, Pauline (1912–)

Parisian. Moved to New York to work with Hattie Carnegie. Trigere worked directly on each model draping, cutting, and making patterns for sleek evening wear. She has received all of the American fashion awards and Hall of Fame recognition.

Worth, Charles Frederick (1825–1895)

The first couturier. An Englishman, Worth worked in Paris dictating fashion and dressing to the supremely born in Europe. His fashion power was notable. A man of genius, customers rivaled for the privilege of buying his limited productions.

Show Personalities

Coward, Noel (1899–1973)

Playwright; authored many sophisticated New York plays. Coward had sophisticated humor, high-society profile, and friends in the theater, art circles, the international set, and the socially prominent and affluent classes. The demimonde of the 1920s and 1930s; New York loved his style.

Fitzgerald, F. Scott (1896–1942)

Author who wrote *The Great Gatsby*. Fitzgerald partied in Paris in the 1920s and 1930s. He belonged to an international social group. His wife Zelda, a party girl, was a chic social character on the Riviera and the Lido who enjoyed fun and drinking at all costs.

The Lido

Group of 1920s' socialities that gathered on the Riviera and the Lido in France. Many international celebrities lived there and had endless glittering parties. Cole Porter and Gershwin played until dawn. Elsa Maxwell organized countless social activities. It was a place of elegance, songs, and custom motorcars.

Porter, Cole (1891–1946)

American composer who wrote "Begin the Beguine" and "Night and Day." Porter had many stage successes, among them, *Kiss Me Kate* in 1948. He was an international presence who partied all over the world in the company of the brightest and richest celebrities.

Swanson, Gloria (1899–1983)

Hollywood actress; Swanson was a glamorous and worldly silent-film star. Her clothes were opulent and her manner was sophisticated.

Tucker, Sophie (1844–1966)

Hollywood glamour actress. Tucker was very popular. She was always dressed in a funny, sensational way. She delivered her off-color sense of humor in a very deep voice. Tucker was a top night club entertainer.

Visual Merchandising

Currie, Robert

A 1970s Director of Visual Planning at Henri Bendel, New York. Currie is the person most responsible for the "New Trend" in window display.

Darcy, Barbara

A 1960s VP of visual merchandising in Bloomingdale's flagship store. Darcy created elegant, new-wave model rooms that showcased interior products.

Hugo, Victor

Visual merchandiser for Halston in the 1970s.

Pratts, Candy

In the 1970s, Pratts designed the forty windows of Bloomingdale's flagship store. Her windows, which were avante garde and were presented as though frozen in time, had curious subject matter.

Spring, Maggie

Employed at the Charles Jordan flagship shoe store, where she created shocking, outrageous anti-establishment windows on the Avenue in the 1970s.

Appendix II

Mannequin Manufacturers and Vendors

ADPI Enterprises, Inc., Philadelphia, PA
American Display Concepts, Inc., Miami, FL
American Mannequin, Inc., Industry, CA
Aurora Design, Duluth, MN
Carol Barnhart, Inc., River Edge, NJ
Barrett Hill, Inc., New York, NY
Barthelmess USA, Inc., New York, NY
Bay Area Display, Inc., San Francisco, CA
Bendies Forms, Inc., Grandy, PQ, Canada
Bon-Art Int., Inc., Newark, NJ
Bottega 565, Inc., Jersey City, NJ
Carrouselle Corp., Atlanta, GA
Champaigne Import & Export, Inc., Miami, FL
Daniels Display Co., Inc., San Francisco, CA
Davila Studios, Inc., Pico Riva, CA
DE Turse Studios, Mississauga, ON, Canada
Decter Mannequin Co., Los Angeles, CA
Design Concepts, San Francisco, CA
Destefano Studios, Inc., Woburn, MA

Discoveries, Inc., New York, NY
Econoco Corp., Hicksville, NY
Robert Filoso Mannequin, Inc., Los Angeles, CA
F. E. Frederick Ent., Pittsburgh, PA
Freedom Display Fixtures, San Francisco, CA
Gemmini Mannequins, Inc., New York, NY
Great Images By Dan Ruerman, Huntington Beach, NY
Greneker/Wolf & Vine, Los Angeles, CA
Gukeisen Display Systems, Vancouver, WA
HGA Products, Inc., Birmingham, AL
Hindsgaul USA, Inc., New York, NY
It Figures Studio, Wilmington, DE
Gordon Keith Originals, Columbus, OH
Kyoya Co., Ltd., Tokyo, Japan
Larosa Mnaichini, Milan, Italy
Lor Sales Co., Brooklyn, NY
MKS Displays, Brooklyn, NY
Morgese Sriano Co., Ltd., Toronto, ON, Canada
Niedermaier, Inc., Chicago, IL
On Display, Phoenix, AZ
Patina Visuals, Inc., Bellevue, WA
Rex Art Mfg., Lindhurst, NY
Adel Rootstein USA, Inc., New York, NY
Siegel & Stockman, Ltd., London, England
Silvestri California, Los Angeles, CA
Societa' Italiana ABC, Cologna Monzese, Italy
Target Midwest, Elk Grove, IL
Tobart Int., New York, NY
Tokyo Mannequin NY, New York, NY
Touch of Class, Sacramento, CA
Vale Display, Moorebank, Australia
Visual Impact Productions, Hayward, CA
Vogue International, Whittier, CA
D. G. Williams, Inc., New York, NY
YLSA Design, Chicago, IL
Zee Studio, Inc., New York, NY

Glossary

Accent Colors—Colors that comprise 20 percent or less of a composition. They are used on accent or small items.

Accessories—Apparel types of accessories are shoes, hosiery, jewelry, handbags, hats, gloves, scarves, hair products, sunglasses, belts, and small leather goods. Bathroom types of accessories are towels and bath mats. Furniture types of accessories are lamps, rugs, flowers, and china.

Acrylic—A petroleum-based product.

Adaptations—Copies of original designs.

Advertising—Activity of communicating and promoting sales messages in media.

Advertising Managers—People who manage the advertising activities of an organization.

Analogous Palette—Color composition based on hues placed sequentially on a color wheel.

Anchor Store—Stores such as Sears at the end of a mall.

Antique—Generally any object that is at least 100 years old.

Apparel Chains—Retail organizations consisting of two or more units.

Apparel Forms—Fixtures for displaying garments, blouses, and shirts.

Apprentice—A VM beginner gaining on-the-job training.

Approaching Color—Often are called near colors. Warm colors such as red appear to be close and green farther away. Cool colors such as green tend to look distant.

Art Deco—Art style in early 1900s, which used stylized geometric shapes in symmetrical patterns.

Associates—Staff, sales clerks, and all store employees.

Assortments—A variety of products massed for marketing.

Atmosphere—Distinctive, emotional mood of retail space; the emotional tone of a work of art, play, or novel.

Backlight—Background light that highlights specific parts of a display from behind the merchandise.

Balance Sheet—Statement showing assets, liabilities, and net worth.

Beam Spread—Width of beams produced by spotlights.

Boutique—Small specialty store featuring designer or craft products.

Branch Stores—Outlying units of a department store that are separate from the flagship store.

Brand Name—Name of product.

Brand Recognition—Identification of a specific product.

Budget Floor—Basement floors in older flagship stores that sell off-price, discount, and promotional products; few exist today.

Bulletin—Large sign holder, 22 inch x 28 inch, used in aisles to herald store events and store information.

CAD—Computer-aided design.

Candlepower—Brightness of a light.

Card Holder—Sign holder.

Central Management—Management activities of a group centrally located in a flagship store or corporate headquarters.

Chain Stores—Several stores owned and managed by the same firm.

Christmas Trim—Total store Christmas decor.

Chroma—Hue intensity and saturation.

Chromatic Distribution—Chromatic value describes red having a medium chroma. Blue has the darkest saturation. The theory is that large areas should be covered with neutrals; small areas, bright intensities; and the smallest areas, the brightest intensities.

Chromatic Value—Reflective properties of hue.

Color—Form of light as reflected from an object's surface.

Color Families—Red, yellow, green, blue, and neutral; designers use color families when creating; each family has a warm and cool variety.

Color Wheel—A circle on which colors are laid out in order to make color relationships and transitions visible.

Complementary Colors—They are shown as opposites on a color wheel. Opposite colors are red and green and yellow and blue.

Composition—An arrangement of line, shape, and other design tools.

Confused Look—Muddled, jumbled, disconcerted store look created by design or merchandising management.

Consumer—Purchases products.

Consumer Publications—Magazines, newspapers, and other print material targeted to the public, such as *Vogue*.

Contrast—Opposite elements in a composition, such as black and white.

Convenience Stores—Convenience-oriented version of limited-line food stores; a convenient shopping place.

Cool Colors—Blue and green and their variations.

Cooperative Advertising—Manufacturers and distributors share advertising costs.

Cornice—An architectural projection. A horizontal band that projects from the top of a window; a horizontal band at the top of the wall face below the ceiling; a projecting horizontal band at the top of the building face under the roof line.

Costume Jewelry—Inexpensive, nonprecious fabricated jewelry.

Country Store—Small stores in rural areas catering to small farm communities.

Couturier—Haute couture designer who manufactures one garment per customer; produces limited runs of sized prete-a-porte.

Creativity—Originating something unique; original thought and expressions.

Cross Merchandising—Mixing merchandise from several different departments to create a life style display. An example is combining wines, table linens, flowers, china, and pottery.

Cubism—Art stressing geometric forms and volume; began in Paris, circa 1905.

Curved Lines—Flowing, soft compositional lines.

Decorative Elements—Accessories and props.

Department Stores—Retail organizations which carry many lines of merchandise and show in separate departments.

Dimmer—Electrical switch that controls light levels.

Discount Specialty Store—A store with a mix of discounted and off-priced merchandise.

Discount Stores—Stores with large assortments that buy off-price and sell at lower prices.

Display Themes—A story told visually by product composition that is material for thought.

Displays—All presentation activities in stores, wholesale rooms, showrooms, and markets.

Dominant Colors—Colors that make up the greatest percent of color in a composition and therefore cover large mass areas.

Down Light—Light beaming down from the ceiling. Up light beams up from the floor.

Edit—Prepare, enhance, eliminate, or add elements in a design to perfect production.

Elements of Display—Fixtures, merchandise, lighting equipment, signs, art, and any other material that contributes to display creation.

Emotional Needs—Consumer benefits that satisfy psychological needs.

Emphasis—Focal point in composition.

Enhancement—Elements such as props, colors, and art that augment or intensify the beauty of another object or composition.

Enhancing Colors—Colors that enhance or flatter each other. Yellow might enhance orange. They are often colors that are next to each other on a color wheel.

Entrepreneur—Owner and operator of personal business.

Face Outs—Water fall or slant, apparel arms that are either mounted on a T stand or on a slat wall. Apparel can be arranged in a frontal manner facing the customer. Rainbow color arrangements of feature apparel are displayed on them.

Fashion Forward—Innovative fashion policy.

Fashion Life Cycle—The introduction, rise, peak, decline, and obsolescence of a fashion; a graph shaped like a bell curve.

Felt—Nonwoven fabric that is 72 inches wide and comes in many clear colors to cover display pads.

Filters—Colored glass and gels that mount on fixtures over clear lightbulbs.

Fine Art—Nondecorative art such as paintings, sculpture, drawings, watercolors, and prints, that is produced according to aesthetic criteria of beauty and meaningfulness.

Finish—A pigment's finish, which is a gloss, flat, semi-gloss, glaze or lacquer. It also is a style such as wood marble faux or color.

Fixture Arrangement—Creating functional retail environments by dividing and allocating merchandise fixtures in store interiors.

Flagship Store—Central unit of a department store group.

Floodlights—Incandescent bulbs for PAR lamps and reflectors that produce wide beams.

Floor Plan—A plan or a drawing of all interior store elements: electrical, structural columns and elements, partitions, and cooling and heating systems.

Flower Theme—Flower arrangements that fit a fashion theme, color, or season.

Foam Board—Lightweight paperboard sandwiched with thin Styrofoam and foamcore.

Focal Merchandise—Feature merchandise that is in the prominent part of a display creating a focal point.

Focal Point—Part of the display that a VM emphasizes; it is most visible and eye-catching.

Font—Set of type of the same style.

Foot-candle—Light falling on an object is measured in foot candles. The Illumination Engineering Society (IES) created a list of foot-candle levels for adequate viewing.

Footlamberts—A measurement of reflected light from an object.

Footlight—Used in a row at stage front in a theater. In display windows, footlights are used on the floor at the front of the display just behind the window glass.

Form—The shape or silhouette of an object. A square form might be a cube and a circle could be a sphere. Forms are mood-creating.

Formal Balance—A design in which equal elements are grouped equally on the left and right side of a composition.

Formula Presentation—Displays styles that have been overused. An example is two mannequins chip flooring and one foamcore graphic backdrop giving the impression that it was created by numbers such as step 1, 2, and 3.

Formula Type Displays—Overusing display design, style, technique, and principle.

Freelancer—Independent fashion or VM professional who works independently for many businesses.

Frieze—Decorative, horizontal architectural band below ceiling line or on building face below roof line.

Gondola—Two-sided multishelved merchandising fixture.

Grid—Composition or floor plan divided equally into parallel horizontal and vertical lines that cross.

Grosgrain—A textile with a silk look created by heavy filler threads and covered with close fine warps producing a distinct ribbed look. The material is used for ribbons and draperies.

Half Sheet—Half of a standard 22 inch x 28 inch cardboard sign.

Halogen—A bright, longlasting quartz lamp.

Hard Line—Merchandise in the home store, such as furniture.

Harmony—Commonality; the assemblage of agreeable design elements.

Hat Forms—Millinery display fixtures.

High Fashion—Costliest of world's most exclusive designers; limited production.

Horizontal Line—Flat surface line parallel to earth.

Homasote—Thick paperboard for panels, partitions, display pads, display boards, display backgrounds, and flooring.

Hot Glue—Glue cartridges heated by an electrical glue gun.

Hue—Basic color names such as red, blue, and yellow.

Hypermarkets—Giant, one-stop shopping store with large assortments of food and apparel; off-priced.

Image—To symbolize and typify a quality of retail with a look and certain merchandise.

Impulse Buying—Buying without planning.

Incandescent Light—Energy flowing through a filament that produces a glow, like the sun heats materials until they glow.

Individual Markup—Describes the markup on one item of merchandise.

Informal (Design)—Emphasis on naturalism and irregularity as opposed to studied organization.

Initial Markup—The first markup placed on merchandise when it arrives in the store.

Interior Display—Presentation designed for store interiors.

Italian Papers—Elaborately printed paper that is 22 inch x 28 inch sheet size, hand painted, faux marble, and fool-the-eye techniques.

Landscape—Art depicting outdoors with trees, lakes, mountains, and woods.

Layout—Arrangement of advertising material on a page; arrangement of fixtures or merchandise in an interior space.

Licensed Brand—Retailers pay fee to buy and stock product.

Licensing—Paying for right to buy and stock trademarks, patents, royalty, exclusives, and other rights.

Life Cycle—Merchandise has a specific length of popularity. The introduction, followed by promotion and strong sales, and the end, when it does not sell and is no longer inventoried.

Light Cove—A row of connected fluorescent lights hidden by a wooden or metal trough distributing a light wash up and down a wall.

Line (of Apparel)—Apparel and other products carried by a vendor or a manufacturer's representative.

Line (of Design)—Design element that creates contour, direction, surface, texture, and mood.

Log—Stylized symbol of identity.

Loss Leader—Product priced below retail to attract customers.

Lowercase—Small, noncapital letters.

Lumen—The quantity of light given off in all directions. Luminaries are lighting fixtures.

Luxe—Luxury products and materials.

Mannequin (Display)—Stylized plastic, wood, fiberglass, plaster, metal, or glass representation of human form; can be realistic or abstract.

Mannequin (Fashion)—Live fashion show or sewing model.

Manufacturer—Produces goods and products.

Manufacturer's Agent—Represents products and lines.

Mark Up—Price added for wholesale to retail.

Markdown—Obsolete or distressed merchandise at reduced price.

Market Segment—Group of customers that responds to merchandise similarly.

Merchandise Signs—Signs describing a product, its benefits, and its price.

Middle Class—Social class in two groups: the upper-middle class (11%): successful professionals, small business owners, managers of large corporations, buy designer products, purchases are symbol for them; lower-middle class (36%): small business people, office workers, teachers, technicians, white-collar workers.

Model (Fashion)—Mannequins or models wearing apparel for show.

Modern Art—Focused on abstract art; centered in Paris in its beginning in 1900s.

Moiré—A textile with a silk-ribbed look created with a water mark texture on its surface. It has an elegant look with a silk-like finish.

Mold—Concave form from which object is shaped; most mannequins are made in molds.

Monochromatic—Composition based on one color.

Mood—Emotional tone of art or design.

Motif—Principal distinct element in design.

National Association of Display Industries (NADI)—VM trade association.

Near Colors—Colors that have approaching tendencies.

Need Satisfaction—Providing products to fulfill customer desires.

Needs—Forces that motivate customers to buy.

Neon—Cold cathode light of many colors and unlimited shapes.

Neutral Colors—Hues that have low chromatic values (beige, gray, coffee, and white).

Off-White—Pure white color that has a touch of tint.

One Hue Palette—The use of one color consisting of many shades in a composition.

Palette—Designer's color choices.

Palette (Art)—Flat surface on which artist mixes colors.

Pastel—Pale versions of all hues.

Personal Needs—Personal satisfaction, self-esteem, accomplishment, fun, freedom, and relaxation.

Perspective—Lines and haziness of colors that create the appearance of distance.

Pica—Typeface measurement of type's width.

Pigment—Dry chemical or organic substance that produces paint when mixed with liquid.

Place—A particular portion of space devoted to retail.

Plannograms—Drawings of slat walls and fixtures that illustrate product placement.

Point—Typeface measurement of character's height.

Price Points—List prices.

Primary Colors—The three pigment colors: red, yellow and blue; combinations of these make secondary colors.

Primary Light—All-over, basic lighting.

Princess Dress—One-piece dress which has a princess inset, short sleeves, bodice with double gore, defined waist, eased skirt, and scoop neck.

Product—Merchandise.

Progression—Arrangement of sizes and items in order of increasing size to create a line.

Prop—A decorative object or merchandise used in a display or store interior to establish a mood or theme. A prop should enhance some quality of the merchandise or store interior.

Proportion—Comparative size relationships; ratios of common sizes.

Pyramid—Broad-based design capped by a central peak.

Quality—An extremely well-produced product without flaws.

Radial Balance—A circular arrangement that guides the eye from a central point, focal point, around the parts of a display. It is an active looking composition.

Ready-to-Wear—Standard-sized, mass-produced apparel lines.

Realism—Art forms that are detailed representations with photographic looks.

Regional (Associate)—In charge of a chain store group.

Regional (Display)—Created for a specific zone or region (i.e., West Coast look or East Coast look).

Regional Malls—Large, covered malls with many small chain stores and four or more anchor stores. Some older regional malls remain open air.

Rhythm—Movement in composition.

Rig—Dressing menswear mannequins and forms.

Rigging—The task of dressing and pinning a man's suit.

Rounder—Round apparel fixtures for large merchandise quantities.

Seamless Papers—Very wide (107 inches x 50 feet) papers that come in many colors; used as inexpensive backgrounds.

Secondary Colors—Colors produced by mixing primary colors.

Secondary Lighting—Spotlights and floodlights increasing highlights, mood, drama, or artistic value.

Shades—The addition of a percent of gray or black to a color; a grayed color.

Shirr—To draw up or gather fabric.

Shirtdress—Shirtwaist, classic dress with long sleeves, buttoned-down front, and shirt-style collar.

Shirtwaist Dress—One piece, fitted bodice belted at waist, long sleeves, front buttons, crisp collar, and made of heavy shirting fabric.

Shopping Environment—Store interiors that stimulate sales through good design and presentation.

Showcase—Display cases that have a glass top and front, wooden or metal sides, and a lighted interior. They protect and show exotic or expensive merchandise, such as fine jewelry, silver, gold, and other rare items. In food stores, showcases are refrigerated, humidified, or heated. They protect and show foods.

Side Fill Light—Secondary light focused on an object from the side to eliminate unwanted shadows.

Silhouette—Profile or outline of garment, art, or drawing.

Silk Screen—Producing color by forcing colors through pro film and silk screen with a squeegee.

Slatwall—Four by eight sheets with horizontal four-inch boards fastened from top to bottom, in a horizontal slat configuration. The boards alternate one in and one out, creating a ridge to fasten small hanging fixtures. Slatwall is constructed of wood or homasote, and covered with Formica. Slatwall provides endless horizontal fixture arrangements, and up and down fixture arrangements are restricted by the four-inch board width.

Social Class—Group of people with equal social positions.

Social Needs—Needs that relate customer's interaction with others: love, friendships, status, and esteem.

Special Event—Activity created for a sales promotion.

Specialty Store—Stores with limited-line inventories that focus on single-style inventories.

Spreadsheet—Data analysis illustrating how business values affect each other.

Store Design—Activity of architects, space planners, and VM designing retail space.

Strip Mall—Shopping center with off-price stores, supermarkets, and convenience stores, organized in rows along busy highways and streets.

Studio—Designer's and artist's workplace; apparel designers call it "atelier."

Style—An elegant, fashionable, or luxurious mode of living; fashion as smartness.

Style—(Merchandise Identification) Features such as style number which identifies a garment.

Stylist—Selects accessories, apparel, and home goods to create fashionable assemblages for promotional purposes in retail, wholesale, and showrooms; in advertising, stylists select models, merchandise accessories, and photo shoot locations.

Stylized—Conforming to a specific style that represents a conventional expression.

Supermarket—Large grocery store.

Superstore—Large grocery-style store inventorying all goods and many services.

Symmetrical—Equal elements balanced equally on right and left sides of the composition.

T Stands—Simple apparel fixtures with posts topped by cross bars; holds fewer than 16 garments.

Target Customer—The customer a retailer wants to attract and sell to.

Target Market—A group of customers a retailer wants to attract.

Target Marketing—Marketing tailored to specific desirable customers.

Task Zone—A work area.

Tempera—Paint that is sometimes water-soluble, with a glue or egg additive.

Tertiary Color—Color made combining primary and secondary colors.

Textile—Woven fabric.

Texture—Tactile quality of an item or an art object.

Tie-Ins—Signs, merchandise, promotions, and advertisements that fit promotion merchandise or display themes.

Tint—Pale color resulting when colors mix with white.

Tonal Value—Strength of color contrasting with black and white.

Trade—Associations, markets, reports, and others dealing with the VM industry.

Trade Publications—Printed media, magazines, and newspapers that provide industry news coverage.

Traffic—Movement of shoppers through a store.

Tri-way—An apparel fixture with three face-out arms; also a rounder split into three adjustable sections.

Trunk Show—Show to which designers or representatives bring lines to store for a short period.

Typeface—The style, character, shape, and design of type; there are typefaces for text and others for display.

Unit—One of a group of stores; coordinate group of apparel.

Upper Class—Two percent of population with wealth and social status.

Upper End Store—Retail stores which carry expensive merchandise.

Uppercase—Capital letters.

Value—The amount of black or white in a color.

Vendor—Manufacturer's representative who sells products to retailers at wholesale prices.

Vertical Line—Top to bottom lines; strong image.

Visual Merchandising (VM)—All presentation activities based on creating sales in businesses, from retail to wholesale.

Wants—Customer needs.

Warehouse—Bulk retailers who sell assorted goods, quantity and giant size packaging, and plain interiors; a building used for storing merchandise until it is stocked in the store.

Warm Colors—Colors range: warm blues, reds, oranges, and yellows through warm greens.

Wash—An all-over, often indirect, lighting technique.

White Space—In advertising design, it is surrounding an advertisement with white space in a way to keep it separate from a neighboring advertisement. In display, it is a way of surrounding a display with empty space to separate it from the neighboring merchandise.

Wholesaler—Businessperson who sells to retailers at wholesale prices.

Window Display—Presentation designed for display windows.

Window Shoppers—Customers who delight at looking at window displays and admiring display art in fashion stores; people looking for new fashion directions.

Wiring Mannequins—Using wires in place of bases and rods to stand mannequins.

Women's Wear Daily (WWD)—Most comprehensive fashion trade publication, providing in-depth apparel news.

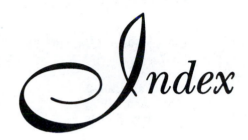

Index